T0288589

By the same author

Hong Kong: China's New Colony
The Years of Living Dangerously: Asia From Financial Crisis to the New Millennium
Market Panic: Wild Gyrations, Risks and Opportunities in Stock Markets
Food Gurus: 20 People Who Changed the Way We Eat and Think About Food

DEFYING THE DRAGON

STEPHEN VINES

Defying the Dragon

Hong Kong and the World's Largest Dictatorship

HURST & COMPANY, LONDON

First published in the United Kingdom in 2021 by
C. Hurst & Co. (Publishers) Ltd.,
83 Torbay Road, London NW6 7DT
Copyright © Stephen Vines, 2021
All rights reserved.

Printed and bound in Great Britain by Bell & Bain Ltd, Glasgow

Distributed in the United States, Canada and Latin America
by Oxford University Press, 198 Madison Avenue, New York,
NY 10016, United States of America.

The right of Stephen Vines to be identified as the author of
this publication is asserted by him in accordance with the
Copyright, Designs and Patents Act, 1988.

A Cataloguing-in-Publication data record for this book
is available from the British Library.

ISBN: 9781787384552

This book is printed using paper from registered sustainable
and managed sources.

www.hurstpublishers.com

This book is dedicated to the memory of Alex Chow Tsz-lok, born in 1997, the year of Hong Kong's return to Chinese rule. He died at the height of the protests in 2019, the first person to lose his life during a demonstration. He was 22 years of age.

CONTENTS

CONTENTS

PART THREE
THE UNEXPECTED AND THE FUTURE

NOTE ON TRANSLITERATION AND NAMES

Mainland China uses a standard form of romanisation for Mandarin, or Putonghua, called pinyin. In this book, all names of Mainlanders, places on the Mainland and transliterations of Chinese regime slogans are rendered in pinyin.

The situation is more complicated in Hong Kong, where the common language is Cantonese—there is no standard form of Cantonese romanisation. Some of this complication is reflected in this book, where names of people and places in Hong Kong are rendered in the standard transliteration used by the Hong Kong government. Frustratingly, this method has never been publicly elaborated; but, especially for place names, it is in common usage. A more accurate and transparent form of romanisation, now widely used, is the Yale method, which I have employed sparingly for transliterated Cantonese speech and slogans.

A majority of Hong Kong people use foreign given names in addition to their Chinese names, either formally or informally. The full Chinese names of the principle characters in Hong Kong politics are provided in Appendix II. In the main text, however, their names are rendered in the form most likely to be recognised by English-language readers.

PREFACE

I moved to Hong Kong in 1987, ten years before the handover to China, as a correspondent for the London-based *Observer* newspaper covering South East Asia. "We're not expecting much out of Hong Kong itself," I was told. "But, it's a good base." To be frank, the paper had generally low expectations of this posting and, in order to persuade my bosses to send me to Hong Kong at all, I had been obliged to transform my full-time job into a part-time position. It gave me the freedom to work for a wide variety of other publications and radio stations, which ended up being far more interesting than I could have hoped for.

Low expectations of Hong Kong have been the order of the day from the time that the British arrived. Lord Palmerston, Britain's foreign secretary when the territory was ceded to the Empire in 1841, famously dismissed Hong Kong as "a barren island, which will never be a mart of trade". He was neither the first nor the last person to underestimate what this barren island could become. Intrinsic to the colony's success was a sense of the possible. It is this sense that has made Hong Kong such a dynamic society.

It affected me more or less from the moment the bulbous Cathay Pacific 747 made the famous sharp turn manoeuvre to line up for landing on the old Kai Tak Airport runway, sweeping gently past the rooftops of the adjacent buildings, now largely torn down, in Kowloon City. Anyone who has made this landing will testify to its drama. But this was just the start—it did not take me long to discover that opportunities abound in Hong Kong.

Having spent most of my working life as a journalist, it had not previously occurred to me that humble hacks could also contemplate being entrepreneurs. Speaking to local reporters, I was impressed to learn about the number of other ventures they were involved in. In London, the only journalists I knew who ventured into business were those who had strayed into the adjacent field of public relations. In Hong Kong, the invisible barrier to a wider horizon simply did not exist, and no one thought it all absurd to contemplate being both a correspondent and a businessperson.

So, just over a year after arriving, I got involved in a retail kitchenware venture. This was followed by starting a number of businesses in the food industry. There is something about the audacity of this place that, despite my primitive technological skills, encouraged me to jump aboard the so-called "dot-com revolution" by founding a content provision company (with, it has to be said, a far more technically savvy partner); the business soared and slumped very much in line with the hype surrounding that strange time. Like so many other people who made their way to Hong Kong, it became for me a place of great opportunity.

Fortunately, this extensive activity outside the world of journalism had the additional benefit of exposure to a far wider range of people and experiences than would have been possible had I remained in the media cocoon. This proved to be invaluable in gaining a better understanding of what was really happening in Hong Kong. I am not embarrassed to say, however, that newspapers were my first love. Yet again, Hong Kong gave me opportunities I very much doubt would have arisen if I had never left London. I was able to become the founding editor of a new daily newspaper, and later helped to establish a satirical news magazine. I have also developed a sideline as a current affairs television presenter. I have every reason to be thankful to Hong Kong.

That said, my plan had been to stay for a couple of years, then make my way back to London. But the Tiananmen Square massacre changed everything. It was, for me personally, a watershed moment.

Even before the fateful night of 4 June 1989, I had learned that many people in Hong Kong were working day and night to support their compatriots across the border during the weeks of protest on the Mainland. The atmosphere was tense but largely positive, as people dared to dream that China—which was poised to take over Hong Kong in just eight years' time—might become a democratic society.

In the middle of the night, reports started coming in that tanks were rolling into Beijing's Tiananmen Square. I was asked by the BBC to contact leading members of the local democracy movement to get some response. Every phone I called was engaged, but persistence finally yielded the information that a rally was being planned. It was just possible, I was told, that something like 100,000 people would take part. They would march from the centre of town to Victoria Park, the largest urban park on Hong Kong island, which has since become ground zero for any protest. I duly filed some reports, thinking it best to leave out any mention of those high numbers, which seemed a bit fanciful at the time.

Hong Kong, then still under British rule, was the only place in China where a demonstration of this kind could be held. Under the arrangements for the handover of power, this right of assembly, among others, was guaranteed for the next fifty years— but who knew whether the Sino-British agreement was going to be worth the paper it was printed on. This uncertainty explained much of what happened in Hong Kong on 5 June, the day after the massacre.

By daybreak, all normal radio programming in Hong Kong had been ditched and replaced by commentary and news of the night's events. In the building where I lived, residents crowded around the doorkeeper's television set on the ground floor. They had their own televisions, but there was an unspoken sense that everyone wanted to share these moments in company. I later discovered that my neighbours were far from unique in their need not to be alone while the unthinkable was happening across the border.

Making my way to the imperially named Edinburgh Place, where the rally was scheduled to begin, it became clear that more or less everyone was headed in the same direction. As the numbers swelled—and then swelled again—it was evident that Victoria Park would not be big enough to accommodate the protestors, and so the gates of the massive race course in Happy Valley were thrown open. A hastily erected stage was filled with leaders of Hong Kong's democracy movement, alongside practically every local entertainment star. They joined together to sing the newly minted Cantonese anthem of the movement, with a title that translates as *All for Freedom*. It would prove to be an important marker for how culture and protest could meld so effectively in Hong Kong.

Precisely how many people joined the demonstration was hard to estimate, but it is commonly assumed that at least 1 million people were present—a record for the time, only to be exceeded in 2019. The pressure of numbers meant a lot of standing around under a burning sun and oppressive humidity. However, patience was the order of the day. There was no need for policing; the self-discipline of the crowd was absolute.

What I learned on that day was that the hoary old myths about Hong Kong were simply not true. It was held to be axiomatic that Hongkongers cared only about money and business, and that they had no time for ephemeral concepts such as democracy and freedom; that, without the steadying hand of the old elite, it would be impossible to get things organised. All these fallacies were effortlessly laid to rest the day after the Tiananmen massacre and, in the years that followed, trampled into the ground.

I had been busy covering protests in places such as the Philippines and Burma/Myanmar, where it also seemed highly unlikely that anything would change. But now, on my own doorstep, something even more compelling was unfolding.

Would this be a one-off? The answer is now clear. Not only was it not a one-off, but the 5 June demonstration presaged the evolution of mass-scale protest in Hong Kong, quite different from the sporadic demonstrations of the past and much more all-encompassing than previous movements. It showed that, when push comes to shove, large numbers of Hong Kong people would be willing to stand up in defence of their home. In 1989 that meant supporting the democracy movement on the Mainland. After the reality of Chinese rule over Hong Kong became clear, interest in the wider Chinese democracy movement dwindled, as it appeared to be far more urgent to defend the freedoms that had been promised, which were in danger of being snuffed out.

A sense of both growing fear and the determination not to bow down without a fight gradually impinged on my consciousness, but these impressions were crystallised into a clearer vision by my experience of being in Hong Kong during the uncertain yet thrilling times of the 1989 Chinese democracy movement. All thoughts of leaving Hong Kong disappeared. I had an opportunity to live through a period of history in the making. Why would I want to walk away?

Reaching back to imperial times, Chinese history has often been repeated. In fact it is crisscrossed with grim symmetry, one anniversary after another being ominously echoed. And so it was in June 2019, when the Hong Kong uprising began, precisely thirty years after the People's Liberation Army ruthlessly extinguished the democracy movement of 1989. The Hong Kong protests of 2019–20 evolved into the most serious rebellion Beijing had faced since that time, and the world waited to see if Hongkongers' audacity would be met with the same violence.

Two years after Britain handed Hong Kong back to the PRC in 1997, I wrote a book entitled *Hong Kong: China's New Colony*. Some critics at the time said that the title reflected excessive pessimism over the future of Hong Kong, insisting that China could not possibly be contemplating emulating the outgoing colonisers once it assumed power. They were right, but for the wrong reasons. As things have turned out, the Chinese Communist Party has not been satisfied with merely preserving the worst aspects of British rule, but—in the style of the emperors who used to rule China—wants to create a vassal entity whose people are expected to tremble and obey.

Three decades after the handover, the streets of the former British colony filled with tear gas, the blast of water cannons and pepper spray, culminating in the summer of 2020 in the imposition of a new National Security Law threatening the whole edifice of civil liberties.

And there was more: at the tail end of 2019, reports had started to emerge of a deadly virus spreading on the Mainland. By January 2020, it was clear that this virus was coming Hong Kong's way. It was a painful reminder of the SARS epidemic that had started gathering pace precisely seventeen years previously, in January 2003. Back then, a so-called super-spreader was admitted to hospital in the nearby city of Guangzhou, infecting many doctors and nurses; a month later, SARS arrived in Hong Kong. It ended up killing 299 people before it was suppressed. The memory of this outbreak is deeply embedded in Hong Kong's consciousness; it helps explain why the efforts of local people have ensured a much lower death toll from the even-more-lethal coronavirus of 2020.

PREFACE

Before the battle against Covid-19 even got underway, Hong Kong was in the midst of another battle: the fight for liberty. Millions of citizens had poured onto the streets to express their yearning for freedom and to preserve Hong Kong's autonomy. Daring to defy the world's most powerful dictatorship, they marched under the slogan "Liberate Hong Kong, Revolution of Our Times!" The protestors' demands have been repeatedly dismissed as "unrealistic", and even those who have expressed some sympathy for the movement have wrung their hands and proclaimed the futility and dangers of challenging the authority of the Chinese Communist Party, which has an ominous track record for dealing with opposition through the barrel of a gun.

The savagery the Party is prepared to deploy against opponents was clearly seen in 1989. Order was restored over the dead bodies of the mainly young men and women who had dared to defy the regime. Now, in Hong Kong, the excruciating fear of history repeating itself lurks ominously in the background. It is hard to overstate the dark mood that overshadows Hong Kong at the time of writing this book, the end of 2020. Never in all the decades I have lived here have I witnessed this level of uncertainty and outright fear. A friend of mine who covered the protests in admirable detail for a number of publications says that, when she's at home and hears a police siren, she always worries that it is headed in her direction. Fortunately, she has remained at home with her family, but a great many other people have been roused from their beds early in the morning and herded off into police vans. Her fears have proved to be far from unfounded because in 2020 journalists joined the growing line of arrestees.

In these pages, I unashamedly reflect a continued fascination with China, a commitment to Hong Kong—a place that has given me so much—and a hope that it can survive in one way or another, despite overwhelming odds seemingly designed to defy optimism.

PREFACE

Many people who first came to Hong Kong with great personal ambition have found that, the longer they stayed, the more they acquired a similar level of aspiration for Hong Kong society as a whole. What for many people started out as a place of transition has been rapidly transformed into a place of permanent settlement, and what flows from that becomes a strong level of commitment.

Hong Kong has been a place of refuge. A place of opportunity. A haven of stability. And a place famously described by the journalist Tsang Ki-fan as "the only Chinese society that, for a brief span of 100 years, lived through an ideal never realized at any time in the history of Chinese societies. A time when no man had to live in fear of the midnight knock on the door."

If British colonialism achieved nothing else, it achieved this. Colonialism also displayed the worst of British racism, bred inequality and instituted an almost farcical reverence for a country far away that, in practice, meant nothing to most Hongkongers. However, almost without the British noticing—and certainly not by design—the people of this former colony have forged a distinct identity, and an increasingly determined attachment to this place that is clearly part of China, but equally clearly apart from it. To understand this is to appreciate the essential background to the events of the uprising that began in 2019.

What all protest movements have in common is that success, or indeed failure, rarely occurs as a result of a single event. It is a process—often with a dramatic conclusion, but usually a conclusion reached via a circuitous route, with the eventual outcome preceded by tortuous ups and downs, and absolutely no guarantees. Hong Kong's uprising is also part of a process; this book represents an attempt to understand that process, and to paint a picture of exactly why and how it happened.

However, beyond the movement itself, something even more profound has also been underway that, I freely admit, did not occur to me when I embarked on this project, probably because close proximity has a habit of obscuring a wider vision. It has become increasingly apparent that what has been happening in Hong Kong has enormous implications for the survival of the Chinese dictatorship. When the uprising melded into the coronavirus crisis of 2020, the challenges facing the Communist Party became that much more profound. Whatever fear prevails in Hong Kong, it has been matched by enormous unease in Beijing. The regime had convinced itself that it was immune to challenges of this kind, yet the world has watched in fascination as tiny little Hong Kong became what many people saw as a beacon of liberty.

This was nothing less than an existential challenge to one-party rule in China. The demise of a dictatorship is often triggered by events not at the centre of power, but on the periphery, and by circumstances that can only be judged as truly significant with the benefit of hindsight. That benefit is not to hand right now, and only a fool or a charlatan would have sufficient confidence to predict how the crisis in Hong Kong will end. But there are pointers, and they are reflected in these pages.

Much of this book is taken up with careful examination of how the Hong Kong uprising began, how it evolved and the impact it has had on the rest of the world. These developments are key to understanding why, in 2021, the seemingly mighty Chinese dictatorship is standing on feet of clay.

Those who insist that the ultimate outcome of the uprising will not be good for Hong Kong have not had the benefit of the sound advice I received from a friend who was to become a legislator. "Never bet against the people of Hong Kong," he counselled. "They will never let you down."

Whatever happens, it is impossible to come away from the events charted in this book without admiring the breathtaking audacity of the people of Hong Kong, their enormous courage and ingenuity. A more detached observer might, at this point, add the words "for better or worse" but I have freely admitted not to be so gloriously detached. My passion for Hong Kong is deep; but not more so than it is for the hundreds of Hongkongers I have talked to, who have made it possible to write this book.

INTRODUCTION

Just twelve months before the Hong Kong protest movement got underway, things had looked so very different for the People's Republic of China. The dictatorship was looking forward to the prospect of triumphalist celebrations in 2019, marking seventy years in power. That was no small achievement: the Chinese Communist Party was on the way to outliving the reign of its mentor, the Soviet Union. At a ceremony in December 2018, President Xi Jinping listed the Party's many successes, asserting that China's status as a world power was now recognised not just by the people of the PRC, but around the globe. He said that China was moving closer to the world's centre stage, widely renowned as a promoter of world peace, contributor to international development and upholder of international order.

Earlier in the year, a more comprehensive account of the Party's many achievements was ponderously spelled out by Premier Li Keqiang, delivering his annual government work report to the National People's Congress, China's rubber-stamp parliament. Sitting behind rows of neatly spaced desks in the cavernous Great Hall of the People, Beijing's handpicked delegates, who are proficient in the art of synchronised hand-clapping, listened attentively as the premier summed up progress made in the past year, set targets for the year ahead and highlighted longer-term goals.

Premier Li's report noted that the economy was firing on all cylinders, achieving an average 7.1 per cent annual growth rate for the past five years. Living standards, he said, "have been constantly improving", with more than 68 million people lifted out of poverty and personal incomes rising by an average of 7.4 per cent over five years. China's plan to become the leading player in global manufacturing, the so-called Made in China 2025 initiative, was enjoying "progress in major projects". And then there was the great success of the ambitious Belt and Road Initiative, which aims to place Beijing at the centre of a massive trading partnership, fuelled by Chinese investment, with physical links spanning Asia, Africa and beyond.[1]

"China," said Li, "has opened its doors wider to the world. This opening has played a powerful role in our own development, and it presents important opportunities for the rest of the world." China was also moving up to its rightful place in global affairs, hosting major international gatherings, assuming leadership on issues such as environmental protection, and at last punching according to its weight in a world hitherto dominated by the American hegemon.

Li was not wrong here: he did not say so, but the Beijing leadership could hardly believe the opportunities created by Washington since 2017, with the Trump administration not only abandoning participation in international bodies and tearing up treaties, but also making a practice of falling out with America's closest allies. China was not ready to declare that it would fill this carelessly created vacuum, but it was not shy in making its presence known. Momentum had been building on this front for several years. President Xi had made the first state visit by a Chinese leader to the United Kingdom in 2015 and had been delighted to note that the British were no longer raising annoying human rights issues, preferring to focus on a "Golden Era" of Sino-British relations. In 2017 Beijing had, for the second time, secured the appointment of its chosen candidate to head the World Health Organization (a move that was to have intense repercussions in 2020). Along the way, Beijing had managed to overcome some long-standing diplomatic problems. China's often tense relationship with Russia had been replaced by the establishment of cordial ties that enabled both nations to work together on wider international issues, notably in the Middle East. China, which once had to rely on Albania as its major ally in Europe, was now making bigger, far more influential friends around the world.

Other tricky issues were also moving in the right direction as far as Beijing was concerned. Taiwan was due to hold a presidential election in January 2020 and there was every chance that the Kuomintang (KMT) would win. The KMT had once been the Communist Party's bitter enemy, but was now its partner in fighting the Taiwan-centric Democratic Progressive Party (DPP). The KMT had scored impressive victories in mayoral elections and found a candidate who was widely expected to trounce the incumbent DPP President Tsai Ing-wen. It seemed that the prospect of taming the island was drawing nearer, reflected in Li's comments that "We have resolutely opposed and deterred separatist forces advocating Taiwan independence." In Hong Kong, it very much looked as though support for the democracy movement had faded following the massive Umbrella protests of 2014. Li reported that "The practice of 'one country, two systems' has been consistently enriched and developed", while "the authority of China's Constitution and the basic laws of the Hong Kong and Macao special administrative regions" had become more evident; overall, "Hong Kong and Macao [had] thrived and remained stable."

There was one line in Li's speech that sounded a different note. It might have been little more than rhetoric, but in retrospect it appears to be prescient. He said, "As the Chinese saying goes, when all is calm forget not danger; when all is well be awake to woes."

Being awake to danger was not much in evidence in the great surge of optimism and self-confidence settling on the Xi Jinping regime. He had been installed in office in 2012 as General Secretary of the Communist Party, and the following year he had become President. Now, in 2018, he had been made president for life. To confirm his dominance, Xi Jinping Thought had been enshrined in the constitution in 2017. Only Mao's ideology had previously held such status; Xi is the most powerful Chinese leader since. Immodestly titled *Xi Jinping Thought on Socialism with Chinese Characteristics for a New Era*, Xi's treatise was designed as the blueprint for enhancing prosperity and, not for the first time, building "socialism with Chinese characteristics". As with Mao Zedong Thought, the primary purpose of this change to the constitution was to make it clear that China's leader was unchallengeable and in control at every level.

As China moves forward, it likes to look back; to reinterpret history to fit prevailing conditions. Like all dictatorships, the Party leadership spares no expense in celebrating landmark moments that affirm its longevity and supposed success. This year, 2018, there were celebrations for the fortieth anniversary of China's programme of Reform and Opening Up to the world; and, before the 2019 celebrations marking seven decades of Communist rule had even taken place, the Party was already looking forward to yet another major event in 2021: its own 100th anniversary.

Preparation for this anniversary entailed a plethora of ambitious goals to confirm the ascendency of the new order. In the space of ten years (2010–20), China intended to have doubled its gross national product and per capita income. To hammer home the progress and power of the new China, the PRC's first domestically produced aircraft carrier had been placed in service, alongside a functioning space station. Developments such as these were important contributions to the "Chinese Dream", a series of goals that would be fully realised by 2049, amounting to nothing less than the "rejuvenation of the Chinese nation", as President Xi described it.

How could it be that tiny Hong Kong threatened to stop this juggernaut in its tracks?

* * *

With a population of 7.5 million, Hong Kong is little more than a pinprick on the surface of the People's Republic of China. After the departure of the British in 1997, Beijing had moved rapidly to make clear that there were limits to the scope of the region's autonomy—judicial independence, for example. This was established via a series of so-called reinterpretations of the Basic Law, Hong Kong's mini-constitution, by the Standing Committee of the National People's Congress in Beijing. In reality, these were nothing less than amendments to the Basic Law that overrode rulings in the Hong Kong courts.

The second decade of Chinese sovereignty in Hong Kong, beginning in 2007, had seen this process of eroding autonomy stepped up, particularly after Xi Jinping came to power in 2012. On the Mainland itself, Xi had barely paused for breath before ruthlessly cracking down on potential and actual opposition, making it crystal-clear that his regime would not tolerate dissent. Inevitably, the hard line across the border had repercussions in Hong Kong. What had begun as a slow drip under Xi's predecessor, Hu Jintao, turned into a flood. There was opposition in Hong Kong, but the Beijing leadership was led to believe by its local echo chamber that Hongkongers were unlikely to put up any significant resistance. This illusion was shattered by what became known as the Umbrella protests of 2014, but they were ultimately put down without a single concession from the authorities.

And that seemed to be that. The opposition appeared to have been humbled, opening the way for more assertive control over Hong Kong. Moreover, it seemed as though this process of fully integrating the former colony into the Mainland could be achieved with minimal repercussions. Foreign countries were viewing Beijing as an ally rather than a rival, the enormous economic power of the PRC bringing with it considerable clout in a great many directions. Things were going so smoothly that the men who ran China thought it was safe to take their eye off the ball in Hong Kong.

This self-confidence was abruptly shaken in 2019, when new Hong Kong protests erupted and quickly escalated in a manner that took both the protestors and the government by surprise. It rapidly became clear that the crushing of the Umbrella Movement had singularly failed to extinguish Hongkongers' willingness to stand up for their rights.

The protests began with opposition to an extradition bill; but, by June, when some 2 million people had poured out onto the streets, the protestors' demands had morphed into far more wide-reaching calls for reform and democracy.

Hong Kong had been promised no change to its political system until 2047 by Deng Xiaoping, the paramount leader of China who had negotiated the handover of power, and gone out of his way to provide assurance that it would not entail a change to Hong Kong's way of life. But, by 2019, Deng had long since gone to meet his great Marx in the sky, and Hongkongers had come to realise that the basic promise of continuity under Chinese rule was worthless.

* * *

This was not how things had looked on the day of the handover. I vividly recall standing in the torrential rain on the Hong Kong side of the border as People's Liberation Army flatbed trucks drove in, delivering troops to replace the British garrison in the early hours of 1 July 1997. They were enthusiastically cheered by large crowds as they sloshed by. The great fears that had prompted a mass exodus in the run-up to Sino-British negotiations for the handover (1983–4) had now given way to a sense of optimism—maybe not euphoria, but there was a sense that things would not be too bad.

It was no small thing for a dictatorship to promise that British-style rule of law would remain intact. Maybe it was always fanciful to imagine that this unique experiment would work—melding the world's largest dictatorship together with a freewheeling society. But Deng, the great reformer credited with opening up the Chinese economy to the rest of the world, had every reason to focus on Hong Kong's contribution to that process.

In its original conception, the Hong Kong experiment was designed to show the world that China was a magnanimous global partner, quite prepared to play along with the rules created by liberal democracies. During the heady 1980s of Reform and Opening Up, Deng decided that there could be no better confirmation of how things had changed in China than to develop the concept of "one country, two systems". With this principle, he told the world that the Chinese were strong and confident enough to accommodate a revolutionary concept that no other dictatorship had even dared to think about. Never before in history had a modern-day autocracy volunteered to incorporate an entity following an entirely different set of rules from those governing the rest of the nation. China even promised to exempt Hong Kong from the nation's ruling ideology.

This was to be no empty promise, but a commitment enshrined in an international treaty signed in 1984 between the outgoing colonial power, Britain, and the incoming sovereign, China. Article 3.5 of this treaty is crucial. It states: "The current social and economic systems in Hong Kong will remain unchanged, and so will the life-style. Rights and freedoms, including those of the person, of speech, of the press, of assembly, of association, of travel, of movement, of correspondence, of strike, of choice of occupation, of academic research and of religious belief will be ensured by law ... Private property, ownership of enterprises, legitimate right of inheritance and foreign investment will be protected by law."

In the early stage of the new regime, there was considerable optimism that these guarantees would hold, and that the delicate balance of "one country, two systems" could be made to work. But the unravelling, which climaxed in 2020, was underway well before then.

Throughout its entire history, the Party has always fallen back on the crude weapons of repression when faced with manifestations of opposition on the Mainland. In Hong Kong, however, that kind of clampdown would be taking place in the full glare of global attention. The former British colony has an importance totally disproportionate to its size. Its survival as an autonomous entity, and the uprising of 2019–20, has been a major test for the Chinese dictatorship, and Hong Kong's high visibility on the world stage made difficult the kind of ruthless repression underway in Xinjiang, another supposedly autonomous region. US Senator Pat Toomey, co-author of the Hong Kong Autonomy Act imposing sanctions in response to the National Security Law, said, "In many ways, Hong Kong is the canary in the coal mine for Asia." He added: "Beijing's growing interference could have a chilling effect on other nations struggling for freedom in China's shadow."[3]

China's leaders were always aware that Hong Kong was going to be in the spotlight, and that what happened there would impact on its relations with the rest of the world. Equally, what happened in Hong Kong would have considerable consequences for the Party's standing at home on the Mainland. Were control to be lost in Hong Kong, and the seemingly impregnable dictatorship exposed as capable of being defied, what signal would this send to the rest of the nation? And to the world?

The message of a brutal crackdown was exactly what many people around the world had always imagined—that China was a bully that could not be trusted to adhere to agreements it had signed. This was bad enough, but what the Party really feared was that its feet of clay would be exposed to the wider mass of people on the Mainland, who might start having doubts over the dictatorship and acting on them. In addition, Xi had to consider his position within the regime itself, where he had established a track record for sniffing out dissent and crushing it. In the febrile world of the Party's upper echelons, jostling for power is a constant preoccupation. This president-for-life, the son of a prominent statesman and the first of the PRC's leaders to have been born into the ruling elite, is all too well aware of how the system works. Xi may well have calculated that the negatives of crushing the Hong Kong uprising were outweighed by the positives of securing his absolute dominance over the nation.

While the leadership in Beijing was still weighing this up, there was a remarkable convergence of political crisis with medical emergency, emanating from the central Chinese city of Wuhan. The initial outbreak of Covid-19 was ominous enough, but things got worse as it morphed into a global pandemic, provoking a massive economic and diplomatic nightmare that no one in Beijing had seen coming. It is hard to exaggerate the extent to which the Party leaders were blindsided in 2019–20, first by the Hong Kong uprising and later by this other potentially lethal challenge posed by the coronavirus.

The Chinese response to mounting international and internal criticism in 2020 has swung between feigned indifference and fervent rebuttal. It is indeed possible that the indifference is real; Beijing may have concluded that, in a hostile world, it needs to meet opposition by becoming as strong as possible, in both economic and military terms.

But the question persisted: how to bring Hong Kong to heel?

* * *

In 2019, many people in Hong Kong feared that the Chinese Communist Party would manifest its strength by sending in the tanks to crush the democracy protests, as they had in Beijing in 1989. But the uprising continued, and the tanks never came.

Hongkongers breathed a collective sigh of relief. They imagined that the former British colony's international prominence, plus the overwhelming popular support for the protests, had saved the day. What no one thought back then was that the men in grey suits—they are indeed all men—would find another, arguably more lethal way of trying to put down Hong Kong's burning desire for liberty.

The optimists had wilfully ignored how the Chinese Communist Party works. Its leaders have long memories and they never, ever tolerate dissent. The men in Beijing were simply biding their time. Instead of ordering a bloody crackdown, they drew up a plan to extinguish dissent by weaponising the law, with the creation of a draconian National Security Law (NSL), which came into force on the eve of 1 July 2020—the twenty-third anniversary of Hong Kong's handover back to China in 1997.

Beijing had been pressing Hong Kong to implement a national security law from day one of that new order. In 2003, the Hong Kong government made an attempt to comply, but was thwarted by mass protests. Not a drop of blood was spilled and it seemed as though the Chinese authorities were prepared to tolerate dissent under one country, two systems. Fast forward to 2019, and the level of protest put the demonstrations of 2003 well into the shadows. The Party's patience came to an end.

INTRODUCTION

Just before the law was enacted, as people were fearfully await-
ing the worst, I went to my local bank branch. Usually, the
smartly turned out staff are all business, and never, ever, talk
about politics. On that day, it took no more than minutes before
the bank official looked nervously over his shoulder and declared,
"I don't trust the Communist Party, but what can we do?" I
doubt he was a frontline protestor, more likely just someone who
was worried and wanted to share his concerns with a non-threat-
ening stranger.

Two days after this encounter, the new law came into force,
dispelling any lingering doubts as to Beijing's determination to
stamp out dissent. On the surface, life as normal continued; but
it is hard to exaggerate the dark cloud that descended. The
promise of allowing Hong Kong a high degree of autonomy
crumbled not so much into dust as into a flurry of paper edicts,
with lethal consequences.

The National Security Law provides for the notorious
Mainland security police to be stationed in Hong Kong. They are
not answerable to local laws. Within days of the NSL's introduction from 1 July, a 33-storey hotel close to Victoria Park—the
historic location for protest rallies—was commandeered and
pressed into service as the new National Security Office headquarters. This Office is headed by Zheng Yanxiong, the former
Party boss in the neighbouring province of Guangdong. He has
a reputation as a hardline enforcer, having put down a widely
publicised democratic revolt in the southern township of Wukan.

Overall the Hong Kong government gave formal responsibility for implementing the law to a new Committee for Safeguarding National Security, theoretically headed by Chief
Executive Carrie Lam, and consisting mainly of officials from
the disciplined services such as the police. However, real power
lies with Beijing's National Security Advisor, in effect a commissar who directs the Committee's activities. This advisor is

Luo Huining, head of the Chinese government's Liaison Office in Hong Kong—as we will see in Chapter 2, this office is widely seen as a shadow government, pulling the strings of the bureaucrats who form the local administration.

The NSL is based on the Chinese legal system, and does away with the safeguards and transparency that are integral to the common law practised in Hong Kong. Instead the law has established the kind of legal framework found in a police state. Special courts have been set up to try cases under the new legislation, and they have been given harsh sentencing powers. Unlike the common law system, which specifies the nature of offences, this Mainland-style blunderbuss covers, without specificity, acts of subversion, terrorism, secession and collusion with a foreign country or external elements, to endanger national security.

This new judicial system is presided over by a panel of judges, handpicked by Carrie Lam under the guidance of "Big Brother from the North". In what are called "exceptional" cases, suspects will be shipped across the border to face Chinese courts, where there is never any doubt as to the outcome of trials. The jurisdiction of the NSL ranges beyond Hong Kong's borders to any crime committed under its umbrella, regardless of where it allegedly occurred. Under it, suspects can be held indefinitely; the presumption of innocence has been cast aside; and there is more, all of which will be familiar to anyone who has had the misfortune to experience how dictatorships work.

Once the law came into force, a truly alarming series of events unfolded in very quick succession. It took no more than hours for the first "national security" arrest to be made. The annual 1 July civil rights rally was banned. The most famous slogan of the uprising—"Liberate Hong Kong, Revolution of Our Times!"—was outlawed, on the grounds that it advocated separatism. The anthem of the protest movement, *Glory to Hong Kong*, was also deemed to be subversive. Public libraries and schools began the purge of dissident books. A high-profile raid was made on a public opinion polling organisation, deemed to have helped democrats organise a primary for candidates in September's upcoming legislative election.

And then the round-up of dissidents began, starting with the arrests of four students formally associated with a disbanded group advocating independence. Liu Xiaoming, China's hyperactive ambassador in London, immediately described those arrested as criminals. Even pretences at the assumption of innocence had evaporated. Arrests have since mounted, with purges of dissidents; the media has been reined in, and even judges, considered to have been "too lenient" in dealing with protestors, have been pushed aside.

On 1 September 2020, Carrie Lam explicitly confirmed the demise of "one country, two systems". She said: "Hong Kong is directly governed by the Central People's Government. In other words, the high degree of autonomy enjoyed by Hong Kong is not full autonomy. The executive power, legislative power, and judicial power are not a constitutional system that separates power from the central government. The rights that Hong Kong enjoys come from the authorisation of the central government."[4]

Arrests continued until the end of 2020 and were rapidly stepped up with an extraordinarily outbreak of activity on 6 January 2021, when some 1,000 police officers were mobilised to arrest fifty-three high-profile democracy activists on charges of subversion. These charges emanated from the holding of an election primary the previous year, designed to select candidates for the planned September 2020 legislative election. For the first time on 6 January, the police also raided and searched a solicitor's office and ordered three media organisations to hand over material to support the arrests. This completed the process of arresting and disqualifying from re-election all pro-democracy members elected to the legislature in 2016, and significantly accelerated the gradual round-up of pro-democracy district councilors. Those who remained on the councils were then put on notice that they too were likely to be eliminated, in a vetting process involving new loyalty pledges.

* * *

The kid gloves have been removed. The price Hongkongers are posed to pay for defying the dictatorship is clearly going to be very high. Yet the price China might be expected to pay in the international community and, possibly, at home is still to be fully played out. The Communist Party and its echo chamber in Hong Kong have been quick to claim victory in suppressing the protests, but history is likely to be a harsh critic of this assumption; the success of the NSL has not provoked a change of heart among the majority of Hongkongers. This is especially true among the younger generation, whose spirit of defiance lingers with extraordinary tenacity.

This book explores the Hong Kong protests, the reasons behind them and their somewhat extraordinary repercussions— because Hong Kong has truly become the canary in the cage. The survival of the Chinese dictatorship may well turn out not to depend on what happens in Hong Kong, and Beijing may manage to contain the challenges from its periphery; but the fractures have been exposed for all to see, demonstrating the brittle nature of Party rule. All dictatorships are strong and seemingly impregnable, right up to the point where they collapse. There is never a comforting interregnum of transition. The Communist Party regime in China is poised to outlive that of all modern-day autocracies, and history may be turned on its head to record that the Party has found the path to survival that eluded other dictatorships. In 2019–20, however, in no small part thanks to events in Hong Kong, this possibility has been placed in question.

INTRODUCTION

It is worth remembering how the Soviet Union, the PRC's mentor, collapsed. It was not in Russia where the seeds of collapse were sown, but in the outer periphery of nations occupied by the Soviet Union. Major uprisings had been put down in Hungary and Czechoslovakia, but with the clear vision offered by hindsight, we can now see that they hammered irreversible cracks into the formidable wall that once held up the Soviet Union.

Even if this comparison is considered tenuous, that is most certainly not the view taken by the Xi regime. Two months after the 2019 Hong Kong uprising began, Zhang Xiaoming, then head of Beijing's Hong Kong and Macau Affairs Office, said that the protests had "obvious characteristics of a colour revolution".[5] In other words, what was happening on the streets of Hong Kong bore a worrying resemblance to the Eastern European protests that brought down the Soviet Union. This parallel has been repeated by Chinese officials time and time again. China's Great Wall is still standing—but its foundations have been shaken in Hong Kong.

PART ONE

THE BACKGROUND

1

AN UNHAPPY FAMILY

China's long history is punctuated by extended periods of division within the nation, rebellions against the centre, and loss of control by the central government. The Communist Party's overriding fear, in Hong Kong as everywhere else in China, is what it calls "splitism". All measures are therefore justified to ensure that Hong Kong, a Special Administrative Region (SAR), nevertheless remains within the fold of a united nation; and to ensure that the virus of liberty does not spread to the Mainland. What matters to Beijing is total loyalty to China, which in turn means loyalty to the Party. As one of the regime's most popular slogans goes: "Without the Communist Party, there would be no New China". The irony is that the Party, born out of a belief in the Marxist slogan "Workers of the world unite", is today an ultra-nationalist organisation paying limited lip service to internationalism, instead burnishing its patriotic credentials as the mainstay of its legitimacy.

The CCP boasts that it has reversed China's dismal history of disunity and created a united, harmonious nation. In the Party's mind, this process has been exemplified by the recovery of

Macau, China's other SAR, ruled by the Portuguese until 1999. The enclave has since been brought under very tight control, in a manner that Hong Kong has not been. If this matter were to be considered in family terms, Macau—with a population of just about 650,000 people—could be considered the favoured son, while Hong Kong would be seen as the troublesome brat.

Much to the delight of Chinese officials, Macau nowadays feels more like a Mainland Chinese city than Hong Kong does. The issue of a distinct SAR identity has been solved in Macau by an enormous influx of Mainland immigrants; unlike in Hong Kong, most Macau residents were born across the border. As a result, Mandarin is much more widely spoken than in Hong Kong. What's more, on the surface at least, Macau has been more compliant in every way. A national security law was introduced there without much fuss. From day one of the handover back to China, Mainland officials were directly installed in the Macau government. And, unlike troublesome Hong Kong, Macau does not have a significant democracy movement, although opposition politics is not entirely absent.

In December 2019, President Xi Jinping pointedly turned up in Macau to preside over celebrations marking the twentieth handover anniversary. Without allowing the words Hong Kong to cross his lips, he showered praise on the people of Macau for their love of country and faith in "one country, two systems", placing their loyalty to Beijing above troublesome matters such as democracy, human rights and freedom. Macau government officials beamed as they were told how successful they had been in avoiding disputes and friction. They had, Xi said, understood the importance of harmony and unity, and had done a fantastic job integrating Macau with the Mainland.[1]

Although Xi alluded to the need for diversification of the economy, he was kind enough not to stress that Macau's business world is dominated by the gambling industry, accounting for over 80 per cent of the SAR's government revenues.[2] As a result, Macau has sped past Las Vegas to become the biggest gambling centre in the world. And, like gambling centres the world over, this business is replete with the criminality of money laundering, loan sharking and high levels of prostitution.

Macau, like Hong Kong, is also part of Greater Bay Area, linking the two SARs with nine cities in Guangdong, supposedly to create an economic powerhouse. And then there's the fantastically ambitious Chinese Belt and Road programme, which is designed to physically link China with some seventy nations in Asia, Europe and Africa. The idea is that Chinese-led trade and investment projects will create a new world order of prosperity. Hong Kong, with its great experience of international trade, is expected to play a major role in this initiative, and endless government propaganda is pumped out highlighting its importance. To put it mildly, implementation of Belt and Road has been patchy, and the tangible benefits of the initiative hardly match up to the rhetoric that surrounds it. In Hong Kong, however, both Belt and Road and, even more importantly, the Greater Bay Area initiative have considerable political importance in forging physical ties to the Mainland and bringing the two closer together.

Hong Kong and Macau have been paying a heavy price for turning the Greater Bay Area into a reality. The world's longest sea bridge, linking Hong Kong, Macau and Zhuhai (the Guangdong border town next to Macau), has cost billions of dollars; a high-speed rail link to Guangzhou, feeding into other Mainland rail lines, has also come with an eyewatering price tag. Both projects establish a very real, tangible link, but have turned out to be white elephants, as neither has even vaguely met the targets set for usage. Nonetheless, more "linking" projects with impressive price tags are in the pipeline, including a new hi-tech city straddling the border between Hong Kong and Shenzhen.

As the official propaganda machine has been put to work to talk up these developments, they have largely been met with indifference by people in Hong Kong. Instead of enthusiasm, there is annoyance over how much all of this is costing. In January 2020, the Hong Kong Guangdong Youth Association, one of many pro-China organisations, published a survey showing that 70 per cent of young people interviewed thought Hong Kong would be better advised to keep its distance from the Mainland. Moreover, in the cohort of interviewees between the ages of 15 and 64, almost 60 per cent said that the Greater Bay Area plan would bring more harm than good to Hong Kong.[3] It is quite surprising that a body such as this should have published findings of this kind, but it reflects the reality: low enthusiasm on the ground for schemes to bring Hong Kong closer to the rest of China.

More broadly, Beijing's process of "reunifying" its peripheries has remained stubbornly difficult. Macau has accepted the imposition of tight control from Beijing, but that task remains to be completed in Hong Kong. And an even bigger gaping hole in the reunification process persists: not only does Taiwan remain stubbornly independent but, to the PRC's fury, it has all the trappings of a sovereign state. To understand how all this has come about, and why it is so troubling for Beijing, requires an understanding of history—which, as ever, shows that unintended consequences have played a major formative role in events, informing both Hongkongers' and China's position in the confrontation of 2019–20.

After the fall of Shanghai to the Japanese in 1937, the most international part of the Chinese nation lost this role; its place was taken by Hong Kong, a tiny dot on the southern periphery, occupied by the British. Most of Hong Kong's territory is attached to the Chinese Mainland; only a small area, the original

Hong Kong, is an island, today housing the government head-quarters and central business district.

Hong Kong became a British colony in 1842 for the simple reason that the ailing Qing Dynasty (1644–1912) decided to hand over this unwanted piece of territory as an alternative to letting the British get their hands on parts of China that were actually considered valuable. The British, for their part, were hardly enthusiastic. They would really have liked to establish a colony in Canton (now Guangzhou); even tiny Macau would have been a better bet for London's imperial ambitions, but the Portuguese were too well established there.

It could even be argued that the colony was largely created by accident, after China started cracking down on the opium traders. In characteristic imperial response, Britain sent out gunboats to defend its drug-trading citizens in the far-flung South China Sea. Captain Charles Elliot, commander of the British force, had no precise instructions from London about what to do, other than to defend British interests. So, in view of Hong Kong's deep and wide natural harbour, Elliot decided to plant the Union flag and claim possession of Hong Kong Island. The foreign secretary, Lord Palmerston, was furious: "You have disobeyed and neglected your instructions", he raged in a letter sent to the now disgraced Elliot. Hong Kong, said Palmerston, was nothing more than a "barren island".[4]

It took another two years before the signing of the Treaty of Nanjing, ending the First Opium War, gave effect to this land grab. Notwithstanding the solemnity of this accord, the first of what China would come to call the Unequal Treaties, the ceding of Hong Kong was of little significance to either of the signing parties. But what were the views of the people who lived in Hong Kong at this time? It was a question that never even crossed the minds of the Chinese and British negotiators who created the colony. Besides which, the population was minus-cule—no more than a few thousand.

Within two decades, however, the new colony's population had grown sixteen times. It was not because those crossing over from the Mainland had any burning desire to live under the British flag. Their main motivation was simply to escape problems in China. The 1850s Taiping Rebellion proved to be crucial in giving a boost to Hong Kong by creating this exodus. It set a pattern of people arriving from China, primarily to avoid chaos and poverty, with little regard or indeed awareness of what the colonial alternative entailed.

This ignorance was also evident among the British, who had no real plan for their largely unwanted possession, aside from the notion of creating a free trade port and a commercial centre. Yet such was the relentless logic of empire that Britain went on to negotiate two other treaties extending its territory in Hong Kong. The third, the 1898 Convention of Beijing, gave the British the largest piece of landmass attached to the Chinese Mainland, which became known as the New Territories. As the New Territories became the biggest part of Hong Kong, continued British rule became unfeasible without this swathe of land. However, whereas the previous agreements had granted Britain the land in perpetuity, this third concession was a ninety-nine-year lease—a time span dreamt up with little thought for what might happen in 1997, when the lease would expire.

Despite the indifference of the people who mattered in both London and Peking, Hong Kong continued to grow, and the full paraphernalia of a Crown colony developed. As the Qing Dynasty slunk into terminal decline, there were many reasons for people to leave the Mainland and try their luck in Hong Kong. Most of them came from the neighbouring Guangdong Province, and a great many thought that the British colony would be no more than a resting place to wait out the storm before returning to a more stable China. But, as China went from crisis to crisis, the exodus to Hong Kong grew, and the authorities on the Mainland were far too preoccupied with a host of other problems to spend time thinking about getting the British to return their territory. Besides which, in a manner that became even more pronounced after the 1949 Communist Revolution, Hong Kong had demonstrated its usefulness to the Mainland as an entrepôt and a place where business could be conducted on behalf of those across the border.

The turning point in the colony's growth came with that same Revolution, which turned the exodus from the Mainland into a flood—one that continues in different ways to this day. In the late 1940s and early 1950s, the arriving refugees were no longer just poor peasants and workers; they had been joined by wealthy people, primarily from Shanghai, who had every reason to fear a Communist regime and every reason to flee, taking as much of their considerable wealth with them as possible. Despite the rapidly disintegrating Nationalist government's half-hearted attempts to regain Chinese sovereignty over Hong Kong in the wake of World War Two, the Communist regime that proclaimed the People's Republic on 1 October 1949 did no more than make nominal protests over continued British rule.

This attitude started to change in the 1970s, as China began opening up to the Western world. However it was the British, rather than the Chinese, who brought things to a head, as it dawned on officials in London that the New Territories lease would be expiring in 1997 and that clarity needed to be obtained over the colony's future.

A crucial meeting was held in March 1979 between China's paramount leader Deng Xiaoping and the Governor of Hong Kong, Murray MacLehose. This was the first time that a Hong Kong governor had meet a Chinese official of this seniority. The British idea was to find a way of extending the New Territories lease, but Deng was uninterested. Instead he delivered a long monologue that focused on the need for Chinese sovereignty to be resumed. He spoke of how a special status would be created for the territory and insisted that Hong Kong's capitalist system would be preserved. This came out of the blue as far as London was concerned, but clearly the Chinese had given considerable thought to the matter. Typically, no one from Hong Kong was involved in these discussions, and when Murray returned to the colony he gave no hint of what was in store. Instead he quoted Deng's remarks about Hong Kong people "putting their hearts at ease", which was taken to mean that the status quo was to be maintained.

Having delivered the bombshell in 1979, China decided to say no more in public until the visit to Beijing by British Prime Minister Margaret Thatcher in September 1982. She was in buoyant mood and very confident of Britain's place in the world following victory in the Falklands War. By now, however, the Chinese Communist Party's plans had solidified and Britain's colonial posturing was of little interest. Beijing was happy to tell the world that it intended to resume sovereignty. Deng spelled out to Thatcher that "On the question of sovereignty, China has no room for manoeuvre. To be frank, the question is not open to discussion. The time is ripe for making it unequivocally clear that China will recover Hong Kong in 1997."[5]

While a certain amount of behind-the-scenes negotiation rumbled along, neither side thought it advisable to let Hongkongers themselves know what was going on. The first direct approach to the people of the colony was made in November 1982, two months after Thatcher's visit to Beijing. Typically, it came in the form of a meeting with one of the colony's grandees, Sir Yuet-keung Kan, who was leading the first mission to China by the Hong Kong Trade Development Council. Kan was summoned to see Xi Zhong Xun, Vice-Chairman of the National People's Congress Standing Committee, to be told bluntly that China would not contemplate a deal over sovereignty and that the return to Chinese rule was set in stone.

Formal Sino-British negotiations finally began in late 1982, which resulted in the Sino-British Joint Declaration on the Question of Hong Kong, an international treaty signed on 19 December 1984 in Beijing. Two months before this, Hong Kong's colonial government embarked on a so-called consultation exercise, with the important caveat making it "clear beyond any possibility of misunderstanding" that the agreement could not be modified. This farcical attempt to pretend that Hong Kong's people had been consulted on their future mainly consisted of regurgitating opinion polls and newspaper articles, alongside consultation with a number of colony notables and civil society organisations. Unsurprisingly, the British government concluded that the agreement enjoyed broad support.

This conclusion was not entirely without foundation, however, because China was making considerable efforts to assure Hong Kong people of its intention to continue business as usual. This pledge was encapsulated in Deng Xiaoping's famous statement at the time of Thatcher's visit that, after 1997, "Horses will still run, stocks will still sizzle, dancers will still dance." Beijing stressed that it had no intention of imposing socialism on Hong Kong and that a system of "one country, two systems" would be put in place, allowing for the resumption of Chinese sovereignty while ensuring that Hong Kong could pursue its existing way of life, within a structure that provided a "high level of autonomy" to what would become the Hong Kong Special Administrative Region.[6]

These promises were enshrined in the Basic Law, a mini-constitution for Hong Kong. There are a number of key "General Principles" outlined at the start of the law, which appear to be unambiguous in setting out how the new SAR was to be governed.[7]

Article 2 is the most important. It says: "The National People's Congress authorizes the Hong Kong Special Administrative

Region to exercise a high degree of autonomy and enjoy executive, legislative and independent judicial power, including that of final adjudication, in accordance with the provisions of this Law."

Article 3 makes it clear that Hong Kong will be governed only by permanent residents of the territory. This is a coded way of saying that Mainland Chinese officials will not be running Hong Kong.

Article 4 states that the "rights and freedoms" of the SAR will be safeguarded. This is the clause dealing with the preservation of the social and political framework that sets Hong Kong apart from the rest of China.

Article 5 explains the "one country, two systems" principle, under which Hong Kong is exempt from practising the socialist system which prevails in China, and "the previous capitalist system and way of life shall remain unchanged for 50 years". Deng Xiaoping added to this by promising that this time limit could well be extended.

However, China's intentions might not have been this simple. The indications are that Deng Xiaoping's original vision of "one country, two systems" was really focused on the toleration of economic, not political, differences between the two systems; he did not dwell on that other profound aspect of allowing two systems to flourish. As the father of China's economic Reform and Opening Up policy, and a believer in the benefits of capitalism for economic development, Deng concentrated on the idea of Hong Kong as a global commercial centre and its ability to contribute to China's development. In fact he believed that a fundamental condition for China to grow and for Hong Kong to prosper was for socialism to be the basis of the economy on the Mainland, and for capitalism to flourish in Hong Kong.

Addressing members of the committee drafting Hong Kong's Basic Law in 1987, Deng said: "Try to imagine what would happen to Hong Kong if China changed its socialist system, the socialist system with Chinese characteristics under the leadership of the Communist Party. That would be the end of prosperity and stability for Hong Kong. To make sure the policy remains unchanged for 50 years and beyond, we must keep the socialist system on the Mainland unchanged."[8]

* * *

Even before 1997, China had begun the process of whittling away its promises. After the handover there was a frenzy of tearing down structural reminders of British colonial rule. The famous red letter boxes, with their royal insignia, were replaced by plain green ones, or painted over; pictures of colonial officials were removed from government buildings; and great efforts were made to liberally sprinkle China's five-star flag around the city. These are essentially cosmetic changes, but reflect the notion that the past needs to be kept under wraps.

More substantial than the colour of letter boxes is the reality that Hong Kong never had an opportunity to elect its own government. As British rule was coming to an end, Chris Patten, Hong Kong's last governor, introduced a raft of political reforms designed to promote greater democracy. In essence he expanded the number of legislators and district councillors elected through a process of universal suffrage. Beijing, however, strongly objected, despite the fact that the Basic Law promises the introduction of universal suffrage. China was prepared to offer elections, but wanted them implemented on its own terms. What this really meant only emerged in 2014, when Beijing offered the people of Hong Kong the opportunity to elect the Chief Executive by universal suffrage—but without a free choice of candidates. Only those approved by the Beijing-controlled Election Committee would be allowed to stand. This, then, was the model for Communist Party-style universal suffrage, and this is what sparked the Umbrella Movement protests, widely said to have failed, but successful in thwarting the passing of a bill that would have brought this plan into law.

Beijing may have unveiled democracy with Chinese characteristics in 2014, but the direction of travel had been signalled for some time. First came the establishment of a Provisional Legislative Council in November 1996, a year ahead of the handover. The main purpose of this transitional legislature was to roll back the democratic reforms initiated by Governor Patten. The council, which met in the border town of Shenzhen, was made up exclusively of Beijing trustees, "elected" by a committee of 400 other trustees. After the handover, it would take over from the colonial Legislative Council and lay the groundwork for the kind of legislation that the central government in Beijing wanted to see implemented. Also in 1996, Vice-Premier Qian Qichen gave an interview to the *Asian Wall Street Journal*, in which he started spelling out what forms of expression would not be tolerated by the new order. There could be no criticism of the Chinese leadership, and no "interference" in Chinese Mainland affairs, such as rallies to commemorate the Tiananmen Square massacre; and the media would have to confine itself to "facts", rather than opinions.[9]

Perhaps more attention should have been paid to a speech that Deng Xiaoping made to the Basic Law drafters back in 1987, when he commented on his famous slogan, *gangren zhigang*, which translates as Hong Kong people ruling (or administering) Hong Kong. In this speech Deng warned that the slogan could not be taken as a green light for self-rule. He said: "Don't ever think that everything would be all right if Hong Kong's affairs were administered solely by Hong Kong people while the central government had nothing to do with the matter. That simply wouldn't work—it's not a realistic idea. The central government certainly will not intervene in the day-to-day affairs of the Special Administrative Region, nor is it necessary. But isn't it possible that something could happen in the region that jeopardises the fundamental interests of the country?"[10]

While warnings of what was to come were there even before the PRC resumed control over Hong Kong, the full reality of what autonomy would look like was only revealed in a series of slow drips, which turned into a flow of direct interventions from Beijing making it clear that Hong Kong's promised "high degree of autonomy" had fast-shrinking parameters.

Within two years of the SAR's establishment, the authority of the courts was severely shaken by the first of, at the time of writing, five "interpretations" of Court of Final Appeal rulings; in all but one case, overruling judgments made in Hong Kong's highest court. The power of interpreting the constitution on the Mainland resides in Article 158 of the Basic Law, but it had been thought that Article 2 (cited above) would ensure that this power would be exercised with great restraint, and confined to matters specifically concerning Beijing's constitutional relationship with Hong Kong. This assumption was killed stone dead with the first "interpretation". In 1999, the National People's Congress Standing Committee, the executive of China's rubber-stamp parliament, issued an edict overturning a Hong Kong verdict on the right of abode for children of Hong Kong residents.

This was followed in 2004 by an "interpretation" of the law relating to the election of the Chief Executive. A year later there was a ruling on how the Chief Executive could be replaced. And in 2016, when the government was looking for ways of overturning the election of democratic legislators, the Standing Committee came up with a ruling on correct methods of oath-taking for office, accompanied by a prohibition on retaking oaths deemed to have been incorrectly delivered. On only one occasion to date has the Hong Kong court itself asked Beijing for an interpretation: a case involving diplomatic immunity over a Congolese mining contract with a Chinese state company.

* * *

Hong Kong is not alone in seeing promised autonomy undermined. Aside from the two SARs, Hong Kong and Macau, China has a history of establishing "autonomous regions" on its peripheries: Inner Mongolia in 1947, Xinjiang in 1955, Guangxi and Ningxia in 1958, and Tibet in 1965. What these diverse places have in common is a complex of ethnicities and a hollow promise of self-government. On top of this, Xinjiang and Tibet are marked by ruthless oppression to extinguish national identities, religious practices and all other forms of distinctiveness seen as challenging the unity of the Chinese state. Under Xi Jinping's rule, China has been unrolling a programme of regulations to "strengthen ethnic unity" while maintaining a focus on the unity of the nation. What this double-speak appears to mean is that the autonomous regions are allowed to engage in harmless efforts to promote tourism and handicraft industries, and even encourage employment of minority groups—as long as none of this undermines the unity of the People's Republic.

The paramount importance of a unitary state with little room for distinctiveness is not an invention of the Chinese Communist Party. On the contrary, it is embedded in Chinese history dating from the Qin Dynasty in 221 BCE.[11] The Communist Party's contribution to the enhancement of a unified China came in the form of acknowledging that cultural differences existed, while creating the illusion of political or governmental diversity. In heading down this route, the Party was emulating the Soviet Union, which also had a highly diverse population, and established fifteen "union republics", all fully furnished with the trappings of what might be described as federalism. But, like their PRC successors, these autonomous regions were nothing but a sham.

The reality is that diversity is only tolerated when it comes in the quiet, apolitical forms favoured by the Party. At major national gatherings, for example, there is always a smattering of participants dressed in colourful "ethnic" costumes; they may even be called upon for a song or a dance. But woe betide any of these "ethnics" if they actually start speaking to each other in their own language, or dare to suggest that their national identity overrides that of the Chinese state. The condescension with which these minorities are treated is nothing short of repugnant.

All of the PRC's autonomous regions started out with a majority of non-Han people, but the Party pursued a policy of making ethnic-minority people a minority in their own regions, settling Han Chinese in these areas to an extent that the original population was overwhelmed. Ethnicity has always been of great importance in China, and even today overseas Han Chinese are treated differently from other foreigners. This also, incidentally, explains why Hong Kong's history of providing permanent residence to people of other ethnicities, notably communities from the Indian sub-continent as well as mixed-race Europeans, is met with a level of incomprehension on the Mainland.

That said, the overwhelming majority of people in Hong Kong, as in Taiwan and Macau, are Han Chinese. These places' differences with the Mainland are not of ethnicity, but of history, culture and way of life. Deng's innovative "one country, two systems" concept was designed to address these differences and offer the special privilege of preserving them.

Yet it is hard to exaggerate the extent to which China has been preoccupied by the issue of reunification of the nation, above all bringing Taiwan back into the fold—and equally hard to overstate the extent to which Beijing's handling of Hong Kong has undermined this primary goal.

Beijing's Taiwan Affairs Office is supposedly working night and day to reintegrate Taiwan into the People's Republic. In a statement outlining its crucial mission, the Office said: "Settlement of the Taiwan issue and realization of the complete reunification of China embodies the fundamental interests of the

Chinese nation. The Chinese government has worked persistently toward this goal in the past 50 years."[12] Indeed, China has made no bones about the fact that Taiwan is the main target of the "one country, two systems" concept, while Hong Kong and Macau are the testing grounds. As the principle was originally conceived to lure Taiwan back into China, its design had to approach the process with kid gloves, given the history of separation from the Mainland and long period of governance by the bitterly anti-Communist Kuomintang (KMT).

Taiwan, which officially calls itself the Republic of China, has all the trappings of an independent state: its own army, own government, own currency, own judicial system and so on. Taiwan has often grown apart from the Mainland, not least during the years 1895–1945, when the island was under Japanese rule. There was then an uncomfortable interregnum from the end of World War Two until 1949. At this point, the KMT was defeated in China's Civil War, and fled to establish a dictatorship on Taiwan; meanwhile, Mao's Communists proclaimed the People's Republic of China on the Mainland. And Taiwan has posed a challenge to the PRC ever since.

In the early days of KMT rule over Taiwan, when defeat on the Mainland was still raw, there was a lingering idea within the party that the Mainland could be retaken. The impossibility of realising this dream led to the establishment of a state that identified itself by its opposition to the PRC, as a "relocated" Republic of China. However, as time went on, the Kuomintang began to appreciate that the basis of its legitimacy could not be grounded in an unrealistic goal of developing a rival China. It made more sense to work hard in developing Taiwan, and finding a way to live with the PRC.

Thanks largely to Chiang Ching-kuo, who succeeded his father Chiang Kai-shek as president in 1978, Taiwan was peacefully transformed into a democracy. Chiang realised that having a mirror-image dictatorship on his side of the Taiwan Straits was as unsustainable as the dream of retaking the Chinese Mainland. The much underrated Chiang ensured that the KMT dictatorship was dissolved and transformed into a democratic party, but he died before his success was sealed with the election of his vice-president, Lee Teng-hui, as president of Taiwan. After leaving office Lee became an outspoken advocate for Taiwanese independence from the Mainland, but his KMT successors would move ever closer to the Communist Party in Beijing.

Given the history, it had seemed highly unlikely that the two parties would ever again find common ground. Nevertheless, this is what happened, as the KMT emerged as democratic Taiwan's bastion of Chinese unification politics, in opposition to the so-called "nativist" parties, which had no desire for reunification. With power moving between the KMT and the Taiwan-centric Democratic Progressive Party (DPP), the CCP realised that their best hope of luring Taiwan back into the fold was to work with the KMT. A democratic Taiwan, offering a quite different alternative, was a far bigger challenge to the PRC than a forever-posturing ROC threatening to invade the Mainland. Over the decades, then, the Kuomintang's stance in favour of reunification led to a significant—though ebbing and flowing—degree of collaboration with the CCP. As we saw in the Introduction, hopes were high in Beijing that the January 2020 Taiwanese presidential election would mark another high point in this co-operation, with a KMT victory.

The DPP's candidate was the incumbent President Tsai Ing-wen. An unassuming and not obviously charismatic politician, she appeared to have every chance of losing her job. The KMT was rising high with a dynamic candidate, Han Kuo-yu, who was polling well and looked set to succeed. He had previously caused something of a political earthquake by winning the mayoral contest in the southern city of Kaohsiung, which had been a DPP stronghold. Han was actively backed by Beijing and even made a visit to Hong Kong, where he was received by Hong Kong's Chief Executive, Carrie Lam. It looked as though the KMT bandwagon was going to be unstoppable.

And that was the case—right up until Hong Kong protests broke out in June 2019. Taiwanese citizens looked on with a mixture of admiration and alarm as mass demonstrations defied Beijing and as the crackdown was rolled out. While Han was slow to respond to this development, President Tsai quickly realised that this was a gamechanger. At DPP rallies she never failed to cite Hong Kong as a reminder of the dangers of "one country, two systems". Part of Tsai's new pitch to voters, outlined in a speech marking Taiwan's National Day in October, was to say: "When freedom and democracy are challenged, and when the Republic of China's existence and development are threatened, we must stand up and defend ourselves." In the same speech, she added: "The overwhelming consensus among Taiwan's 23 million people is our rejection of 'one country, two systems,' regardless of party affiliation or political position."[13]

The KMT had never quite embraced the concept of "one country, two systems", but never outright rejected it either. Now the party found itself in a quandary, made all the more acute through the second half of 2019 as the Hong Kong uprising developed and Tsai's ratings steadily improved.

Chinese officials, who are hardly experts in the business of democratic elections, anxiously observed developments in Taiwan and were very unsure how to respond. A Communist Party Central Committee meeting held shortly before the election offered a distinctly conciliatory approach to Taiwan, saying in an official communiqué: "When national sovereignty, security and developmental interests can be guaranteed, after peaceful reunification, we will fully respect our Taiwanese compatriots' societal system and way of life, while fully safeguarding our Taiwanese compatriots' private property, religions and legitimate rights."[14] But, days before the poll in January, Xi Jinping adopted a rather more aggressive tone, insisting that reunification was inevitable. He added, "We make no promise to renounce the use of force and reserve the option of taking all necessary means."[15]

Tsai Ing-wen could not have dared wish for a better vote-getter than the Chinese Communist Party. Eventually, the KMT was forced into an outright rejection of "one country, two systems", but to no avail, as Tsai scored an easy victory at the polls. When the dust of the election settled, Tsai emerged as the greatest beneficiary from the Hong Kong uprising. Her victory was achieved precisely because people living in an atmosphere of freedom decisively rejected the idea that their society should become anything like Hong Kong. And, as we shall see in Chapters 9 and 10, events in Hong Kong went a long way in bringing Taiwan back into the embrace of the international community.

Final ignominy was inflicted on the defeated KMT presidential candidate Han in June 2020, when he was also kicked out of office as mayor of Kaohsiung, after a highly unusual referendum. Beijing's disquiet over these results was intensified by the glee with which Tsai's re-election was received in Hong Kong. Those involved in the democracy movement had seen images of their protests flashing up on screens at DPP rallies; they had heard leader after leader denounce "one country, two systems", and had been impressed by the warmth shown them by the Taiwanese.

* * *

When Xi Jinping came to power in 2012, there had been some hope that he would follow in the footsteps of his father, Xi Zhongxun—a close associate of Deng Xiaoping known for his reformist views. This has proven to be wishful thinking in the extreme. According to Richard McGregor, a veteran observer of Chinese politics, the Xi regime has "gone back in time, with echoes of the Maoist era, a period of ruthless purges, ideological education, loyalty tests and personality cults".[16]

McGregor goes further, pointing out: "Gradually, and then in a rush, Xi has ditched or unwound most if not all of the political advances that had been considered instrumental to modern China's success. Not only did Xi upend the system at home. Xi's China is now playing a different game abroad as well."[17] As far as Hong Kong is concerned, Xi has had equally forthright ambitions: to end the "high degree of autonomy" that China's leaders were clearly now regretting despite having granted in the first place.

With the benefit of hindsight, we can see that the key to the Xi regime's intentions in the SAR was made clear in a Chinese government white paper published in 2014—the same year as the proposal for a Beijing-controlled Chief Executive election. This paper gave the first indication of a hardening of the Party's approach to Hong Kong, referencing its "comprehensive jurisdiction" over the territory. In the years that followed, which saw a succession of unprecedented pronouncements on the matter, it became evident that this white paper had been a signal of Beijing's intention to whittle down Hong Kong's freedoms. In 2015 Zhang Xiaoming, the director of Beijing's Central Liaison Office in Hong Kong, airily dismissed the notion that there could be such a thing as a separation of powers in Hong Kong. The executive, legislature and judiciary should, he said, come under the power of the Chief Executive. Only sovereign states, he argued, could enjoy the luxury of separation of powers.[18]

However, it was not until October 2019, with the uprising in full swing, that the Party finally spelled out what this actually meant for Hong Kong, and how Beijing's thinking had evolved. This followed a meeting of the Communist Party Central Committee, the fourth plenary session of the 19th Central Committee (apologies, but these cumbersome formulations are the bread and butter of China's bureaucratic system).[19] A subsequent press conference gave Shen Chunyao, director of the rubber-stamp parliament's Legislative Affairs Commission, the opportunity to elaborate on what had been decided about Hong Kong.

What Shen said marked a sharp departure from previous policy in a number of worrying ways. According to the former journalist Willy Lam, Shen's message was that Beijing would have authority to "exercise full control over all aspects of policy-making" in Hong Kong.[20] Lam, an adjunct professor at Hong Kong's Chinese University, is one of the foremost China analysts in the territory. He viewed this meeting, with its unprecedented degree of focus on Hong Kong, as a seminal moment in the evolution of China's policy towards its wayward Special Administrative Region. Among the significant decisions taken were that the National People's Congress Standing Committee, in other words the ruling body of China's "legislature", would have greater powers to "interpret" the Basic Law. What this actually meant, to go by the previous "interpretations" detailed earlier in the chapter, was amendments to the mini-constitution, allowing the committee to impose legislation that it feared might not be passed by Hong Kong's own Legislative Council (Legco). Now, said Lam, it was likely that these powers would be used to bypass Legco entirely, and enforce a national security law by way of such an "interpretation". He was right, as this was precisely what happened almost a year later.

Shen also signalled that tighter control would be exercised over the appointment and removal of Hong Kong officials. This was despite all previous assurances that Beijing's nominal power of confirming appointments would be precisely that: nominal. There would also be a stepped-up programme of national education to "increase national consciousness and patriotism". And further measures would be taken to escalate the integration of Hong Kong's economy with other parts of southern China under the Greater Bay Area scheme. Just as significant as what Shen mentioned was what was omitted from official accounts of the meeting's proceedings. There was no mention of "Hong Kong people running Hong Kong" or of a "high degree of autonomy", both mantras that had previously been repeated extensively whenever the SAR was under discussion.

It is not clear how long this policy was in the making, but the eventual public airing of the new direction in autumn 2019, with the uprising in full swing, explained perfectly why, as weeks dragged on into months of protest, the Hong Kong government had not shown the slightest intention of engaging in talks with the protestors, nor contemplated meeting any of their demands. The hardest of hard lines was in force. However, as the Communist Party has repeatedly demonstrated, it is always possible to go further, beyond whatever hard line happens already to have been in force.

In November 2019, this was made explicit in relation to the judiciary. The trigger was a Hong Kong High Court decision to overrule the Lam government's imposition of emergency powers to outlaw the wearing of face masks, which were being used by the protestors to deflect the effects of tear gas and disguise their identities. Zang Tiewe, a spokesman for the legislature's Standing Committee (NPCSC), immediately issued a statement castigating the court for not complying with the Basic Law and ignoring the sole right of the NPCSC to interpret SAR law. He said, "Whether Hong Kong's laws are consistent with the Basic Law can only be judged and decided by the NPCSC. No other authority has the right to make judgments and decisions."[21]

Although it had long been feared that Beijing was prepared to slash away at the foundations of Hong Kong's independent legal system and ignore Article 2 of the Basic Law, this determination had never before been made explicit. It prompted Andrew Li, a former Chief Justice who rarely comments on such matters, to say: "The statement appears to suggest that the Hong Kong courts have no power to hold Hong Kong legislation to be invalid on the ground of inconsistency with the Basic Law. If this is what was meant, it is surprising and alarming."[22]

Questioning the independence of the judiciary has continued, amidst fears that China will directly intervene in the matter of judicial appointments, supposedly undertaken by an independent body whose recommendations are submitted to the Chief Executive. This political supervision of the judiciary deepened with the introduction of the National Security Law in July 2020. As we have seen, the NSL empowers the Chief Executive to select judges for cases brought under the law.

As for the independence of the legislature, always limited as we'll see in Chapter 2, again Article 2 of the Basic Law has been brought into question—in this case as early as 2004, when the Hong Kong and Macau Affairs Office in Beijing made its views known on the Chief Executive's annual policy address, a policy statement entirely confined to Hong Kong's internal affairs. A far more forceful intervention was made in April 2020, when the Office expressed strong concern over the way that the Legislative Council's House Committee had fallen into stalemate, effectively stalling the passage of legislation. It went further, accusing the opposition legislator Dennis Kwok, acting chairman of the committee, of allowing filibustering, making him liable to prosecution for misconduct in public office, a very serious criminal offence. Kwok was subsequently disqualified from standing for re-election, and later expelled from membership of the legislature.

This blatant attack on a member of Legco might have caused Beijing's puppets in Hong Kong to pause and reflect. On the contrary, they released a flurry of supporting statements, from the Chief Executive downwards. Carrie Lam said: "When the Legislative Council is almost malfunctioning ... I find it only legitimate for them to express concern."[23] More worryingly, Tam

Yiu-chung, who ranks as the seniormost Hong Kong representative in China's legislature, insisted that "one country, two systems" should not be understood as confining Beijing's statements of its position to matters such as national defence or political reform.[24]

Lurking in the background to all these direct assaults on Hong Kong's autonomy, which came thick and fast during the 2019–20 uprising, was a pattern within the administration of second-guessing the leaders in Beijing and self-censoring for fear of provoking the bosses' ire. Senior government officials in Hong Kong are constantly looking over their shoulders, a habit that has become endemic. The rot started with Tung Chee-hwa, the first chief executive of the HKSAR (1997–2005). Tung, a former shipping tycoon, became an ultra-loyalist after his company was bailed out by China. As Chief Executive, he employed the worst management style: micro-managing combined with indecision. According to officials who worked with him, he was forever referring decisions to the Central Liaison Office, to an extent that even they became exasperated.

In this, Tung established a pattern of deference that has been followed by his successors. All matters of importance now coming before Hong Kong's Executive Council are accompanied by a note on "Mainland implications" or, where there are greater doubts, "possible Mainland objections". It is hard to establish when this precise practice began, but its existence demonstrates that the government, down to the most minor parts of the bureaucracy, is constantly looking to Beijing on matters of policy.

More than this is the depressing willingness of Hong Kong's establishment to go along with this process of undermining autonomy. It is very hard to find an example of any senior official prepared to stand up for Hong Kong's interests in the face of Mainland pressure. This supine attitude was laughably underlined in November 2015, when Hong Kong faced China in a FIFA World Cup qualifier. Asked which team he was supporting, the deeply unpopular Chief Executive Leung Chun-ying ducked the question on grounds of sensitivity. In a subsequent Facebook post, he congratulated both teams for "giving it [their] all". Irony aficionados will note that the final score in this game was a sterile 0–0 draw.

* * *

In May 2020, all previous Mainland attempts to diminish the reality of Hong Kong's promised autonomy were entirely over-shadowed by a seemingly sudden decision: to entirely bypass the Hong Kong government and legislature by having the NPCSC impose from Beijing a wide-ranging national security law. This may not have been quite as out of the blue as it appeared—there was intense impatience and a sense of bewilderment among Chinese officials over the fact that, two decades after the hand-over of power, the SAR had still failed to introduce such legisla-tion. The failure to act added to Beijing's suspicion that Hong Kong people not only lack patriotism, but are intransigent and deficient in their understanding of the Motherland.

Shortly after Carrie Lam was appointed Chief Executive in 2017, she met President Xi Jinping in Beijing. Yet again, he emphasised the need for Hong Kong to get this law on the statute books. Lam's decision to start the ball rolling with an ill-fated extradition bill in 2019 (see Chapter 5) was initially regarded with indifference in Beijing, but this turned to anger when it became clear that the uproar provoked by this bill was delaying introduc-tion of the much-more-important National Security Law.

The full impact of the NSL in Hong Kong is yet to be seen, but it is very clear how the Chinese regime has used supposed threats to national security as a pretext for extinguishing all opposition on the Mainland. Laws of this kind were used against the Nobel Peace Prize laureate Liu Xiaobo, against lawyers who have defended dissidents, and in myriad other ways against those involved in even minor protests throughout the country. Like all dictatorships, the PRC is obsessed by questions of national security. It is paranoid about what it sees as attempts to undermine or overthrow the government. And, again in common with other regimes that outlaw all forms of dissent, the Chinese state allows no space for legal opposition, turning those who question the government into threats to state security.

In Hong Kong, though, there had been space for a legal opposition, and sufficient freedom of speech to allow criticism. This difference has been a source of perpetual concern to the leaders in Beijing, even though Hong Kong's autonomies are guaranteed under the Basic Law. It is very hard for people who run a one-party state to understand how a free society operates, or to appreciate the thinking of citizens who have experienced a heady diet of liberty and are reluctant to change it for something else. So, in the unhappy relationship between Hong Kong and the Mainland, suspicion mixes freely with incomprehension, and produces the kind of frustration that boils over.

Hongkongers, on the other side of this tempestuous relationship, return the suspicion and lack of understanding in spades. Moreover, they have a history of looking down on their Mainland counterparts. They have been richer and better educated, have enjoyed a vastly superior standard of living, and have definitely harboured something of a "country bumpkin" attitude towards their Mainland counterparts. This was fostered by the fact that a great many Hongkongers were materially supporting both their relatives and others in the Mainland, as disaster after disaster afflicted people on the other side of the border. Of course this support was welcome, especially during acute periods of distress such as the three-year Great Famine which began in 1959, and the Cultural Revolution that swept through the PRC in the late 1960s, murdering, imprisoning and adding to impoverishment.

The resentment of Hongkongers has not changed as the Mainland itself has grown richer. As the writer and journalist Lee

Yee explained, this relative prosperity did bring a change in the relationship, but not a favourable one. He wrote: "As the country grew and its economy boomed, China reversed its stance and began despising Hongkongers, claiming the prosperity and robust economic development of Hong Kong was a 'hand-out' from the Mainland."[25] Whichever way round things are viewed, it hardly makes for a comfortable relationship. The Party's narrative focuses on Hong Kong's intransigence, accusing its people of having a "colonial mentality" or "Western-looking mentality"—a theme that has been taken up enthusiastically by foreign apologists for the Chinese government.

In a sense, this narrative is true, because Hongkongers have been far more exposed to international thinking and ways of doing things than Chinese on the Mainland. So there is a real gap in attitudes. But what is not politically convenient to mention is the fact that, given exposure to free and open societies, Hongkongers are far more likely to choose liberty over a tightly controlled dictatorship. In Beijing's eyes, this simply denotes a lack of national pride. Seen from this perspective, it is little wonder that so much suspicion lingers over the people of Hong Kong.

Despite endless and even herculean efforts by Beijing to portray the relationship with Hong Kong and indeed Taiwan as akin to that of a happy family, the reality is somewhat different. Maybe the happy family has actually been achieved in Macau, but Macau's compliance has only been secured by literally changing the composition of the population, importing a vast number of Mainlanders. There is a hint here of Bertolt Brecht's famously satirical remarks about the Communist Party of East Germany: "the people had lost the government's confidence / And could only regain it with redoubled effort. / In that case, would it not be simpler if the government simply dissolved the people and elected another?"

2

A FARCICAL POLITICAL SYSTEM

The words "not fit for purpose" are barely adequate to describe Hong Kong's political system, which has dysfunctionality at its very heart. This helps to explain both why the uprising that began in 2019 kept escalating, and why there was no means of achieving de-escalation through negotiation with the authorities. Hongkongers have long known that the system was incapable of reflecting their views. This made some citizens feel helpless, others simply cynical; and, as the uprising demonstrated, a great swathe of the population was downright angry.

Dating back to the British colonial era, the structure of government and politics in Hong Kong was cobbled together with smoke and mirrors, giving an outward appearance of democracy and accountability belying the reality of autocratic government hamstrung by inherent contradictions and obstruction. Under Chinese rule, this level of dysfunctionality has actually increased, as real power has been taken away from the organs of government in the SAR to give greater control to Beijing.

There is, or at least was, a pervasive myth proclaiming Hongkongers' lack of interest, and reluctance to get involved, in politics. Some commentators insist that this is because Hong Kong people care only about money; others maintain that, among the older generation, memories of the Chinese civil war have left politics widely regarded as a dangerous business yielding few benefits. This myth, largely cultivated by Hong Kong's elite, has been used to justify the lack of democracy and to impose a political system almost aggressively designed to exclude public participation. However, the idea that popular political activity barely existed before the 2019 movement is simply untrue. Protest against the governmental system has a long history in Hong Kong. What has changed with the new generation of protests is that relatively passive expressions of political involvement have been abandoned, and replaced by an explosion of activity on the streets.

The now defunct Hong Kong Transition Project, which conducted intensive public opinion surveys from 1989 to 2012, found that interest in politics was very high. The project's founder, Michael DeGolyer, told me that their findings showed that the "the idea that Hong Kong people are politically apathetic is just not true". His surveys recorded unusually high levels of newspaper readership, with heavy interest in political news, strong attendance at meetings discussing public affairs, very high levels of donations to political causes and significant participation in demonstrations.[1]

* * *

So, Hongkongers are far more politically engaged than is commonly assumed—but they are faced with a system that makes participation very hard to achieve. As a result, Hongkongers' consistent interest in politics does not necessarily translate to an interest in the operations of government. It may be argued that the SAR's formal political structure is largely irrelevant, because real power in Hong Kong lies with organs of the Chinese state. This fact has not gone unnoticed by the local population. Despite promises enshrined in the Basic Law that Hong Kong people would be allowed to rule themselves, Beijing has installed a control system that increasingly operates as a command centre. At the apex of the Mainland control system is a centre located in Shenzhen, just across the border from Hong Kong: a pleasant lakeside location called the Bauhinia Villa. The villa complex has been there for some time and was used as a crisis centre during the 2014 Umbrella Movement.[2] As we shall see, in late 2019 it achieved new status as the highest-level base for Beijing to oversee the work of Hong Kong's administration during the uprising.

Day-to-day operations, meanwhile, are directed by the Hong Kong and Macau Affairs Office, under the powerful State Council in Beijing. Its most senior officials have access to China's top leadership. However, most of the heavy lifting is left to the innocuously named Liaison Office of the Central People's Government in Hong Kong, generally simply known as the Liaison Office. This institution, housed in a vast austere building bristling with security apparatus, occupies a large chunk of land close to the city's historic centre. Inside are a warren of departments that closely mirror the work of Hong Kong government departments. Elsewhere is a hive of activity concerned with purely Party work.

Before the handover, Beijing's coordination and liaison work was undertaken by a branch of the New China News Agency (Xinhua). This use of a media organisation was a convenient fiction, studiously overlooked by the British, who knew full well that this state-controlled body was effectively China's base in Hong Kong, with growing powers and prominence as 1997 drew closer. The Liaison Office, which came to assume Xinhua's functions and more after the handover, was not necessarily intended to be the command centre that it has since become. However, due to the incompetence and perpetual shoe-shining efforts of all the Chief Executives installed since the creation of the Special

Administrative Region, the Liaison Office's workload has grown, and it has taken a far more assertive role in directing the work of the Hong Kong government, as well as the wide network of United Front and ancillary organisations. United Front activity is common to all Communist Parties, following the Leninist principle of gathering a large outer circle to act as supporters for the core of the Party. How it operates in Hong Kong is explained in more detail below. The office worked hard, too, on developing amenable relations with the tycoons who had the ability to enhance the material life of its Mainland cadres.

It also appears to be the case that the Liaison Office has embarked on a property-buying spree in Hong Kong, purchasing 757 by 2020, according to research by the now dissolved pro-democracy Demosisto party.[3] This is curious, and, as ever, the purpose of these purchases has not been clarified. But it is another indication of the extent to which China's point men in Hong Kong have dug themselves firmly into the fabric of society. The swagger and general arrogance of the office's staff grew as SAR government officials, most of whom were trained in the old colonial school, showed how easily they could be pushed around. Everything that was important, and much that was not of very great importance, was brought to the attention of the Liaison Office.

Article 22 of the Basic Law makes clear that "No department of the Central People's Government and no province, autonomous region, or municipality directly under the Central Government may interfere in the affairs which the Hong Kong Special Administrative Region administers on its own in accordance with this Law." However, in April 2020, the Liaison Office discovered a way of circumventing this apparently clear restriction with a spot of double-speak, declaring that this office, and its Beijing-based counterpart the Hong Kong and Macau Affairs Office, could not be considered "departments" in Hong Kong, as they had the authority to represent the PRC's government directly. The Liaison Office went further and declared that it was entitled to exercise its power to supervise what was happening in Hong Kong, and to make statements on issues ranging from the SAR's relationship with Beijing to the "correct" implementation of the Basic Law; the "normal functioning" of the political system; and other "important matters pertaining to the overall interests of society".[4]

The Hong Kong government appeared to have been taken unawares by this new interpretation of the Liaison Office's role, having stated previously that this office was governed by the rules of the Basic Law's Article 22. When this was flatly denied in Beijing following the April pronouncement, it took no fewer than three contradictory statements from the Lam government in the space of 24 hours to clarify the new situation—and, of course, to offer support for the change of direction while denying that such a change had taken place. The Hong Kong and Macau Affairs Office embellished its own statement, insisting that the central government had the right to "exercise full governance" over Hong Kong. It explained that granting a high degree of autonomy to Hong Kong did not mean that Beijing does not have, or will abandon, supervisory power: "The central government must ensure that the relevant authority is properly exercised."[5]

Things were very different in the early days after 1997, when lines of communication were extended to the opposition camp. However, with growing confidence in the likelihood of putting down the dissent, the Liaison Office increasingly disdained contact with the opposition and focused attention on the government, its supporters and the United Front organisations, whose loyalty was long-standing. As a result, the upsurge of protest in 2019 caught the Liaison Office by surprise, and its staff compounded their ignorance of the situation by issuing airy assurances to their bosses in Beijing that the uprising would soon fade: the silent, pro-China majority would assert itself, and the government would be able to claw back the initiative. In other words, Beijing's men on the ground had no idea what was going on.

The straw that broke the camel's back was the November 2019 district council elections. When the expected victory of the pro-China candidates turned into a shattering defeat, scapegoats had to be found, leading to the dismissal and demotion of those running the operation. As we shall shortly see, the ramifications of this have been profound.

* * *

Meanwhile, the creaky, dysfunctional system of formal government, exercising a much-circumscribed degree of autonomy from the PRC authorities, is still just about adequate to keep the wheels of officialdom turning. It is worth detailing how this structure works, despite or rather precisely because of its weaknesses: the sham nature of Hong Kong's political system is a constant source of irritation, a reminder of how Hongkongers have been denied the promise of representative government and key to understanding why so many have taken their frustration to the streets.

At the apex of the system is the Chief Executive (CE), who selects an Executive Committee (Exco)—a purely advisory body, bereft of any form of election, whose operations are shrouded in secrecy. Most of the time, Exco exists to endorse whatever the CE wants it to endorse; and to provide an opportunity for handing out status-enhancing positions to leading members of the pro-China camp. As we have seen, Hong Kong's first Chief Executive Tung Chee-hwa set the tone for how business was to be conducted in the SAR. Tung had been invited to join the colonial Executive Committee by the last Governor, Chris Patten, as a way of trying to get the pro-China camp on side. It did not work and Tung, who must have been well aware of the futility of this tactic, never made similar overtures to his own opposition when he was in office. His successors have all managed to lure one or two opposition figures into the new Exco, but these members never manage to rise above the level of nominal "outsiders"; they have had no visible impact on policy.

Indeed, the CE is not obliged to accept any advice proffered at these meetings; nor is it constitutionally necessary to refer even the most important decisions to Exco at all. Under Carrie Lam, installed as CE in 2017, not only is Exco bypassed, but Lam herself, as she openly admits, has not been consulted by Beijing about far-reaching decisions, not least the imposition of the National Security Law from July 2020. Since the 2019–20 uprising in particular, Lam, the person supposedly in charge of Hong Kong's government, has been reduced to little more than CENO—Chief Executive in Name Only.

A career bureaucrat, Lam is often mockingly referred to by the Chinese media as "Hong Kong's Deputy Mayor". She told a Mainland television interviewer in August 2020 that she did not consider herself "to be a person who understands politics very well, I am an administrator".[6] She appears to have had any scrap of charisma surgically removed; and is simply incapable of dealing with people who challenge her opinions, or subordinates daring to disagree. In public she has a robotic manner of speaking, and even in extreme circumstances, highlighted by the coronavirus crisis, has failed to display empathy. When 1 million people poured onto the streets to protest her plan to promote extraditions to the Mainland, her first response was to say that they would be ignored. When, shortly afterwards, the crowd swelled to some 2 million, she simply said that they did not understand the situation. We will see in Part Two how this was received by the public.

No expertise in political leadership is required to understand how tone-deaf Lam can be. Yet she gives every impression that the views of others are irrelevant, as she has few friends and, more importantly, few personal allies, who in most political systems give leaders the backing they need to operate successfully. Instead, Carrie Lam owes her position solely to the men in Beijing who installed her in office, and who can remove her any time they want to. She has masked this insecurity by becoming increasingly strident, and by an increasing tendency to appear and even speak in the stilted manner of senior Party cadres.

To be fair, Lam has always been faced with an impossible task. Hong Kong's system has the trappings of accountability and some flickering means of constraining the government; but it is mainly a simmering swamp of inaction, with much floundering punctuated by bursts of authoritarian rule. Amazingly, this had sort of worked, as long as Hong Kong offered its people the prospect of progress, and a way of life superior to that found on the other side of the border. However, as the SAR's economy has slowed and the political system has appeared to be heading toward convergence with the Chinese dictatorship, the inherent inadequacies of the regime have become increasingly apparent.

When the incoming Chinese sovereign inherited the political system devised by the British, it looked as though it was ideal for its purposes. The most attractive feature of the colonial system, as far as the Party was concerned, was that all power resided with the Governor, primarily accountable to his bosses in London; the new regime merely needed to substitute the word Beijing for London. Thus the Basic Law spells out thirteen all-embracing powers bestowed on the Chief Executive. They clarify the incumbent's dominance in the government, yet all four CEs who have come into office since the creation of the SAR have been failures, and the likelihood is that their successors will follow in these dismal footsteps if the "system" remains intact.

A crisis of administration might appear to be a somewhat arcane matter, with little relevance to the majority of people— but in Hong Kong it has produced dire consequences.

They are everywhere to be seen, but are most evident among the one in five people who live below the poverty line, in a society where wealth is flaunted and reaches dizzying levels among the elite.[7] Then there's the shocking failure to tackle the housing crisis. This persists not because of inadequate financial resources of the state, nor, although this is the excuse made, because of a lack of land. Meanwhile, officials have access to a seemingly end-less slew of cash, which is frittered away on massive white ele-phant projects. We will come back to Hong Kong's crisis of inequality in Chapter 3.

This stark neglect of the interests of ordinary working peo-ple has been able to thrive in a system of unelected government with minimal accountability. It is one of the worst legacies of British colonialism.

Despite initiatives to reform the system dating back to the end of World War Two, reform was staunchly resisted by both the local elite and the old Colonial Office in London, which cher-ished the political process, widely used in other colonies, giving all power to the Governor. While other colonies underwent dras-tic political reform to prepare for independence, self-government was never on the cards for Hong Kong. Even after the Colonial Office was absorbed into Britain's Foreign and Commonwealth Office, which was marginally more open to change, substantial transformation was deemed to be out of the question. Governor Patten, who was genuinely interested in political reform, could do no more than tinker with the system, bringing in a modicum of greater election; but, as we saw in Chapter 1, by this time it was far too late, and these reforms were overturned on day one of the new order in 1997.

Because the CE is given enormous power under the Basic Law, Beijing—back in the 1980s when it cared about these things—paid special attention while drafting it to creating a mirage of an electoral system, one that would suggest the Chief Executive emerged through a democratic process. The sham starts with every CE earnestly claiming to have a democratic mandate. The reality is that this mandate comes from a 1,200-strong Election Committee (up from an initial 800 members), carefully designed to "elect" whoever Beijing chooses for the role.

The committee is made up of four, equally balanced sectors. The first supposedly represents business—the industrial, commercial and financial community. The second covers the professions. The third could be described as covering "civil society", a hotchpotch of labour, social services, and religious, agricultural, sports and cultural representatives. The fourth sector is the one Beijing likes best, as it consists of the fully house-trained Hong Kong members of Mainland political bodies: legislators and district councillors, alongside the reptilian Heung Yee Kuk, an advisory body supposedly representing indigenous Hongkongers—unless they are women, whose interests are ignored by the Kuk.

In theory, these four sectors broadly represent the Hong Kong people, yet only a tiny fraction of the public are allowed to choose the committee members, and those who do are given a far from equitable voting system. The Election Committee that installed Carrie Lam in office in 2017, for instance, was chosen by 246,440 electors—but half of the seats on this committee were filled by the votes of just 11,340 people. To put this in perspective, in the education sector (one of the rare constituencies permitted a broader voting base), 80,643 people elected just thirty, or 2.5 per cent, of the committee's members. By contrast, the agricultural and fisheries sector was given twice as many representatives: sixty uncontested seats for just 154 voters. So, when it comes to anointing the leader of Hong Kong, the sectors with minuscule electorates have together eight times the voting power of the few constituencies where something resembling a competitive election takes place.[8]

Lam ended up securing just 777 votes from the committee's 1,200 members—in other words, an endorsement from less than 0.01 per cent of Hong Kong's population. This is the kind of election favoured by the Chinese Communist Party.

* * *

That limited concept of democracy also extends to the Legislative Council, or Legco, where elections are important to the administration for no other reason than the cloak of respectability they are supposed to give to Hong Kong's political system. Despite this uneven playing field, election campaigning also provides a major opportunity for political debate and mobilisation of support. But in terms of functionality, the legislature itself is starkly powerless, except in the important matter of passing budgets. Legco members have no power to introduce legislation without the CE's permission, and increasingly fewer powers of scrutiny over government action or law-making.

Half the seats in Legco are occupied by the so-called functional constituencies, with an electorate numbering no more than 250,000; 4.5 million voters are confined to the other half of seats, comprising geographical constituencies that represent districts.[9] In order to pass any binding resolutions in the legislature, a majority must be secured from both sides of the chamber. This often resulted in stalemate until, as we shall see later, all but two opposition members either resigned or were kicked out.

The functional constituency half of Legco is little more than a motley collection of rotten borough constituencies, and trade and social group representatives. Only nine of the thirty functional constituencies enjoy anything resembling recognisable elections. That leaves 80 per cent of the seats to be chosen by tiny electorates. Chicago's infamous gerrymanderers would have given their right arms for a system like this. The tiny "rotten borough" functional constituencies restrict voting to either corporate representatives, or individuals who supposedly represent their sectors. To see how this works, consider some of the more blatant examples: the retail and wholesale constituency, representing one of the biggest workforces in Hong Kong, has just 5,997 electors, no more than 5 per cent of the total number of people employed in this sector.[10] They elect a single member. This gives all workers in the retail and wholesale trade the same level of representation as the rural Heung Yee Kuk, whose legislator is chosen by just 155 voters, and the agriculture and fisheries constituency (160 voters); these two constituencies do not even bother to hold elections, because there is no contest.

The most democratic part of the Legco election system lies in the geographical constituencies. However, even here, another exquisite form of ballot-rigging comes into play: a transferable vote system that ends up giving seats to candidates who win comparatively few votes. This system was deliberately designed by the colonial authorities to ensure that those considered pro-establishment candidates in those days would win seats—it was assumed that, in a more open contest, the opposition would always prevail.

It may be imagined that this level of rigging in Hong Kong elections would be more than adequate for those in power to keep control. But, as the 2019 district council polls demonstrated, even this system was not sufficiently fireproof to prevent a democrat victory. So, in October 2020, the government introduced proposals to allow Hong Kong residents living on the Mainland to vote. This involved some 333,000 electors in neighbouring Guangdong Province, who, it was assumed, would vote for pro-China parties.[11] Hitherto, local electoral law only allowed votes physically cast in Hong Kong; there is not even a system for postal ballots. This new expansion of the electorate puts part of the poll beyond the control of the SAR's authorities, and will ensure that campaigning to a significant section of voters is restricted to pro-China parties. After all, there is no way that the Mainland authorities would allow democrats to cross the border to campaign among Hong Kong residents.

* * *

The bizarre nature of the election system for the legislature has given rise to the creation of political parties that are in many ways equally bizarre.

In most places, political parties are pretty much a routine fixture. Not so in Hong Kong, where parties are technically not allowed to exist—they have to register under company laws. In practice, however, during the later colonial era the British authorities turned a blind eye to their operation, following the evolution of elections in the mid-1980s. Despite this, the logical step of creating a legal framework for the operation of political parties has never been taken. This ambiguity reflects the greater ambiguity towards the Hong Kong political process as a whole. Although parties have no legal status, the Lam government still managed to ban the pro-independence Hong Kong National Party in 2018.

In 2016, following the last Legco elections before the uprising, eighteen different parties were represented in the chamber. By far the largest—in terms of seats, membership and financial resources—was the Democratic Alliance for the Betterment and Progress of Hong Kong (DAB). It claims to have over 42,000 members and had thirteen seats in Legco, plus two in Lam's Exco from 2017. Before the shock result of the 2019 district council elections, the DAB also had the highest number of councillors, and controlled the majority of the councils. Most of the party's founders and the people who still determine its policies are members of Hong Kong's underground Communist Party. In 1992, local Party members, on orders from Beijing, formed the DAB in a classic United Front manoeuvre: creating a party under the PRC's control, yet sufficiently distant to give the impression of independence. As it has grown, this pro-China party has largely shed its working-class roots and become heavily reliant on tycoons for financing.

The DAB's current leader is Starry Lee, in all probability not a Communist Party member. Born in 1974, she certainly qualifies as young among the sea of ageing men who dominate the DAB—but Lee is a dreadful public speaker, and an accountant by trade, embracing all the glamour and excitement associated with that profession. In functional terms, however, it's not crucial for Lee to be either charismatic or a Communist Party member. In all important matters the Party still pulls the strings; what matters is that she does what she is told.

Closely allied with the DAB is the Federation of Trade Unions, another United Front body but with more obvious workerist interests. It remains closer to its Communist Party origins and, as the name suggests, also operates as a trade union organisation.

This raises the obvious question of why the Hong Kong branch of the Communist Party refuses to emerge from the shadows. Although the Party was never much of a mass organisation in Hong Kong, it had influence far beyond its relatively modest membership. Its finest moments came during the Japanese occupation of Hong Kong in World War Two, when the Communists formed the core of both the armed and passive resistance to the occupiers. Its most infamous moments came during the Cultural Revolution-inspired riots of the 1960s, causing vast disruption and loss of life in the then colony. For most of its history, the local party has operated under the umbrella title of the Hong Kong and Macau Work Committee of the Chinese Communist Party, although even this name was never openly acknowledged.[12] But why so shy?

One answer is simple: if the Party were to operate openly in Hong Kong, this would have a wider impact on formalising the existence of parties in the SAR. Moreover, the reluctance to allow the Party to appear in the full light of day demonstrates an awareness of public unease over the Communist Party. Why rock that boat, when the Party can still maintain control and indeed work successfully through its complex United Front network? Maybe, however, the most compelling reason for subterfuge lies in the difficulty of shaking habits of secrecy and deception that have prevailed since the local party's forerunner, the minuscule Marxism Research Group, was established in 1920. This laid the ground for Hong Kong's elaborate framework of front organisations: trade unions, schools, neighbourhood associations, social clubs, publications and media companies, bookstores and even sporting clubs. In other words, the Hong Kong Communist Party (which never uses this name) developed on classic Leninist lines—hardly surprising when the mother party on the Mainland owed its structure to work undertaken by emissaries from the old Soviet Union, who dictated much of what happened in the crucial early years of the Chinese Communist Party.

United Front tactics have been at the core of Communist Parties' operations ever since they were devised by Lenin and his inner circle of Bolsheviks. What is unusual in Hong Kong is that the United Front operates on two tiers. One is directly under Party control, and then there is an outer tier of political parties, prominent individuals and a myriad of organisations. This tier does not fall directly under Party discipline, but maintains a high level of interaction with Party organs, albeit usually through Mainland government channels. Most of the time, the relationship is quite relaxed, and nudged along by all manner of carrots. The stick lurks in the background, but having to bring it into play would be viewed as a sign of failure.

Arguably, there is also a third tier of the United Front in Hong Kong, seen in the even more detached parties that form the wider loyalist camp. The Liberal Party, for instance, illustrates the complexities of operating at this level. It is one of the longest-standing pro-China organisations in Hong Kong and was formed to promote the interests of the business community. It has often demonstrated a degree of independence that greatly displeases its handlers in the Liaison Office, but these Beijing officials are loath to cut the party adrift, both because of its longevity and standing in the community and because maintaining the unity of the establishment camp is seen as a prime objective.

Other parties in the loose pro-China orbit largely exist to promote the ambitions of their founders, which creates a set of problems familiar to anyone with experience of dealing with large egos. A prime example is the party founded by the intensely ambitious former Security Secretary Regina Ip, who was widely known as "Broomhead" due to a rather unfortunate hairstyle. Ip is prone to veering off script in order to win popularity: though a member of Exco, she is a constant critic of the Lam administration. As with Starry Lee, however, what matters from Beijing's point of view is that, when push comes to shove, Ip and others in the broad pro-China camp will fall into line, a compliance assured either through appointments to prestigious Mainland organisations, or by threats of isolation that would reduce their chances of holding office.

Despite these complexities, the pro-China camp is better financed and better organised than the opposition, though pro-democracy parties enjoy greater popular support. The longest-established and largest of these is the Democratic Party, which was founded in 1990 as the United Democrats of Hong Kong, bringing together a number of well-known campaigners. Two of the party's key founders were Martin Lee, known as the "Father of Democracy" in Hong Kong, and Szeto Wah, a wizened former school teacher. Since 1990, other opposition parties have emerged: these include the Civic Party, the Labour Party and the more radical League of Social Democrats. The league's founder, Leung Kwok-hung, is better known as "Long Hair" for his trademark look: his locks are accompanied by a Che Guevara t-shirt, non-violent principles and, often, a beer and a cigarette. Though he continues with dogged persistence to attend more protests than most people could contemplate joining in several lifetimes, he has regularly been expelled from Legco and jailed; his career as a legislator is effectively over.

Indeed, opposition party members often pay a high personal price for their adherence to these parties and, although they can achieve employment through election to Legco and the district councils, prominent involvement in opposition politics usually entails financial sacrifice.

At a more extreme level, Beijing's alarm over the development of democratic party politics reached new heights after the foundation of the Hong Kong National Party in 2016. This was the first party to advocate independence for Hong Kong, with a membership numbering no more than two dozen people. Not only was it minuscule, but it also had little connection with the mainstream democracy movement. However, Beijing chose to focus on this tiny group as part of a narrative accusing the pro-democracy camp of trying to prise Hong Kong away from the Motherland.

As we shall see in Chapter 8, the reality is that there has been little support for independence among Hong Kong democrats, but there is support for freedom of expression to allow such views to be aired. In fact, views like those of the National Party had been aired for many years, with very few people paying any attention. Nevertheless, in 2018 legislation was drawn up to ban the National Party, the first time that this has happened in Hong Kong: by contrast, the British never banned the underground Communist Party in Hong Kong, even after the deadly riots of the 1960s. This was because its existence was constantly denied, and because the colonial authorities took the pragmatic view that forcing the Party deeper underground would also make it harder to control. But pragmatism had ceased to be the order of the day in the corridors of Carrie Lam's government.

On 14 August 2018, Andy Chan, the party's deceptively meek-looking founder, was invited to make a speech at the Foreign Correspondents' Club, a venue that prides itself on providing a platform for all newsworthy points of view. What he said that day largely overlooked the party's independence stance, focusing instead on support for democracy. As Chan put it, "in reality, what the National Party is chasing after is no different from what many Hongkongers wish for: the dream of democracy."[13] What followed was a furore led by Chinese officials and just about everyone else on the pro-China side of the fence, accusing the FCC of supporting an illegal organisation (which the party wasn't, at the time of the speech) and of supporting separatism. Calls were made for the club to be evicted from its premises and Victor Mallet, a *Financial Times* correspondent who happened to be chairing the meeting, was effectively kicked out of Hong Kong, as his visa was not renewed. He has subsequently been barred from entering as a visitor. The National Party was banned shortly after Chan's speech. The ban was upheld after legal appeals in February 2019, and Chan was arrested more than once during the uprising.

This was all very much a sideshow, but a sideshow with important ramifications. For a start, the much-cherished idea of Hong Kong being a haven for freedom of expression was dealt a body blow with Mallet's expulsion, the first time such a thing had happened to a foreign correspondent working in the territory. Expulsions of this kind are hardly unknown on the Mainland, and now the SAR had the dubious privilege of falling into line. Secondly, a political party was being banned, purely on the basis of its views and not because of any previous unlawful activity.

As the crackdown in 2020 deepened, it was not just the more extreme wing of the opposition that faced jeopardy; previously legal activities such as standing for election were also thrown into doubt. In the past, the authorities had been happy to sit back and watch Hong Kong's democrats undermine their own potential and squander support with competing candidates standing for election, even though what separates them is often little more than a question of personality. What changed in 2020 was that a determined effort was made to overcome these divisions, with the holding of a mass election primary to decide who would run for Legco in September. The alarming success of this operation contributed to the Lam government's decision to stall the election for at least a year. It also explains the wider crackdown on those in the democracy camp who had previously won elections.

What is interesting is that, in both camps, political ideology plays a very minor role in mainstream party politics. Some of the smaller parties do have a more ideological inclination. The FTU, for example, looks to its trade union roots to be a workers' rights advocate, while the relatively new Labour Party is self-consciously social-democratic in orientation. The main parties, however, are more obviously defined by their attitude towards China. Take the patrician Martin Lee, son of a Kuomintang Lieutenant General: in another political system, Lee would be considered a conservative right-winger, but in Hong Kong he is viewed by the pro-China establishment as a dangerous radical. His Democratic Party is a coalition of old-style conservatives like him, alongside liberals and social democrats, who put aside any ideological differences to focus on the cause of democracy. On the other side of the fence, most DAB members readily identify with the Chinese Communist Party, yet have little interest in Marxism. Many are barely aware of even its basic tenets, but acutely aware of the career opportunities offered by DAB membership.

Perhaps the most lasting impact of the 2019–20 uprising has been the extreme polarisation of Hong Kong politics. Two colour-coded camps have emerged: blue for the pro-China supporters and yellow for the opposition. Like all shorthand, this lacks a degree of subtlety, but it does provide a useful model for discussing post-2019 politics. For ideology is also notably absent from the protest movement, which is largely defined by what it opposes—the Chinese Communist Party and its echo chamber in Hong Kong. The uprising has been focused on creating a democratic Hong Kong as its core belief, a vision that is open to many interpretations.

This explains why the younger generation has been slow to get involved in traditional politics. The formation of Demosisto, a party founded by Joshua Wong and Nathan Law and others in 2016, was an exception among the galaxy of organisations and ad-hoc bodies established during the uprisings of both 2014 and 2019–20. The newer protest movement tends to be suspicious of political parties and wary of leaders. Its members are proud of their spontaneity and ability to act without a central controlling structure; and they have been dismissive of the value of electoral politics in a largely rigged system. As the protests mounted in 2019 and the Legislative Council building was sacked, then entirely shut down, it appeared that the legislature was even more irrelevant than usual. Even the pro-democracy Legco members, who actively supported the uprising, were forced to take a back seat, as those on the streets made it clear that they did not want legislators to speak on their behalf. They could help, but could not lead.

Thanks to the crackdown on all forms of dissent, the division between the democrats in Legco and the protestors has narrowed, as the streets have cleared and the onslaught on the Legco opposition has intensified. In November 2020, the police arrested eight members as a result of an unruly session the previous May. A number of those arrested had been charged before. In fact, by the time this happened, a staggering 86 per cent of the twenty-nine opposition legislators had been either expelled from the legislature, disqualified from running for re-election, or arrested.

A bigger blow was to come later the same month, with the expulsion of four other Legco democrats on orders from Beijing, and threats of yet more expulsions to come. At this point, all members of the opposition in Legco, bar two, resigned. This has left the chamber more or less entirely in the hands of the pro-China camp.

Beijing's intervention was on the grounds that these lawmakers had broken their pledge to uphold the Basic Law, and it was made clear that this was only the beginning: even more candidates would be disqualified from standing for election; district councils, the civil service and indeed the entire public service of the SAR would continue to be purged.

Whatever differences may have existed between so-called moderate democrats and the more hardline street fighters quickly evaporated amidst these developments in late 2020, as Beijing was effectively declaring that opposition would no longer be tolerated, in any form. The implications of this are still sinking in at the time of writing. On the surface, it appears that a triumphant pro-China camp, plus a few "moderate" opposition figures, will now be the only legitimate political force in Hong Kong.

However, the pro-China politicians had more than their own share of problems. At the height of the protests, they simply disappeared from sight, fearing attack if they appeared in public. As the pressure mounted, they were supposed to support Chief Executive Lam, who herself disappeared from view for large stretches of time, only to reappear seemingly armed with fresh instructions from Beijing, which could not be questioned. This created a painful dilemma for the pro-government camp, as they no longer wished to be identified with the floundering administration. Instead of offering support to Lam, pro-China legislators started openly criticising her. They did so because, despite the enormous flaws in the system, they still needed to get elected in constituencies where gerrymandering was insufficient to guarantee results.

Officials from the Liaison Office spend a vast amount of time issuing instructions and "guidance" to their loyal acolytes. They are also responsible for drawing up the list of suitable candidates at election time, in order to eliminate competition within the pro-China parties. During the uprising, the Liaison Office supplied supporters with the official narrative of what was going on, and expected them to faithfully regurgitate the Party line on demand. I have been told by a number of the camp's leading members that they had bombarded the Liaison Office with requests to distance themselves from the government, until finally being given the nod to do so. Lam was effectively abandoned because, in the brutal world of Communist Party politics, individuals are always dispensable, however loyal. They can be summarily dismissed from office, disciplined, or even abused if it serves the greater good of the Party.

In short, Hong Kong is stuck with an institutionally dysfunctional political system, headed by a leader who has lost public credibility and the trust of her own camp, leaving her solely dependent on the support provided by her bosses in Beijing. For the time being, Lam has been allowed to linger on while a replacement is sought. This support she enjoys from her controllers hangs by a small thread that can be cut at any moment. As Lenin graphically described a similar situation, it is akin to a rope supporting a hanging man. Meanwhile, even the government's supporters in Legco have been permitted to edge away from identification with the Lam administration, and since 2019 have ceased describing themselves as "pro-government", preferring to be known instead as members of the pro-China or "pro-Beijing" camp.

With the uprising escalating by late 2019, the Chinese leadership moved decisively to sideline Carrie Lam, as Vice-Premier Han Zheng was put in charge of Hong Kong affairs and installed at that charming Beijing command centre, the Bauhinia Villa in Shenzhen. Han, a survivor who has prevailed through Party infighting since Jiang Zemin left office in 2002, is now close to Xi Jinping and very much seen as the President's man. Chief Executive Lam has been summoned regularly to see Han at the villa, and its apparatus has garnered increasing importance, with vice-ministers from China's State Security Ministry, Public Security Ministry and Cyberspace Administration despatched to Shenzhen to join the inner core now handling Hong Kong affairs.

Reuters, which broke this story, reported that Xi was receiving daily written briefings from the Bauhinia Villa, revealing both the degree to which Hong Kong has moved to the top of the Party's agenda and the importance of officials given command of the situation. The existence of the Villa as the centre of operations has not been acknowledged by the Chinese government. But Han Zheng is visibly in charge, and makes occasional weighty pronouncements on Hong Kong.

What remains unknown is whether Beijing always intended to exercise such a tight grip on the affairs of its supposedly autonomous Special Administrative Region, or whether the Xi regime has been driven to exasperation by either Lam or the Liaison Office leadership—or, more probably, a combination of both.

In any case, in brushing aside the tattered remnants of autonomy belonging to the Hong Kong administration, Beijing has created even more reason for the protest movement to pursue its goals, pouring oil on the fire that continues to burn even after the crackdown of 2020. Moreover, by cracking down hard on all forms of opposition, be it street violence or participation in elected bodies, the authorities have underlined their fundamental inability to cope with criticism, and eroded the grounds for pursuing peaceful protest.

3

A MALFUNCTIONING ECONOMY

The last thing anyone was expecting in Hong Kong in 2019 was an outbreak of Marxist thinking from Beijing, in a way that actually struck a chord with many people in the SAR. Yet, as the protests mounted, and in a desperate attempt to switch the focus from politics and disenfranchisement onto other territory, the Party suddenly remembered that inequality and poverty might possibly be bothering Hongkongers. They had some reason to do so because Hong Kong is a deeply unequal society and, while it is famous for producing some spectacularly rich people, many are left behind.

The Party had hitherto shown not the slightest interest in reviving notions of class struggle in Hong Kong. On the contrary, it had been happily repeating the famous Deng Xiaoping slogan of "To get rich is glorious". An editorial in the *Global Times* back in 2015 underlined this view: "Jealousy and discontent are not the dominant sentiments when the Chinese public sees [that] an increasing number of mainland billionaires are included in the rich list and outshine their counterparts from Hong Kong and Taiwan. Instead, most feel happy and proud over the surge in so many business tycoons. This is a healthy and active attitude."[1]

This editorial was part and parcel of a wider official narrative extolling the virtues of free enterprise as an engine for growth. Euphemisms abound to explain the Mainland's chosen path of a "socialist market economy", and the compatibility of "socialism with Chinese characteristics". What is really happening, of course, is capitalism with Chinese characteristics. This involves freedom to operate private companies, but a forthright advocacy of capitalism sits uncomfortably with the keepers of the Marxist faith; so private enterprises are routinely described as "non-public" companies.

In Hong Kong, where capitalism has long flourished and the retention of a capitalist system is enshrined in the Basic Law, the market economy can be more open, and the tycoons who dominate it have long been accustomed to being lauded by the regime. Indeed, Party leaders have routinely made local business leaders their first port of call when visiting the SAR. Beijing even went so far as to engineer the appointment of a tycoon, Tung Chee-hwa, as Hong Kong's first Chief Executive. That did not turn out so well—his utter ineptitude culminated in an attempt to force through national security legislation despite significant public opposition; he blundered into a number of other problems after this before "resigning" in 2005. But Tung's cautionary tale did not deter the Beijing leadership from making sure that Hong Kong's richest people (and their sons) were installed across all major Mainland political advisory bodies. The Party and the fabulously wealthy of the SAR appeared to be enjoying a prolonged honeymoon.

However, the honeymoon came to an abrupt end in September 2019, four months into the uprising. The leaders in Beijing were becoming increasingly frustrated by the seemingly never-ending protests, and alarmed by the Lam administration's evident failure to do anything about it. They particularly disliked the way that the protestors' narrative of a struggle for freedom was increasingly gaining traction not just in Hong Kong but elsewhere in the world. What was needed, the regime concluded, was a new narrative to deflect all this talk of freedom and democracy—concepts that severely undermined the Party's legitimacy.

At this point, someone in the bowels of Zhongnanhai, the hub of China's government, must have remembered the dusty old texts littering their bookshelves by Karl Marx and his associate Friedrich Engels. Why no one had thought of this before is a mystery, because Marxism offers a ready-made explanation for why people rise up against their governments in capitalist societies: it is the product of class struggle, the historical imperative for the broad masses to defy their masters in the search for economic and social equality. Maybe I'm getting a bit carried away here, but this old-school Marxist thinking has clearly been behind the evolution of a new narrative designed to explain away what was happening in Hong Kong. The Party preferred the idea that Hongkongers were not struggling for political liberty, but protesting against economic inequality.

The first hint of the new line came, as it often does, from Hu Xijin, Chief Editor of the *Global Times*, in a blog post lambasting Hong Kong's "extreme capitalist system" while criticising the local government for neglecting livelihood problems. In a pointed criticism of the Lam administration, he contrasted its lack of attention to social matters with the way that the central government in Beijing "would long ago have acted to tackle the profound housing and social welfare issues that Hong Kong faces".[2] Then the Party's official mouthpiece, the *People's Daily*, piled in: "For the sake of the public interest, it is time [property] developers show their utmost sincerity instead of minding their own business, hoarding land for profit and earning the last penny."[3] This was followed up by the *Global Times* reporting that "Hong Kong developers have drawn harsh criticism in mainland media and social media amid rising social tensions that fueled months of anti-government street protests in Hong Kong."[4]

The main target of the new anti-capitalist rhetoric from Beijing was the "Big Four" families who dominate the local property market. They have made vast fortunes out of a system where the government—the sole supplier of new land for development—organises these sales in such a way that few developers outside their charmed circle could compete (at least until Chinese state corporations got involved; see below). The "Big Four" are Henderson Land Development, founded by Lee Shau-kee; New World Development, founded by Cheng Yu-tung; SHKP, run by the Kwok family; and CK Asset Holdings, founded by Li Ka-shing. Li may no longer be Hong Kong's richest man, but he remains the most powerful of the tycoons, once widely known as "Superman" by a legion of faithful shareholders and other admirers. Known for his guile, he embodies Hong Kong's classic rags to riches story, having started out as a penniless immigrant who began his empire with a plastic flower business.

As of 2019, these four conglomerates collectively held some 83 million square feet of land in land-scarce Hong Kong.[5] Throw in a couple of other companies, Wharf and Sino Land, who are close to the "Big Four" but not quite there, and you have a list of nearly everyone who really mattered in Hong Kong property development before Mainland property developers entered the picture. The power and wealth of this property oligopoly is such that it rode through the 1997 handover without blinking. If anything, the oligopoly's influence has increased under the new order. Its leaders have had better access to the top echelons of power in Beijing than many senior Hong Kong government officials. Often the tycoons have acted as sounding boards and offered advice to the Party, not just about Hong Kong, but also about how China's economy could operate in a more capitalist manner.

It is hard, therefore, to quite imagine their shock when they were suddenly castigated in the official Chinese media in the autumn of 2019. This was followed up by the Liaison Office egging on the local cheerleader chorus to solemnly affirm their newfound disgust for the way that the stinking rich behaved in Hong Kong. The tycoons' first response was to get their minions to draft full-page newspaper advertisements pledging loyalty to Beijing and opposition to the protest movement. This was rapidly followed up with offers of land for social housing and suitably humble declarations of self-criticism for having neglected the social implications of their businesses. Only Li Ka-shing opted for a more subtle reaction, but ambiguity was not what Beijing was looking for—a fresh volley of criticism was fired in his direction.

However, the outbreak of Marxist-style rhetoric was never really meant to sink the rich, nor indeed to inch Hong Kong towards some form of socioeconomic equality. Its sole aim was to promote a new narrative that would move attention away from the protestors' calls for freedom, toward the safer ground of economic issues. The best indication of this is that, although this outbreak of Marxism lingered in Beijing and the pro-China camp, all further action towards curbing the power of the property oligopoly quickly disappeared.

* * *

Nonetheless, there are solid grounds for asserting that inequality and a lack of social welfare in Hong Kong are pressing issues. These problems did not trigger the protests, nor were they the main focus of attention during the uprising; but the Party cannot be faulted for choosing Hong Kong as the place to rediscover its Marxist roots. Income disparity in the SAR is at world-record-breaking levels: on average, the richest 10 per cent of households earn forty-four times more than the poorest 10 per cent.[6]

It's worth noting in parenthesis that, although living standards have clearly improved for many people on the Mainland, this vast chasm between rich and poor is mirrored in China's "socialist" system, where, according to the latest figures, 40 per cent of Chinese households survive on an average annual income of 11,485 yuan (US$1,621), while the top 20 per cent enjoy an average annual disposable income of 76,404 yuan—almost nine times higher.[7]

Inequality and grinding poverty in Hong Kong have real implications, most notably in terms of housing conditions. In the SAR, the average home size is just 430 square feet. That's the average—many families lucky enough to secure public housing are living in 220 square-foot apartments, while others have to find a way of surviving in tiny subdivided apartments of just 132 square feet or less.[8] Even relatively comfortable middle-class families consider 700 square feet the most they can aspire to owning or renting. Even this size, one third bigger than the Hong Kong average, compares unfavourably with most countries. In Britain, where average home sizes are modest by international standards, the average is still some 818 square feet.[9]

Despite the poor quality of the housing stock, Hong Kong has some of the world's most expensive real estate. Housing poverty is perhaps the most obvious symbol of the great divide between rich and poor, with the possibility of home ownership little more than a dream for most people. Successive governments have talked about fixing the Hong Kong housing problem, and there is an extensive public housing programme, but the authorities have little to show for their efforts. The ever-inventive sloganeers of the protest movement were quick to seize on this issue, with a piece of graffiti neatly combining protest against the housing crisis with defiance towards the police. It read: "7K [HK$7,000] for a house like a cell and you really think we out here are afraid of jail?"

Housing, or lack of it, is only the most visible aspect of social policy failures that have carried through from colonial times. The number of impoverished Hongkongers is staggering. At the start of 2019, they accounted for 20.4 per cent of the population, with acute poverty concentrated among the elderly: a breathtaking 44 per cent of those aged above 65 are living below the poverty line.[10] Despite the enormous prosperity to be found in Hong Kong, the streets are still populated by elderly people pushing around carts filled with cardboard waste, which they trade for pennies at recycling depots. Some are too proud to claim any form of government welfare or to ask for help from their families; others are claiming social assistance, but the sums on offer are so small that they fail to cover the most basic of living costs.

All in all, 1.41 million people in the SAR are living in poverty, according to government figures.[11] This statistic is questioned by Law Chi-kwong, the minister responsible for labour and welfare.[12] He argues that, once government assistance to the poor is taken into account, that headline figure is more or less halved. This is a debatable view, and somewhat bizarre coming from the minister responsible for providing the figures in the first place. What Law does not dispute is that the poverty level is too high, and has been that way for decades.

Despite holding some of the biggest fiscal reserves in the world and consistently producing budget surpluses, the SAR is highly reluctant to commit itself to lasting poverty alleviation measures, such as the introduction of a state pension or other forms of consistent, substantial assistance that would assure a decent standard of living. Instead, all administrations since the handover have favoured a plethora of one-off schemes and payments of so-called "fruit money". The lack of a sustained poverty alleviation programme is defended by protestations that the government cannot do more, because the public has no appetite for a welfare state. This aversion to social welfare was also prevalent in the British era, using the excuse that Hong Kong had always got by on the plucky self-reliance of its people, and that welfarism was an anathema to this society.

Although the protests that began in 2019 were not directly motivated by concerns over poverty or inequality, these deep-seated and long-standing grievances fed into the picture. One of many fascinating byproducts of the uprising was the bringing together of all social classes. As ever in protest movements, the bulk of the leadership was middle-class; but, out on the streets—especially once the protests spread away from the centre of town into working-class areas—much of the heavy lifting was carried out by people from low-income backgrounds. They might not have been propelled onto the streets to protest against inequality, but they were acutely conscious of the way society was organised, perpetuating poverty and injustice. Hong Kong's large underclass understood that an unelected government was unlikely to accommodate their needs.

Radicalised working-class young people on the frontlines found themselves thrust together with middle-class people, who were able to learn a great deal from them about the reality of life at the bottom of the pile. "To be honest, I hadn't really met that many people from poorer backgrounds before the protest movement," I was told by a university student who described himself as coming from a "not rich, but middle-class" background. He was not alone: a growing awareness of poverty in Hong Kong is often mentioned by protestors of a similar class when they talk about their experiences at demonstrations, and this has repercussions for politics in Hong Kong that have yet to develop.

In the meantime, following the official logic that economic discontent lay at the heart of the protest movement, the government launched two major so-called relief packages to put money into people's pockets. Economic relief packages were welcomed both before and after the outbreak of the coronavirus, but the handouts did little to lower the political temperature. This rather crude attempt first to bribe the Hong Kong electorate ahead of the November 2019 district council polls was widely seen for exactly what it was. The move might have been consistent with the strategy of reducing the uprising to a primitive form of economic determinism, but Beijing's dalliance with Marxist concepts during the protests was never serious.

* * *

What was serious, and having a profound effect on Hong Kong's overall economy, was the complex and fast-changing economic and financial relationship between Hong Kong and the Mainland, which also did much to determine the political relationship. Hong Kong's once dominant role in the Mainland's economic affairs has undergone profound shrinkage. In this new situation, Mainland officials are far less likely to pay attention to their Hong Kong colleagues, whose previous high standing was heavily informed by the importance of the SAR to China's development. Moreover, now that Chinese companies are increasingly playing a major role in the Hong Kong economy, with a growing reliance on funds and other resources from the Mainland, what was once seen as the swagger of Hongkongers has pretty much disappeared.

Like a perennially anxious orphan, concerned over being abandoned by its adopted parents, Hong Kong has long been preoccupied by whether it is "serving" the Mainland's interests. Government officials, business leaders, media pontificators and many in between have agonised for years over this question. Was Hong Kong doing enough to promote economic growth in China? Was Hong Kong the key entrepôt for China's trade with the rest of the world? Would China be able to enter the international financial system without help from Hong Kong? And, most importantly, did any of this make Hong Kong sufficiently relevant for the Mainland's purposes?

In 1987, when I first arrived in Hong Kong, I kept being told that the key to preserving Hong Kong's distinctiveness from its

incoming sovereign was to ensure its continued economic usefulness to the Mainland. The highly complacent view in business
circles at the time was that plucky little Hong Kong had the
upper hand in this relationship. Fast forward to now, and in
some respects the SAR is indeed useful, continuing to provide
vital services to the Mainland—but its crucial role in China's
economic development is much reduced, and its importance
within the overall Chinese economy has shrunk significantly. In
1993 Hong Kong's GDP was equivalent to 27 per cent of the
entire PRC's. By any standards, this was an extraordinary figure
for such a tiny place. By 2018, that figure had contracted to
around 3 per cent.

Another measure of how things have changed is that in 1997,
at the time of the handover, something like half of China's overseas trade went through Hong Kong; now, it is less than
12 per cent.[13] In the heady days of Reform and Opening Up,
overseas companies wanting to get into the Mainland economy
generally did so via Hong Kong. The British colony provided all
the essentials for doing business in China: banking, accounting
and legal services were there and, most importantly, so was the
knowhow. Hong Kong businessmen were the pioneers setting up
companies in the PRC as the economy opened to foreign investment in the 1970s, and even by the end of the 2010s some
60 per cent of direct investment into the Mainland still flowed
through Hong Kong.[14]

Nowadays, much of this so-called direct investment comes
from Mainland companies based in Hong Kong recirculating
funds to take advantage of incentives available to inward investors.
This business is so well established that it even has its own name:
"round-tripping". However, a significant proportion of this
Mainland investment does remain in Hong Kong, where it is
invested in local businesses. From the 1980s, Mainland companies, notably the CITIC conglomerate now known as CITIC

Pacific, gingerly dipped their toes into the territory's economy. That timid entry quickly turned into a flood as businesses lined up to make their way across the border, opening swanky offices in pricey locations and sending hundreds of thousands of people to work in them. These Chinese companies are in the SAR for a number of reasons, primarily to provide a base for their activities in the rest of the world. They can also raise money for overseas investments, not least by tapping local banks. It is not only private Mainland companies using Hong Kong as a base. Three of the biggest state-owned enterprises—China Merchants, China Resources and China Travel Service—have relocated their headquarters to the SAR. Fifty of the ninety-six companies managed by the State-Owned Assets Supervision and Administration Commission have at least one subsidiary listed in Hong Kong.[15]

Corporations from across the border have moved to become major players in Hong Kong industries from construction and telecommunications to travel and trading. For instance, Chinese banks control twenty-four of the 193 licensed banks in the SAR as of October 2020.[16] Mainland companies have also started to challenge the big players in property development, to the extent that most of the local players find it expedient to partner with them in new projects. Companies such as China Vanke, China Overseas, Shimao Property and Poly Property are now well-established bidders in the land auctions that trigger all property developments in Hong Kong. In 2016 and 2017, Mainland property developers, sometimes in co-operation with local companies, purchased 40 per cent of the residential land at these auctions and contributed 65 per cent of the capital involved in the transactions.[17] This is remarkable because Chinese property developers only entered the market in 2011. According to research by the property agents JLL, one in ten privately built new homes in Hong Kong was expected to come from Chinese developers by 2019.[18] And when it comes to the business of building these projects, big Mainland companies invariably also figure large in the mix of construction companies doing the work. Strangely, or maybe not, the Party's criticism of property developers overlooked the operations of Mainland companies.

Property development is the biggest target for Mainland company investment in the SAR, but Mainland investors have also shown interest in a wide range of other sectors, making them the second biggest source of direct foreign investment overall. The consequences of this scale of Mainland intervention in the economy have been enormous—not just in business, but also because of its impact on Hong Kong's power structure.

Beyond direct investment in the SAR, we can also see this ever-growing presence in the stock market. One in every two companies listed on the Hong Kong stock exchange is Mainland-linked, and the benchmark Hang Seng Index largely consists of Mainland companies, which account for almost 77 per cent of the exchange's total capitalisation.[19] A commonly cited statistic is that, since 1997, Chinese companies have raised US$335 billion in capital through Hong Kong stock market listings, a figure that is still growing fast. What started out as a handful of Chinese listings has been transformed into a state of affairs where these companies can dictate terms to the Hong Kong stock market and have the muscle to secure exemptions from the rules.

In other words, it's the relatively recently arrived Mainland entities operating in Hong Kong who are now calling the shots. The Hong Kong stock exchange is under constant pressure to establish links and support the work of the two Mainland stock exchanges. In 2016, the Shenzhen–Hong Kong Stock Connect scheme was launched to draw more international capital into the Chinese market. This was followed by a connect scheme for Shanghai. Great claims are made for the success of these projects, but the suspicion lingers that much of the money raised comes from Chinese companies taking advantage of the preferential arrangements in order to bring capital back to the Mainland.

This shift in power at the stock exchange is reflected throughout the Hong Kong economy: investment banks, big law firms, the major accountancy companies and so on are now highly dependent on their Mainland clients. They have therefore had to learn how to behave in what is politely described as a "Mainland way" and, in so doing, have discovered that rules previously requiring scrupulous adherence have become flexible. Where this did not work, regulations have been changed to make the Mainland companies feel more comfortable. This has had the effect of undermining the integrity of Hong Kong's way of doing business, which both makes local professionals uncomfortable and impacts on the SAR's credibility as an international business centre.

And then there's the whole business of placing well-connected Mainlanders, often from families of senior Party officials, on the staff of local companies. Many arrive fresh from overseas business schools and universities with vaguely plausible claims to well-remunerated employment; but no one is under any illusion as to the real reason for their presence in the office. One lawyer with a mid-sized firm specialised in corporate law, and heavily dependent on Mainland business, told me that his office always has at least one of these "princelings" on the premises. "Mostly they are useless," he says, but the boss dares not fire them or even allocate much work to them, lest they complain to their relatives.

In October 2019, the German newspaper *Süddeutsche Zeitung* published a story based on a mass of internal documents, collected over a fifteen-year period, describing how Deutsche Bank in Hong Kong had won business in China by hiring more than 100 relatives of senior Chinese Party members, and showering them with lavish gifts and treats such as golf outings.[20] The German bank is hardly alone in this kind of behaviour.

Hong Kong business has learned to live with the presence of Mainland companies, but is finding it a lot more difficult to cope with the Chinese government in its role as a regulator. This is part and parcel of the control exercised over the SAR from Beijing that has caused such enormous resentment across Hong Kong society.

The extent to which this is so is most compellingly illustrated by what happened in August 2019 to Cathay Pacific, Hong Kong's de facto airline flag carrier. Cathay is especially vulnerable to Mainland control because not only is 30 per cent of its equity owned by Air China, the PRC's flag carrier, but the Chinese aviation authorities effectively control the airspace Cathay uses—not just to service Mainland destinations, but also to travel further afield, as planes taking off from Hong Kong fly over Chinese territory. Cathay's parent company Swire, one of the old conglomerates dominant in colonial Hong Kong, remains a major player in SAR business, although in November 2020 the parent company's shares were taken out of the benchmark Hang Seng Index for the first time in history. Moreover, Swire is highly susceptible to the whims of the Chinese government, given its Coca-Cola franchise on the Mainland, alongside a massive aircraft maintenance operation and property development projects.

As the Hong Kong protests escalated, the airport was occupied in August, amid widespread expressions of support from both ground staff and aircrew. The Chinese regime was incensed, but also saw an opportunity to hit back at a company it perceived as being "soft" on protestors. Melvin Swire, the company's chairman and, as his name suggests, a member of the company's founding family, was forced to fly to Beijing and engage in a humble act of abeyance, apologising for staff who had commented positively on the uprising. He was told that in future all crew members flying into Chinese airspace had to have their names submitted for checking, and anyone accused of supporting the protests would be banned. China's Civil Aviation Administration warned that Cathay needed to take firm action against staff who had participated in "radical activities", and Beijing insisted on sacking staff who had supported the movement in word or deed, including in private posts on social media.

Though Swire initially resisted this political interference, ultimately tens of staff were fired or forced to resign for supporting the uprising. Even this was not enough: the chairman was also told to purge Cathay's top management as punishment for their apparent transgressions. Rupert Hogg, the Chief Executive Officer, and Paul Loo, the chief of Cathay's customer and commercial office, were forced to resign, allegedly to take responsibility for lapses in flight safety and security. The reality was underlined when news of their departure was broadcast on Chinese state television before it was made public by the company itself. More widespread purges of Cathay staff continued after Hogg and Loo had gone, and the chairwoman of the company union was summarily kicked out.

What happened at Cathay sent a clear signal to all companies doing business with the Mainland. There were many reports of sackings by other companies fingering staff known to have supported the protests. China's principle of Party before profit is well known. Within state-owned enterprises, this principle is explicit: in a rare example of transparency, the CCP Central Committee published new regulations in January 2020 spelling out the Party's primacy in the operations of such enterprises. Among other stipulations, state enterprises must include recognition of the Communist Party in their articles of association, and a Party organ must be created in any state firm employing more than three Party members. "All major business and management decisions must be discussed by [this] Communist Party organ before being presented to the board of directors or management for decision." Moreover, state enterprise chairmen must be the Party secretary for these units.[21]

Later in the year, in September, the Party doubled down on enforcing its presence throughout the business sector, with a series of announcements outlining how private sector companies were expected to play their role. Among other things, this included the need to recruit Party members for advisory bodies, particularly in the technology sector, offering, in return, an expectation of more state aid.[22] Then, in November, the Party underlined its determination to impose control over the private sector in a manner unambiguously signalling to the rest of the world that even the biggest non-state companies with a high international profile need to keep in line. Ant Group, part of the Alibaba empire controlled by Party member Jack Ma, was two days away from launching what would have been the world's biggest-share Initial Public Offering, when the authorities ordered it to be pulled. The Group then came under investigation by no fewer than four government regulators, followed by a slew of investigations into the operation of Alibaba itself on grounds of anti-trust violations. It now seems clear that this flurry of activity was sparked by Ma's criticism of the Chinese banking system, and suggestions that business was being held back by the way that financial institutions were controlled. Many commentators have noted that Ma's main offence seems to have been getting too big for his boots, necessitating a sharp reminder that the Party always calls the shots.

* * *

Even though Hong Kong's presence has diminished within the Chinese economy, there are still ways in which the SAR continues to play a key role. As we shall see in Chapter 11, Hong Kong's really irreplaceable function for the Mainland's leaders has little to do with wider economic considerations, but is linked to their personal financial interests, something which is rarely discussed. Hong Kong, under its new masters, has travelled some way from being the Chinese economy's indispensable "growth factor", or the necessary facilitator bringing the Mainland's economy into the wider world. The boot is now on the other foot, and even the grandest of local entrepreneurs have learned that the correct response to being asked to jump on demand is: how high?

In short, Hongkongers have long had good reason for economic discontent, and were anxious about the shadow of the Mainland looming ever larger over their economy. And, as we saw in Chapter 2, they were faced with a political system that had no way of adequately accommodating their views. On top of all this was another part of the equation explaining the background to the uprising, as we shall see in the following chapter: the unfolding of a new sense of Hong Kong identity.

4

CHINA'S NIGHTMARE

THE BIRTH OF A HONG KONG IDENTITY

At the heart of the 2019–20 democracy movement lies the iden-tification of people in Hong Kong as Hongkongers. This sense of a specific Hong Kong identity had been growing for some time, but it took the uprising to both crystallise awareness of it and firmly establish its political importance.

In August 2019, when the protests were intensifying, Chief Executive Carrie Lam infamously claimed that the protestors represented a "small minority of people" who "have no stake in the society which so many people have helped to build, and that's why they resort to all this violence and obstructions [sic] causing huge damage to the economy and to the daily life of the people".[1] Her remarks provoked a furious backlash, because at the heart of the protest movement is a tenacious sense of attachment to Hong Kong as their home, and a strong commitment to its future as a free society. The people on the streets most definitely thought they had a stake.

A year on, Lam was no longer talking about Hongkongers having no stake in society, but criticising them for excessive concern. She said: "There's a recent trend in Hong Kong, where people over-emphasize local culture."[2]

The reality is that, whether the people had "no stake" in Hong Kong or were excessively emphasising its individuality, the people who shout loudest about their loyalty to the new order and stand stiffly to attention when the Chinese national anthem is played are ambiguous at best, and hypocritical at worst, in their attitude towards the SAR. They flaunt their Chinese patriotism while, much more quietly, going to considerable lengths to secure a means of exit from the nation they proclaim to be so close to their hearts. Almost without exception, members of Hong Kong's ruling class have prepared elaborate escape routes for themselves and their money. Their families have foreign passports, are educated abroad and have sizeable assets overseas.

This simmering hypocrisy starts at the very top of the government. Each one of Carrie Lam's predecessors as Chief Executive ticks these boxes. Lam herself has—or at least had—a way out by virtue of the fact that both her husband and her two sons hold British nationality. She herself was a British national up until 2007, when she relinquished her overseas citizenship—a requirement for the top job.[3] Nor is she alone in the current administration: two of the officials who have been at the centre of government attempts to put down the protests also have escape routes to democratic countries. The security minister, John Lee, is a former high-ranking police officer who stumbled out of his bureaucratic cocoon into the spotlight during the uprising by parroting the rhetoric of the force's leadership; he can claim British citizenship, as both his wife and two children are UK citizens. Justice minister Teresa Cheng was lured into government service by Lam after many other members of the legal profession made it clear that they did not want to serve under her. She has the right to emigrate because her husband has a Canadian passport. And the studiously low-key Tam Yiu-chung is the sole Hong Kong member of the PRC's parliamentary executive, making him the seniormost Hongkonger in China's national decision-making—he has two sons safely tucked away in Australia. So, if anyone could be described as lacking commitment to Hong Kong, surely it is the ruling elite; not the ordinary people who took to the streets to preserve a way of life they value. Unlike the rich and powerful, most protestors weren't spending their time devising an escape route.

Beijing views their strong sense of Hong Kong identity as a dangerous manifestation; but the majority of Hongkongers, while cherishing the distinctiveness of Hong Kong, are not looking to separate themselves from China and create an independent nation. And, just to be clear, contrary to repeated claims by Chinese officials and their supporters, there was no call for secession or independence in the protestors' demands. Most of all, pro-democracy Hongkongers harbour a feeling that was summed up by a young protestor I interviewed during the airport protests. He said, "I just wish they'd leave us alone." But leaving citizens to their own devices is not the way of the Chinese Communist Party.

The struggle for a sense of identity as Hongkongers is something that has been slowly building, to the point where the majority of people now identify themselves as part of a distinctive entity that may well not be a nation-state, but has a distinctive culture and way of life. Regional divisions and hostilities are common in a great many countries, and indeed in parts of China; the problem in Hong Kong is that these either emerge in ugly street confrontations between Mainlanders and Hongkongers, or are unrealistically ignored.

There is a long history of mutual suspicion between Cantonese and Northern Chinese. Not only do they speak very different languages, they also tend to look different. While power resides in the north of the country, it is unsurprising that so few Cantonese have any part in national authority. It is worth remembering that one of the reasons why Beijing selected Tung Chee-hwa as Hong Kong's first Chief Executive is that he is not Cantonese. Born in Shanghai and very much part of Hong Kong's elite Shanghainese community, he made Chinese officials feel more comfortable than any of the possible Cantonese contenders for the post.

One of the most important aspects of Hong Kong culture and pride is the Cantonese language. Its importance nationally can be judged by the fact that the first Chinese republic was actively toying with the idea of making it the national language, not least because it was the mother tongue of Sun Yat Sen, the republic's founding president. Yet the official line in China is that everyone should speak Mandarin and that the nation's other languages are mere dialects. Thus China's most avid supporters in Hong Kong want the official language of instruction in schools to be Mandarin, also known as Putonghua (which translates as "the common people's language"). They also think that Hong Kong's use of complex Chinese characters needs to be replaced by the standardised simplified characters used on the Mainland. But Hongkongers view their written version of Chinese with pride, and note that Mandarin, a northern language, has a rather shorter history than Cantonese. What's more, Hong Kong Cantonese is the same but somewhat different from the Cantonese spoken in Guangdong Province: it is richly embellished with a distinctive slang, has its own words for a great many things, mixes in a form of English, and comes with an accent clearly identifiable to native speakers.

So, the fight for Hong Kong identity is very much a struggle to preserve the language, and the culture that flows from it. As the protests developed in 2019, there was a growing backlash against Mandarin. This was part of the process of defining Hong Kong by emphasising everything that distinguishes it from the Mainland. A friend recalls going to a Hong Kong democracy concert in New York headlined by the pop star, actress and democracy activist Denise Ho, who is trilingual in Cantonese, Mandarin and English. When she started speaking in Mandarin to address "our friends from the Mainland", the crowd started booing and jeering until, by force of personality, she got them to simmer down, explaining the importance of getting all the people of China onside. They sort of got it, but the loudest cheers came when she reverted to Cantonese.

When I've spoken especially to younger Hong Kong people, most of whom can in fact manage pretty good Mandarin, they have often told me unprompted, even well before the uprising began, that they will never speak the language again.

* * *

The Hong Kong University Public Opinion Programme has been tracking the question of identity for a long time, and found that by 2019 a majority of people identified themselves as Hongkongers (53%). This was a dramatic increase from just two years previously, when only 37% identified this way. Up until 2018, the largest cohort said that they had a mixed identity, both Hongkongers and Chinese—they represented 43% that year. This percentage dropped to 36% the following year.

The really bad news for the Party, which counts instilling pride in the nation among its priorities, is that even in 2017 only 21% of those surveyed identified as Chinese, a figure that dropped sharply to 11% in 2019. The news got even worse when researchers asked respondents whether they were proud of having become citizens of China in 1997. A mere 27% answered "yes" to this question in 2019, compared with 71% saying "no". Unsurprisingly, those who considered themselves to be either Chinese or of a mixed identity were concentrated among people aged 50 or older. Among the young, aged 18–29, practically no one identifies as Chinese. Indeed, three out of four younger people describe themselves as Hongkongers. Moreover, a paltry 9% of people in this age group said they were proud of being Chinese nationals.[4]

In the wake of the Hong Kong protests—albeit not definitively because of the protests—there was also a sharp upturn among people in Taiwan identifying themselves as Taiwanese, as opposed to "Taiwanese and Chinese". In a survey conducted by the Pew Research Center in October 2019, 66% of interviewees declared themselves to be Taiwanese, whereas only 28% said they had a dual identity. Among those aged 18–29, the level of identification as Taiwanese shot up to 83%.[5]

It is also interesting to note that, despite a century and a half of British colonial rule, most Hongkongers never considered themselves to be British. Some carried British passports, or the strange demi-passport marked "British Dependent Territories Citizen". This passport, later changed to designate "British Nationals Overseas" (BNO), was held by over 300,000 Hongkongers before the imposition of the National Security Law from July 2020, but it was little more than a line on a travel document. In response to the NSL, Britain decided to offer BNO-holders, potentially amounting to some 3 million people, the right of settlement in the UK. At this point, applications for the passport surged—but, again, this cannot be taken as a sign of identification with Britain. Many who had not previously bothered obtaining a BNO passport were now looking for a means of escape, and were just as grateful to other countries opening their doors, such as Canada and Australia.

Indeed, Britain had no previous intention of transforming a large swathe of BNO-holders into citizens, even though at the time of the handover there was pressure for the UK to do so. As we have seen, Britain's ambivalence towards its former colony is very long-standing, and in part explains why the government in London was not overly bothered by the fate of the people they were leaving behind in Hong Kong—the first and only British colony handed over to a sovereign state without the consent of its people, who had neither demanded the end of British rule nor expressed a desire to be ruled by a dictatorship.

Even if Hongkongers didn't necessarily view the handover with relish, it equally cannot be said that this was because they felt particularly British. In other British colonies, notably India, the British were keen to evoke in their subjects a sense of loyalty to the "Mother Country", and to foster what were considered to be British attitudes, not least British sport in the form of cricket. In Hong Kong, however, efforts to instil a sense of "Britishness" were made half-heartedly, if at all. At heart, Britain had long viewed its presence in Hong Kong as no more than transitory, and was never enthusiastic about fostering a British identity while ruling the colony. This, combined with the UK's fear of furnishing Hongkongers with British passports in 1997, has meant that, by and large, the impact of colonialism on issues of identity has been far less significant than might be imagined.

This is not to say that a century and half of British rule failed to leave any impression on the complexity of factors that have forged Hong Kong identity. Of course it did. Among the complications inherent in "Hongkongness" is the fact that, until 1997, the people who governed Hong Kong were of a different race and spoke another language. In the colonial era, Hong Kong people needed to learn English if they aspired to success in this strange place. With the transfer of sovereignty in 1997 came another linguistic and cultural challenge, with the use of Mandarin as the crucial official language alongside Cantonese and English, and the need to master it for the same reasons that English had to be mastered.

But Hong Kong identity is not as British as Party supporters claim. They taunt Hongkongers for having failed to shake off their colonial mindset. It is interesting to note that this claim is also made about the people of Taiwan, who are damned with the suggestion that a long Japanese occupation gave them a "Japanese mentality". Some of this is little more than name-calling, but most of it reflects an insecurity among those who passionately believe in the hegemony of the Chinese nation and fear that differences among the people will lead to chaos. They do not see diversity as equating with strength.

* * *

Yet diversity is precisely what has contributed to the evolution of identity in Hong Kong. Up until the 1970s, the majority of the colony's population had been born on the Mainland; in other words, most people were immigrants. However, the 2016 by-census, the most recent with a breakdown by place of birth, showed that around 60 per cent of the population was born in Hong Kong. The share of the population born locally continues to grow. In 2016 the demographic shift was moving fast: while only a third of those aged 65 and above were born in Hong Kong, while over 90 per cent of Hongkongers under 15 were locally born.[6]

This major shift helps explain changing attitudes towards identity, which fuelled the 2019–20 uprising. A society largely composed of immigrants tends to have low expectations of government support and a strong belief in the ability of individuals to overcome adversity. Once the immigrant majority gives way to a majority of locally born, there is a rising demand for government intervention to address inequality. An academic study published in 2015 found that almost 58 per cent of those questioned in the SAR supported government mitigation of income disparity, whereas only 13.6 per cent opposed state intervention. The authors saw this as part of a rising trend away from the laissez-faire attitudes that have long been held to be dominant in Hong Kong.[7]

The democracy activist Joshua Wong, who was born in 1996, is seen by many people as the face of the movement. Bespectacled, skinny and with a tendency to speak in a staccato manner, he is not at first sight the most obvious of leaders; but his combination of extraordinary energy and determination demands attention. He has eloquently expressed why Hongkongers of his age are "struggling to carve our place in the world and develop an identity in our own image. More and more we look to our pop culture, language, food and unique way of life as the foundations of that self-image."[8]

It is not axiomatic that younger, Hong Kong-born people are the only ones protesting. The uprising's bigger rallies always saw high levels of participation from all age groups. Nevertheless, the younger generation were to the fore and, in the most general terms, it is possible to state that the bedrock of the pro-China camp is the older generation, who both identify more with the Mainland and are acutely aware of the kind of chaos they have experienced in their earlier lives as a result of political change.

Although the demographic changes are significant, Hong Kong retains the characteristics of an immigrant society today, because the majority of Hong Kong families are still rooted in people who arrived after birth: even those born in the territory have parents or grandparents born on the Mainland.

In crude terms, Hong Kong—like most immigrant societies—has seen the first generation experience difficulties integrating, some finding it hard to learn the new language and tending to gravitate towards communities of fellow immigrants. In Hong Kong, language was less of an issue than it may be elsewhere; but it did mean that first-generation arrivals from non-Cantonese-speaking regions tended to keep together, producing the emergence of individual districts heavily populated, for example, by Shanghainese or Fujianese. The second generation, by contrast, are unlikely to have linguistic or social adjustment problems and are much keener to integrate. They have hardworking parents as their role models, but may not be quite as driven to succeed. By the third generation, there is much less awareness of the place of origin. The generation now coming to the fore in Hong Kong is marked by even greater levels of integration into the host community, and a closer sense of identification with the place of their birth. No longer sharing their forebears' attachment to the Mainland, the new generation insist on their Hongkongness, and have markedly less enthusiasm for visits to their ancestral homes on the Mainland, which are highly valued by the older generation. Little wonder, then, that the issue of identity in the SAR remains complicated.

This is not a situation exceptional to Hong Kong: it is in the nature of many immigrant societies around the world, most of them created through colonialism, for subsequent generations to identify more strongly with the place than the original incomers. Even in other immigrant-based nations such as the United States, it took a while for something called an American identity to emerge. Crucially, however, places like the USA have found a way of accommodating an American identity that is compatible with immigrants' identification with their country of origin— hence the proliferation of dual identities, African American, Irish American, Italian American and so on. This duality is a sign of a country comfortable in its own skin, able to acknowledge and celebrate diversity while maintaining "Americanism" at its core. The United States is not unique in this respect; many other countries value the contribution made by diversity as a consequence of immigration and actively nurture both a sense of belonging and pride in their citizens' other backgrounds.

The problem in Hong Kong is that the new master does not encourage a sense of belonging in Hong Kong. It insists that citizens of the People's Republic of China are Chinese and nothing else. There was a time when compromise on this absolute position was possible, as many people in the 1970s, '80s and '90s identified as Hong Kong Chinese, or some other mixed variation. But even this was not acceptable to the Party. Considerably less acceptable is the new situation of people simply calling themselves Hongkongers, which is viewed as a dangerous manifestation of a lack of patriotism.

Moreover, the question of identity has become intensely political, because the Party insists that loyalty to and support for the PRC is of paramount importance, and cannot tolerate this being "qualified" by any other kind of loyalty. It is notable that members of the Hong Kong opposition are routinely described as "traitors" in the Mainland media, because opposition is seen as an act of turning one's back on the nation and undermining it. In his book, *Unfree Speech*, Joshua Wong recalls that, when he spent time in jail after the Umbrella Movement, older prisoners would routinely shout the word at him.

It would be wrong to say that Hong Kong people, even those most strongly opposed to China's political system, have no pride in the Chinese nation, which is not to be equated with pride in the Chinese Communist Party. There was, for example, a surge of national identity when Beijing hosted the Olympic Games in 2008. In the same year, Hongkongers dug deep into their pockets to support the victims of the devastating earthquake in Sichuan Province. They also celebrated the heroism of rescuers on the scene. However, Beijing's determination to politicise these events and transform them into a narrative of support for the Party quickly led to the dissipation of patriotic sentiment.

People who identify themselves as Hongkongers are also making a political statement, indeed a highly charged one. This is why one of the most popular t-shirts seen at the protests bears three Chinese characters that translate as "Hong Kong Person", and it is why one of the most popular slogans of the movement is "Hong Kong is not China". Maybe what this slogan also means is that there is a new generation in Hong Kong defining themselves more clearly by what they are not rather than by what they are.

As we shall see in Part Two, prior to 2019 younger members of the democratic movement had been impatient with older members keen to commemorate the 1989 Tiananmen Square massacre as part of their concern and engagement with the democracy movement on the Mainland: "What's it got to do with us?" That question deeply troubled the founders of the Hong Kong movement, such as Martin Lee and the late Szeto Wah; but, as the uprising developed, views converged, with the older generation of protestors coming to share the emphasis on Hong Kong, and more young people coming to appreciate the mutual relevance of the two struggles. Interviewing young people at the protests, you often hear them saying things like "Only my parents care about the Mainland", and "I was born here; I don't care what happens on the Mainland." But Beijing's increasingly harsh crackdown on the movement, and particularly its clueless response to the emerging Hong Kong identity, have ironically turned indifference toward the PRC into alienation and anger.

The Party has little idea how to combat either indifference or alienation. It seems to think that these problems would fade away if only schools could more thoroughly indoctrinate impressionable students. Sometimes Chinese leaders believe that attitudes can be changed by dangling the inducement of greater prosperity through greater integration with the Mainland. But this offer has few takers in Hong Kong. So, like all dictatorships, where the carrot does not work, the Chinese state falls back on the option of the stick. The Party's local cyphers call for greater punishment to be inflicted on protestors, for those supporting the opposition to be weeded out of the workplace, and for draconian action to reduce freedom of expression. They want non-patriotic teachers kicked out of schools and replaced with real patriots who will embark on intensive indoctrination as a substitute for liberal studies classes, which are held to be responsible for school students developing foreign ideas.

There is little place for internationalism or diversity in China, and so the concept of people in Hong Kong being Hongkongers is dangerous and needs to be suppressed. Hongkongers, for their part, have seen the Party's intolerance as reinforcing the very values that set them apart from the Mainland. So, if nothing else emerges from the protests of the 2000s, it will be a strengthening of what might be called Hongkongism. A politically charged concept with enormous social implications, and a vicious circle of mutual incomprehension.

PART TWO

THE UPRISING

5

HUBRIS

To understand how the 2019–20 protests came about and what triggered this unprecedented outpouring of discontent requires a look at the four-year period of official hubris that stoked the pent-up fury unleashed in June 2019. In other words, what happened after the 2014 Umbrella Movement was extinguished.

This movement grew out of a civil disobedience initiative called Occupy Central, designed to oppose government plans for reforming the election system, allegedly to promote democratic development. When the plans were finally tabled, it became clear that the price for granting elections of the Chief Executive through a process of universal suffrage was that only candidates endorsed by Beijing would be on offer. It was hard to say what annoyed people most. Was it the plan itself? Or the suggestion that Hongkongers would be too stupid to notice that they were being given a vote for the sole purpose of installing someone with a mandate from Beijing?

The Umbrella Movement that took to the streets outside the government complex in the centre of town in September 2014 was more radical than the protests envisaged by the Occupy

Central organisers. It was so called because of the distinctive presence of thousands of (mainly yellow) umbrellas, deployed as a somewhat inadequate barrier against tear gas. Hundreds of thousands of mainly young people who had never before joined the democracy movement were mobilised.

The protest lasted for seventy-nine exhausting days. By the time it ended, 955 people had been arrested. However, the authorities were careful to draw out actual prosecutions; a drip-drip process eventually brought all the high-profile leaders to court. In all, over 300 people were eventually charged—less than a third of those arrested, and a mere fraction of the more than 10,000 arrests that would be made during the 2019–20 uprising.[1]

Top of the list for prosecution were Joshua Wong, who was arrested alongside Nathan Law and Alex Chow; this is the most famous trio of young democracy leaders. The original founders of the non-violent Occupy movement that morphed into Umbrella were brought to trial much later. Academics Benny Tai and Chan Kin-man, alongside the cleric Chu Yiu-ming, were jailed for various offences connected with their leadership role (Chu's sentence was suspended). Another six prominent leaders were convicted at the same time: three former and current legislators, two student leaders and a well-known political activist. These convictions were drawn out over a long period and meant, for example, that Wong was still in jail when fresh protests broke out in 2019, while others like Benny Tai were sent to jail during the later uprising for offences committed in 2014.

What the 2019 movement took from these arrests is that it would be better to have no readily identifiable leaders who could be targeted and removed, leaving the movement rudderless. This was one of many lessons learned from the Umbrella Movement, as we shall see in the next chapter; but, in the intervening years, some momentum was lost. Large street protests went into hibernation after the Umbrella Movement was crushed, and demoralisation set in as the government embarked on a steady flow of measures to hammer home the point that opposition was futile. This hard line in Hong Kong emanated from an increasing crackdown on protest in the Mainland, where President Xi Jinping was moving the goalposts for toleration of dissent into a very narrow space.

A year after the Umbrella protests ended, it became clear just how far the Chinese authorities were now prepared to upend what they regarded as restraint in dealing with Hong Kong. Hitherto, dissident activity in Hong Kong connected to the Mainland had been given considerable leeway, and the existence of a physical border between the two ensured that dissidents had no fear of being plucked off the SAR's streets and despatched to the other side of the border. There had been rumours that this kind of "restraint" might be coming to an end, but these fears morphed into shocking reality in 2015, when the people running a shop called Causeway Bay Books were abducted and bundled over to the Mainland for interrogation.

This was one of the few bookshops carrying a comprehensive range of works criticising the Communist Party leadership, sometimes in lurid and fanciful detail. It had been the case that activity such as publishing dissident works could be conducted safely in Hong Kong, but it rapidly became clear after the abduction that this complacent assumption no longer held. More worryingly, but perhaps unsurprisingly, the Hong Kong government refused to lift a single finger to protect the rights of its citizens who had been seized. The last of the five men abducted to China, Gui Minhai, remains in detention at the time of writing. He is a Swedish citizen who, unlike the other four men seized in Hong Kong, was snatched in Thailand without any legal process.

Having noted the relatively muted response to the removal of the booksellers, the Chinese authorities subsequently succeeded in shutting down other publishing companies and booksellers, and even managing to ensure that local printers would no longer produce politically sensitive books. There was also polling evidence suggesting that the government and its supporters were winning over popular opinion; this appeared to be confirmed in byelections that followed the 2016 Legco election giving victory to pro-government candidates.

In January 2017, the Chinese authorities launched an even more high-profile abduction, not least because the victim was a prominent billionaire: leading businessman Xiao Jianhua, seized at the five-star Four Seasons Hotel, in the centre of Hong Kong's financial district. No charges were laid, at least in the public domain, but rumours of his involvement in an intra-Party struggle were rife, alongside shadowy accusations relating to stock market manipulation. However, what seems to have sealed his fate was an interview in *The New York Times*, published in 2014, giving details of assets he had purchased from Xi Jinping's sister and her husband, reflecting their considerable wealth. As a banker, among other things, Xiao was privy to a great deal of information concerning the financial dealings of Party leaders.

As with the booksellers, Xiao's abduction didn't produce sufficient kickback to unduly concern the authorities. Indeed, the general level of protest in the SAR was well down on previous years—the mood of despondency in the democracy camp seemed to be as unshakeable as the sense of victory among the government and its allies. This emboldened them to move from what they saw as winning the argument to punishing their opponents. In the year following the result, six democrats who had managed to win seats in the legislature were expelled for "improper" oath-taking. Even more disappointing for the democrats was that in two of the byelections following these expulsions, pro-China candidates overturned the previous democrat victories. Subsequently, another two democrats were expelled from the

Legco. By 2019, almost a third of those elected on the democratic ticket had been removed.

The pro-China majority in the legislature saw this as a green light to set about changing the rules of procedure, to limit debate and thwart questioning of officials. There was little that the democrats could do aside from filibuster, which had the look of desperation and provided ammunition for the government, which mounted a campaign decrying the obstructionist tactics of the opposition.

Less visible was an underground white terror running through public institutions, notably universities, where academics associated with the opposition found themselves losing their jobs, being denied tenure and forced into early retirement. This clampdown in the education sector became even more evident during the uprising: at the end of 2019, school teachers started to be suspended for taking part in demonstrations, after anonymous informants unearthed their private online posts supporting the protest movement. In the civil service itself, those who had demonstrated their closeness to the PRC moved to pole position for rapid promotion, and official advisory bodies that were supposed to provide independent advice on public policy were shorn of members associated with the democrat camp—a sharp reversal from the days when these bodies provided a rare forum for co-operation between all shades of opinion.

Months into the uprising, the mood in the pro-China camp was described by Jasper Tsang, who is widely recognised as being one of the most articulate and open-minded members of the pro-China camp. A former Legco president and former headmaster of a Beijing-backed middle school, he is also undoubtedly a member of Hong Kong's underground Communist Party. Interviewed by the *Hong Kong Free Press* in November 2019, Tsang said that, until the uprising, "many of my colleagues in the pro-government camp thought that we were winning victory after victory". He added something that few others on his side of the fence would be prepared to admit: that this hubris was making the people angry.[2]

* * *

The democracy movement may have suffered electoral setbacks in 2016, but it had also been tentatively showing renewed signs of life earlier in the year, with the so-called Fish Ball Revolution. This was not an overtly political movement in the sense of the Umbrella Movement, but it reflected activists' growing realisation that opposition required a broader social base, and had to get more deeply involved with the needs of the underprivileged. One of the ways that Hong Kong's underclass managed to make a living was by operating unlicensed small-scale businesses. For instance, selling fish balls on the tightly packed streets of Mong Kok, a largely working-class area. Street food-hawkers were being rounded up by the police for not having a licence, and violent clashes followed.

One of the people who emerged as a leader of this resistance was Edward Leung, back from the United States, where he had been studying at Harvard. In 2018, Leung would be jailed for six years following his conviction for rioting and assaulting a police officer in 2016. Known as a "localist", someone advocating Hong Kong concerns and intent on preserving the SAR's autonomy, Leung is a quiet, studious and somewhat austere-looking person, not at first sight a charismatic character; but he comes alive when addressing people through a microphone. He declared his intention to run for Legco in 2016 under the slogan "Liberate Hong Kong, Revolution of Our Times!" This slogan managed to capture the mood that was to erupt with the 2019 protest movement. Since the imposition of the new National Security Law in 2020, chanting Leung's slogan has been grounds for arrest. Although Leung himself is still confined to jail, both his words and his image have often been seen throughout the protests. In many ways, he became the hero of the uprising.

Ultimately, Leung was disqualified from running in 2016, even though he had taken part in a byelection earlier that year. In the midst of fighting his disqualification, he wrote on Facebook: "Those in power do not want me in Legco, but even if I need to crawl into it or roll into it, no matter how, I have to enter the system."[3] This was accompanied by what became known as the "DQing" of five others, who were also barred from running on grounds of suspected sympathy with separatist views. Disqualification of this kind had not been used before as a method of "screening out" candidates with unacceptable political views.

In 2017, Carrie Lam was "elected" as Chief Executive, replacing Leung Chun-ying. Leung, a hardliner with an extraordinary knack for making enemies even among people who would otherwise be expected to support him, had landed himself in Beijing's bad books not just because the Umbrella Movement had emerged under his watch, but also because of his failed attempt to bring in a national education curriculum after taking office in 2012. Democrats saw this imposition of a new curriculum as little more than an attempt to force schools to teach the kind of propaganda commonplace across the border. Leading the successful protest against this move was Joshua Wong, then just 15 years old. It was a humiliating defeat for Leung, but his strong "patriotic" credentials had saved him back then; they could not do so again after the 2014 protests. The excuse for ending his tenure after one term, originally supposed to be two, was Leung's sudden discovery of pressing "family reasons" for not being able to continue. As a face-saver, he was made a vice-chairman of the National Committee of the Chinese People's Political Consultative Conference, a post carrying considerably more prestige than power. As he made way for a new CE, it was widely imagined that no one could possibly be as unpopular as he had been. Enter Carrie Lam.

A civil service lifer, Lam arrived in office steeped in the belief that the government always knows best, and a firm conviction of the need to conscientiously serve those in power. Her competence as a bureaucrat is in sharp contrast to her almost aggressive lack of political talents and unwillingness to learn any of the basic skills of leadership, most notably that of empathy. Even those close to her are somewhat taken aback by her adamant refusal to take advice from colleagues or listen to anyone aside from Beijing emissaries. It should be noted that, of all Hong Kong's rulers, only the last colonial Governor, Chris Patten, managed to leave office with ratings higher than when he started out. Painfully aware that—despite his lifelong experience as an elected politician—he was an appointee in Hong Kong, Patten had approached his governorship as if it were an elected office. Often seen on the streets, he made endless efforts to reach out to opponents and worked hard to promote democracy prior to the handover; Beijing remains deeply resentful of his enduring popularity in the SAR. By contrast, all three of Lam's predecessors as Chief Executive since the handover have left office with ratings well below the high levels they had enjoyed at the start of their tenure, and Lam herself set new lows. But she entered the scene promising Beijing a safe pair of hands that would get the job done.

With zero experience of grassroots politics, Lam arrived at the top with very little of the ideological baggage that had weighed down her predecessor. Her mission, as dictated in Beijing, was unmistakeable: to consolidate the defeat of the opposition and, among other things, get back on track the introduction of a national security law, as set out in Article 23 of the Basic Law. Lam was given credit for not rushing ahead with this, on grounds that when Tung Chee-hwa had attempted it in 2003, this had provoked mass demonstrations leading to his resignation. (Just to complete the dismal history of Chief Executives, his successor, Donald Tsang, was jailed for misconduct in public office, albeit released on the technical grounds of a mistrial, without the substantive offence being considered again.)

Lam let her masters in Beijing know that, although the national security legislation would be put on hold, they were to rest assured that she would be no pushover for the opposition. On the contrary, she had plans to keep them in their place, and would show her resolute determination in reminding Hongkongers who was in charge.

One of the first indications of how she would go about getting this job done came from a totally unexpected quarter, when Lam suddenly announced that a branch of Beijing's Palace Museum was to be opened at the new cultural complex being built in West Kowloon. The museum is seen by Beijing as part of its cultural mission to foster patriotic awareness of China's history. It has long played a role in Chinese politics, not least when most of its treasures were shipped to Taiwan by the retreating Kuomintang. Not only did Lam not even consult the organisation responsible for the complex, but she made sure that she would not have to go to the legislature for funding, as the money would come from the powerful Jockey Club. The horse-racing body is the sole legally recognised gambling institution in Hong Kong; in return for this enormously lucrative privilege, the club is expected to fund numerous government projects. Lam subsequently explained that she had rushed through her plan in secret because she wanted to avoid an "embarrassing situation" that would have arisen had the public been given an opportunity to oppose the project.

The museum served two important objectives for Lam. First, it demonstrated to her masters in Beijing that she could get things done, and with speed. Second, a venue for Chinese treasures (albeit, as it has turned out, not of the first order) affirmed her willingness to be at the forefront of efforts to promote patriotism. But what it also showed was that Lam has very little time for consultation, and a firm conviction in the rightness of her own views. Rather astonishingly, she chose to put her indifference to others' opinions on record a year later, in a joint interview with "trusted" journalists. The Chief Executive explained that she was "immune" to criticism, arguing, "Why allocate and spend time to read, to listen [to critics] and to be unhappy? Why not just don't read and don't listen ... no matter how [they] berate me, it won't affect my work."[5] Not only was Lam uninterested in listening to opposing views, but she had no hesitation in trampling over procedures that got in her way. Building around the new museum was to take place at breakneck speed, very much at the expense of other developments in the long-planned cultural complex.

By 2019, Lam was feeling increasingly secure in her position, and seemingly enjoying a good rapport with Beijing. She was keen to consolidate this level of approval and equally keen to show her opponents that they had failed.

Rumbling in the background, but from an unexpected quarter, were flickers of defiance that needed, in her view, to be stamped out. Hong Kong football team supporters had been making a practice of booing the *March of the Volunteers*, China's national anthem, at international games. This insult to the state was the kind of thing that sends Mainland officials into a frenzy. So, in January 2019, Lam introduced a national anthem law, modelled on Mainland legislation, carrying severe penalties for showing disrespect towards the anthem and specifying how and when it should be performed. A combination of mockery and concern greeted this proposal, but, again, it seemed as though the CE would have no problem getting it on the statute books before the end of the year. Its passage was in fact stalled by the 2019 protests, a turn of events Lam certainly didn't see coming, but it was finally pummelled through Legco with minimal debate in June 2020.

* * *

The introduction of the national anthem law stirred the democratic camp but, yet again, not sufficiently to provoke widespread protest. The real bombshell, which at the time appeared to be barely fizzling, came a month later, with a proposal to amend the Fugitive Offenders Ordinance and the Mutual Legal Assistance in Criminal Matters Ordinance. These amendments would allow ad-hoc extraditions to jurisdictions with which Hong Kong did not have existing rendition arrangements, including Mainland China, Macau and Taiwan. This, in other words, was the infamous extradition bill that became the focus of the 2019 protests.

What happened next is detailed in the following chapter, but let's pause to consider why on earth Carrie Lam thought it would be a good idea to introduce this legislation in the first place; and to consider whether she was doing little more than following instructions from Beijing.

The pretext for the bill's sudden introduction was the murder in Taipei of 20-year-old Poon Hiu-wing by her boyfriend Chan Tong-kai, 19; the young couple were Hong Kong residents who had gone to Taiwan for a holiday in February. The following month, Chan, back in Hong Kong, reportedly admitted to the murder, but was arrested on separate charges of theft and money-laundering. The Taiwanese authorities requested his extradition to face murder charges for a crime on their soil, but the Hong Kong authorities were unprepared to co-operate, citing the lack of an extradition treaty, accompanied by strict adherence to the Beijing line, which insisted that Taiwan could not be treated as a jurisdiction apart from the Mainland. At this point, Lam declared that the enactment of the extradition bill was urgent for humanitarian reasons and at the behest of Poon's family.

The reality was that previously such cases had been dealt with by discreet co-operation between the two authorities, but in the new atmosphere the Hong Kong government had other objectives. Indeed, their actual disinterest in securing justice for the Poon family became crystal-clear after Chan was released from jail in October 2019, where he had been serving time for the other, lesser offences. Again Taiwan pressed for his transfer to face charges, but the Lam government insisted that this could only happen if its own police force delivered him to the island. By this point, Taiwan was in the midst of a presidential election campaign, and the Tsai government was also keen to play politics, insisting on its jurisdiction and right to collect the suspect from Hong Kong, which is the norm in cases of murder elsewhere in the world. At the time of writing, Chan remains a free man living in Hong Kong under police protection. In October 2020, he made a determined attempt to return to Taiwan, but the complicated politics of the Taiwan–Hong Kong relationship stymied his efforts.

As demonstrations against the extradition bill progressed through spring 2019, even the government ceased pretending that its timing was primarily linked to the Taiwan murder case. Instead there was a widespread belief that Lam had acted under orders from Beijing. This impression was reinforced by the Mainland propaganda machine and its echo chamber in Hong Kong, whose members were unceasing in extolling the virtues of the legislation and stressing its urgency. Pro-China legislators told me that officials from the Central Liaison Office had been pressing them to ensure the bill's smooth and speedy transit through Legco.

However, as protests mushroomed, Beijing—while still supporting the legislation—saw the need to ensure that blame for the unrest fell squarely on Lam's shoulders. It is certain that the Chief Executive sought approval for her move prior to announcing it: approval is most likely to have come from the highest level, meaning Han Zheng, the most senior official presiding over Hong Kong policy.[6] But the Chinese government bluntly denied being responsible for the bill's initiation. The ambassador to London, Liu Xiaoming, who frequently performs the leading role in defending his country's policy to the overseas media, was first in line to tell the BBC in June: "As a matter of fact, [the] Beijing central government gave no instruction, no order about making [the] amendment. This amendment was initiated by the Hong Kong government, it was prompted by a murder case in Taiwan."[7] Although Liu has proved himself to be a slippery customer when explaining Beijing's actions, on this occasion there is considerable evidence that his denial of a direct intervention was honest. Lam herself also stressed that she was acting on her own initiative.

The more I have researched the question of where responsibility lay for introducing this legislation, the more it has become clear that just one person, Carrie Lam, both initiated and relentlessly pursued this proposal. That Lam's plan backfired is not entirely her fault. No one in her advisory Executive Council challenged the move; the serried ranks of government supporters in Legco also offered unqualified support; and the bulk of Hong Kong's traditional media gave their backing. Predictably, it was only after things turned nasty on the streets that many of these enthusiasts claimed to have had misgivings from the very beginning.

Melinda Liu, a veteran journalist who has covered Chinese and Hong Kong affairs for decades, put together a convincing picture explaining the timing of Lam's move: "Lam was in a rush because she'd hoped to curry favor with senior officials in Beijing around the time of the [PRC's seventieth] anniversary ... Lam reportedly had been impressed by the kudos Beijing showered on Chinese anti-graft investigators who'd managed to wangle the return to the mainland of a number of allegedly corrupt fugitives who'd fled overseas."[8]

Jasper Tsang of the pro-China camp has also reflected on Lam's mood at the time: "She was very proud of her accomplishment, and she perhaps had not expected the strong opposition from the [democrats], who were determined not to let [the bill] go through Legco. This made the central government angry. It didn't think the bill was so important, but then it became a matter of governance. Beijing said that if the government was tabling a bill, it had to pass it, and it was giving it all the necessary support."[9]

"What you have to understand," a government insider told me, "is that this was all about Article 23." He was referring to Beijing's determination to have national security legislation placed on Hong Kong's statute books as soon as possible. As we've seen, Lam was acutely aware that Tung Chee-hwa's previous attempt to achieve this had led to his downfall, and so she had adopted an approach of biding her time, moving forward with other measures to steadily demoralise and neuter the opposition to the extent that they would be too weak to mount an effective response. This slow but steady policy also had the merit of demonstrating to Lam's bosses that the aims of asserting control and drawing the SAR closer to the Motherland could be achieved in a number of other ways.

And so Lam brought forward this extradition bill in February 2019. At first it looked as though the government would be successful in burying this move under a mass of legal jargon, deliberately overlooking the implications of this unprecedented measure to allow renditions to the Mainland, something that had been explicitly rejected when the Basic Law was being drafted.[10] Some unease was expressed early on over the provision giving power to initiate extraditions to the Chief Executive, rather than the courts, but officials argued that such decisions could still be challenged within the court system.

What sparked rather more suspicion was Lam's insistence on the urgency of getting this law passed before the end of the year. Although there was widespread scepticism over Lam's continued insistence that her primary concern was related to the Chan murder case, the first protest against the bill, a march held on 31 March, attracted minimal interest. Surprisingly, and unexpectedly, the chief murmurings of dissent at this early stage were concerns expressed by business organisations, who were waking up to the dangers the legislation posed to their members doing business on the Mainland.

As mentioned above, the reasons for these concerns were sparked when in January 2017 billionaire Xiao Jianhua, head of the Tomorrow Group conglomerate, had been seized at the luxury Four Seasons Hotel, ferreted across the border, and subsequently disappeared into the black hole of the Chinese judicial system. At the time of writing, he has yet to re-emerge. The business community, which had shown no real concern over the fate of the Causeway Bay booksellers, now realised that, when billionaires could be lifted off the streets, there might indeed be a problem. These misgivings came to a head in 2019 when Carrie Lam started pushing her extradition bill, and normally tame business organisations popped their heads above the parapet. Most pointedly, the legal profession in Hong Kong was also expressing alarm. In early April, when the pro-China majority in Legco ensured that the bill's first reading was passed, warning noises started emerging, most emphatically from the Hong Kong Bar Association.

On 28 April, more than 100,000 people joined a protest against the bill, many of them influenced by the decision of Lam Wing-kee to seek asylum in Taiwan. He was one of the abducted booksellers who had returned to Hong Kong, but he had become very uneasy over the risk of being handed back to the Mainland.

Opposition elsewhere was mounting over fears that the new law would deliver a body blow to the safety of local residents, who had developed a tenacious attachment to Hong Kong's legal system. No one needed to spell out how different this was from the system that prevailed on the Mainland, where defence lawyers are put in jail, where torture and prolonged detention are used to extract pre-trial confessions, and where practically every single person appearing in a court of law is certain to be convicted.

In Hong Kong, an independent judiciary was still in place. Due process was guaranteed and there was full expectation of decent treatment for suspects. Indeed, the existence of Hong Kong's independent legal system formed a central pillar of reassurance for the people of the SAR. How, they asked, would this survive if there were to be arbitrary removal of suspects to the Mainland? That fear of the knock on the door in the middle of the night, highlighted by Tsang Ki-fan, very much looked as though it would be making its way to Hong Kong if this law were to be passed.

The trickle of concern that emerged in April became a flood in May, as more and more organisations and individuals from all walks of life started expressing their disquiet. The Lam government fuelled these concerns by suddenly withdrawing the legislation from Legco's Bills Committee, where opposition lawmakers were guaranteed to thwart progress. The effect was to bypass intensive scrutiny and place the bill directly before the full council, where a pro-China majority was guaranteed to pass the legislation without a lot of questions. Unsurprisingly, this manoeuvre did little more than confirm suspicions about the proposed law.

On 30 May, it finally occurred to the government that something needed to be done to lower the heat. It announced that amendments would be made to the bill, largely designed to remove those involved in the commercial world from its scope. Carrie Lam was still working on the assumption that she could somehow bamboozle the legislation through Legco, so long as the business community had been placated. As ever, she simply did not appreciate what was happening in the wider world of Hong Kong.

Business organisations, never natural allies of anti-government protests, did indeed breathe a sigh of relief, although some, notably the American Chamber of Commerce, remained worried. But the more important effect of the amendments was to give the impression that the bill was being skewed so as to ensure a safety hatch for the rich and powerful, while everyone else's concerns were being ignored. Thus Lam's adjustments to the legislation not only failed to quell the protests, but did a great deal to ensure even more widespread opposition. Matters came to a head on 9 June, when an estimated 1 million people joined a peaceful protest. It was either as big as or bigger than the 1989 Tiananmen protest. How could it be ignored?

At first there was silence from the government and then, astonishingly, on the following day Lam announced that not only would the bill be going ahead, but she was ensuring that its progress through the legislature would be accelerated, with the tabling of a second reading in two days' time. The Legco president, Andrew Leung, confirmed that the bill would be brought back to the chamber on 12 June, and that he was imposing a draconian 66-hour time limit on debate, so as to ensure that the law could be enacted by 8pm on 20 June. Even more amazingly, Carrie Lam then decided to compound things by making a tearful television appearance, in which she spoke of how much she had sacrificed for Hong Kong, insisting she would not sell it out. People watched this performance open-mouthed. The interview ignited a frenzy of activity on social media even as she spoke, expressions of incredulity flooding in as the broadcast ploughed on.

But Lam was not done. She ensured that this mood of incredulity turned to anger when she referred to the 1 million of her fellow citizens who had taken part in the march as spoiled children. "If my son was stubborn," she said, "and I spoiled him and tolerated his stubborn behaviour every time, I would just be going along with him."[11]

A civil servant who had worked closely with Lam told me, "That's typical Carrie; she always thinks she's right and she never listens."[12]

The anger that the Chief Executive generated with this outrageous response transformed what had hitherto been a peaceful protest into far more violent action—an uprising that would be countered by an outburst of police violence not seen since the Cultural Revolution-inspired protests of the 1960s.

6

BE WATER

Bruce Lee—the American-born, Hong Kong-raised martial arts film star—was an unlikely source of inspiration for the uprising, yet so he has proven to be. Lee's statue, in fighting pose, stands on Hong Kong's harbourfront and, although he died in 1973, he remains a major cultural influence, reflecting some of the ambiguities which lie at the heart of Hongkongers' struggle for identity. This is because Lee, son of a Cantonese opera star, was both very much a local icon and an international figure. He was torn between America, the country of his birth, and Hong Kong, where his career was launched, but which proved too small to accommodate his ambition for international stardom.

In a famous interview, Lee explained his tactics as a fighter and his attitude to life: "Be formless, shapeless, like water. Now you pour water into a cup, it becomes the cup. You pour water into a bottle, it becomes the bottle. You put it into a teapot, it becomes the teapot ... Be water, my friend." This idea caught the imagination of the 2019 protestors, who had learned, from the experience of the Umbrella Movement, that they needed a smarter approach. To "be water", or *jouh seui* in Cantonese, was the order of the day: flexibility rather than a rigid structure, and rapid adaptability in response to whatever was happening. As a result of this way of thinking, the 2019–20 uprising saw a whole new style of protest emerge.

The first indication of the growing strength of the mass movement came on 4 June, the anniversary of the Tiananmen Square massacre. In retrospect, it is possible to say that it provided a bridge between what had already become Hong Kong's biggest protest movement, and what would become something very different, albeit with shared objectives.

In 2019, this date marked the thirtieth anniversary of the massacre, and Hong Kong remained the only place in China where it was commemorated on an annual basis—with a sombre gathering at Victoria Park, where survivors of the massacre spoke, music was played and leaders of the democratic movement delivered eulogies to those who had died at the Square. For many years, the keynote speaker was Szeto Wah, the former leftist who had helped to form the Democratic Party with Martin Lee. The late Szeto, who died in 2011, was a wizened former school-teacher, steeped in Chinese history and with a fine sense of oratory. He embodied Hong Kong's traditional pro-democracy movement, a movement with a visceral connection to democracy fighters on the Chinese Mainland. Other members of his generation were very much concerned with the fate of China as a whole, and saw the struggle for democracy in Hong Kong as being part of a movement embracing the entire nation.

Unfairly, perhaps, their decades of political activism had contributed to a sense of alienation expressed by the new generation, whose entire focus was on Hong Kong. Most of the youth in the democracy camp of the 2010s had not even been born at the time of the massacre, and saw little point in joining the annual commemoration. Indeed, the numbers of people who showed up had been dwindling. Some of the new activists had actively boycotted previous 4 June rallies, on the grounds that it had nothing to do with them. But in 2019 attendance at the commemoration swelled to 180,000 people. The pending extradition legislation had provided an explicit link to the Mainland and gave many of those who had dismissed this event a reason to think again. Instead of the older activists who had predominated on the platform in previous years, the majority of those on stage this year were young. They talked about the connection between their situation and that of the students and others who died at Tiananmen.

From a damp and uninviting patch of lawn somewhat distant from the main stage, I observed parents telling their children why they had come to Victoria Park. The familiar faces of the old-style democrats were submerged in a sea of younger faces. And, as if to make the point that this year was different and more serious, a couple of Mandarin-speaking men in ill-fitting suits hovered close to where I was sitting. They did not join in the chanting and singing—undercover members of the Chinese security services were there for another purpose.

Just over a week later, on 12 June, thousands of people responded to a call to surround the Legislative Council, where the extradition bill was being propelled at high speed towards the statute book. This protest came just days after the massive 9 June demonstration, which had been marked by its peaceful nature. But what happened on 12 June proved to be a turning point in the tenor of Hong Kong protest. By mid-afternoon, when I reached the site of the demonstration, the barrage of tear gas cannisters had become so intense that the stench and burning impact of the gas reached the underground area of the Admiralty Mass Transit Railway station.

Outside the station, there was a tense standoff between protestors and police clad in Darth Vader-style black riot gear. An estimated 5,000 riot police faced the demonstrators. The level of violence they used was extensive, and some seventy people were injured. As events played out, they were closely followed on numerous social media channels and seen on live television late into the night.

Some protestors had come prepared, and others moved deftly among the crowd dispensing face masks, which I quickly discovered were inadequate to dispel the choking and stinging impact of the tear gas. A friend who had turned up in her working clothes was knocked to the ground by a tear gas cannister. She was immediately surrounded by people helping her to get back on her feet. As tears streamed down my face, someone appeared at my side with saline solution and water to ease the impact of the gas. This level of mutual concern and co-operation was to become a hallmark of the 2019–20 movement.

Meanwhile, mainly younger protestors had started erecting barricades, and were hurling all manner of objects at the police. The response was rapid: more tear gas was fired; bean-bag rounds and rubber bullets were aimed at the crowd, including at those not taking part in any kind of violent activity; and then out came the truncheons, beating whoever happened to be in the way. By the end of the day, more tear gas had been unleashed than during the entire period of the Umbrella protests. Stephen Lo, the Commissioner of Police, declared the protest to be a "riot", justifying a violent response from his officers. (Five days later, he conceded that not all those involved in the demonstration had been rioters.)

We didn't know it at the time, but on these streets on 12 June a pattern of demonstration and police retaliation was being established that would remain little changed in the months to come, except that the level of violence—on both sides—was to intensify many times over.

Hong Kong had a long history of peaceful protest, which was how the Umbrella Movement had begun; it had then evolved in another direction as the authorities made clear that they were determined to tackle protests in a much harsher manner than previously. In 2019, this harsh approach deepened, and the Hong Kong police moved into full battle mode. Over the course of the year, a new array of weaponry would be introduced, supposedly for defensive crowd control, but very often deployed against fleeing protestors and fired into peaceful crowds, something I have witnessed on many occasions. Speaking to people at the 12 June rally, I was somewhat taken aback by their firm conviction that the level of violence would escalate. "It will definitely get worse," said a man in his late twenties, who was pressing me to take a face mask and goggles for future use.

Young people in the crowd—some very young, in their mid-teens, who had never been on a demonstration before the start of these protests—were talking about the need to sacrifice their personal safety for the future of Hong Kong. "I don't care what happens to me," said a female student. "But you might be arrested or injured," I suggested. She shrugged this off, replying, "If we don't succeed, what future will there be for Hong Kong? I can't worry just about myself."

As the protests dragged on through the summer, it became clear that the level of exhaustion was extreme. Many protestors were no longer sleeping for more than a few hours a night. Those with jobs were juggling something like a nine-hour working day and another nine hours of participating in protests. One of them, employed at a well-known five-star hotel, said that his entire life was now consumed by the movement: "I get up, go to work, finish work and come on the streets. I do nothing else."

I kept hearing the words "It's now or never" to explain why these Hongkongers were so determined to take part in the protests and see them through. The elaboration of the movement's five demands was to come later, but even at this stage, it was clear to me that the movement had moved beyond the single aim of thwarting the extradition bill.

Meanwhile, behind the scenes, there was even more frantic activity within the Lam administration. A senior civil servant has told me that he attended numerous meetings during this time at which government leaders gave solemn assurances that, although the situation was indeed "difficult", the protests would soon pass. Business leaders and members of pro-China parties were less convinced, and were pressing the government for decisive action. It later transpired that Carrie Lam had belatedly realised that sitting out the protests would not work. On 14 June, she travelled to Shenzhen to meet Chinese Vice-Premier Han Zheng at the Bauhinia Villa. The *Sing Tao Daily*, which has become one of the best sources of "official" leaks from the Chinese government, reported that she was using the meeting to seek permission to suspend the bill.[1] The same-day leaking of this request marked the start of a process whereby Chinese officials distanced themselves from responsibility for initiating the extradition bill.

On her return from Shenzhen, Lam convened a late-night meeting of her senior officials, ending at midnight. They were told that passage of the bill would be suspended, and that an announcement would be made the following day. This is precisely what happened at 3pm on 15 June. Lam, however, made it clear in this briefing that the bill was not being withdrawn, merely suspended. Yet again, she demonstrated her extraordinary ability to ensure that, no matter how bad things were, she could make them worse. The Chief Executive proceeded to express her sorrow over her failure to convince the public of the need for the legislation. It was a return to her familiar refrain: that the public's lack of understanding was the root of the problem.

As I have found, speaking to Lam, particularly in the context of a media interview, is a strange business. She makes no attempt at establishing any kind of personal rapport, gives every impression that talking to you is a waste of time, and makes it clear that questions she dislikes are based on ignorance. She lacks any kind of empathy; what instead shines through is her absolute conviction that she is right at all times. Over many years of interviewing politicians, I have found that even the least skilled will try charm or use wit when confronted with questions they don't like. Lam ignores tactics of this kind and has developed something of a martyrdom complex. She stresses how hard she works, her commitment and devotion to duty. On one extraordinary occasion, when talking (she thought in private) to a group of business leaders, she complained about how the protests had made it impossible for her to visit her hairdresser. When a recording of this meeting leaked, she simply could not understand why it was met with such a barrage of derision and contempt. She was, to use her own, often repeated words, prepared to "accept responsibility" for the unrest—but this acceptance of responsibility was always accompanied by explaining that trouble had only arisen in the first place because of the public's "lack of understanding".

To absolutely no one's surprise, then, Lam's "suspension" of the extradition bill did nothing to placate the movement. The already febrile atmosphere became even more intense with news that Marco Leung Ling-kit, a 35-year-old protestor, had either fallen or committed suicide after hanging a banner on a walkway connecting the upmarket Pacific Place shopping centre and the Admiralty Centre, where the 12 June demonstration had been held. His yellow raincoat bore the Chinese characters for "Carrie Lam is killing Hong Kong".

Leung's shocking death intensified the protests to a degree that could not possibly have been anticipated. On the following day, 16 June, an estimated 2 million people—in other words, a quarter of Hong Kong's population—poured into the streets. In proportionate terms, this was not only by far the largest demonstration ever seen in Hong Kong, but among the largest ever seen anywhere in the world.

With few exceptions, the 16 June marchers wore black, to commemorate Leung's death. Black was then to be adopted as the colour of all subsequent demonstrations. It was at this stage that what became the five demands of the movement started to emerge, with calls for the extradition bill to be withdrawn, not suspended; for an investigation into police violence and an end to the official practice of classifying demonstrators as rioters. There were also calls for the release of those arrested. Later, the demand for free elections under universal suffrage was added. One demand, however, was rarely heard again: for Carrie Lam to step down. As one protestor said to me, "Why bother with her? She doesn't matter and even if she goes they will probably put in someone worse."

As the 2 million march showed, Hongkongers were not yet ready to give up on mass peaceful protest. However, it had taken a sharp outbreak of violence to secure the climbdown over the now suspended bill. As a famous slogan first daubed on the walls of the Legco building said: "It was you who taught me peaceful marches did not work."

While all this was going on, the government's supporters were in a state of considerable disarray. Following the lead from Beijing, they began distancing themselves from the Lam administration. They started darkly muttering about betrayal after the bill was withdrawn without their prior knowledge. It left them looking foolish for having wholeheartedly backed Lam. For years, Hong Kong's pro-Beijing camp had been claiming that its views had the support of a "silent majority", a point they tried to prove on 30 June by organising a "pro-police" rally. Despite extensive backing from the mainstream media, and the bussing in of many participants, no more than 100,000 turned up. That would have been an impressive number in previous times, but was now a mere shadow of the democrats' mobilising power.

As we've seen, what had once been known as the pro-government camp was now in full retreat from this designation, preferring to be known as "pro-China". However, in the short-hand most widely used for the uprising, its members were simply described as being the "blue" camp, facing off against the "yellow" camp of the protest movement. (These colour codes are a bit confusing, as the protestors always wore black following Leung's death—the yellow is their political identifier.) Devastating for the blues was that the yellow camp could always mobilise more people than they could dream, and was forever coming up with new forms of protest that sometimes led the pro-China camp to cry foul, or, at others, to make a half-hearted attempt at emulation.

The new democracy movement was self-consciously determined to be different from what had gone before. Hitherto, for example, protests had been focused on the centre of town. In the case of the Umbrella Movement, this had involved primarily a seventy-nine-day occupation of the streets surrounding Hong Kong's government and legislative complex. It had seemed like a good idea at the time, but exhaustion had set in and, inevitably, this large, static demonstration dwindled. Worse had followed as the movement's leaders were picked off and sent to jail, in a long-drawn-out process of trials and convictions. Recrimination among the protestors had been widespread, albeit kept largely below the surface. This led to a period of reflection by members of Hong Kong's democracy movement. Much of this process was conducted through an ever-burgeoning online discussion forum called LIHKG, where ideas and tactics were shared and where, as the protests of 2019 grew, a virtual command post was established, despatching protestors to various parts of town. LIHKG was also a way to raise resources, not just financial, but also material and in the form of expertise.

There was also the question of leadership, arising from a backlash against the democracy camp's previous reliance on a "big platform" where the leaders stood and told everyone else what to do. Many LIHKG users asked: why rely on a smallish number of leaders who could be singled out and arrested, when the movement could create an organic leadership that was hard to identify, and which drew its strength from democratic discussion that could be quickly translated into action? Whether consciously or, more likely, unconsciously, this concept of non-centralised leadership has characterised a number of other new protest movements around the world, most notably the Black Lives Matter movement, which embraces a number of distinctive personalities, but no central leader telling everyone what to do. As the 2019 protests developed, the Telegram messaging app, more secure than the LIHKG forum, was brought into play for discussing specific tactics and deployment.

This is not the first time that social media has had such a central role in protest movements. The Maidan uprising of 2014, in the Ukraine, has also been called the Facebook Revolution, because of the network's mobilising role. Facebook was also a central player in the Umbrella Movement, not least as a means of providing news once the protests spread beyond the centre of town. What has been different about social media this time around, though, is the extent to which it has served the role of organiser in Hong Kong. As a command post without a commander, LIHKG, Telegram and other online discussion boards were never going to neatly devise plans or provide a clear picture of how decisions came to be made. This is why it is hard to pinpoint exactly how a consensus emerged among the protestors that not only was it tactically smart to launch guerrilla protests in any number of different places, but it was also politically smart to involve people in their own localities.

The result was that one of the most significant aspects of the protestors' ability to "be water" was this realisation that they didn't need to rely on protests in the centre of town. An early indication of this realisation came with the emergence of Lennon

Walls in every district. These walls, named after the Beatles' John Lennon, were inspired by the 1968 protests in Czechoslovakia (known as the Prague Spring), during which citizens posted messages of defiance and works of art aimed at the Soviet-backed regime. A version of the first wall still stands in Prague, the capital of what has become the Czech Republic, and it now features an image of Marco Leung, the first fatality of the Hong Kong uprising. Hongkongers have not been slow to emulate forms of protest seen elsewhere in the world, and they first latched on to the Lennon Wall idea during the Umbrella Movement, when part of the government compound was plastered with tiny post-it notes, pieces of artwork and a colourful array of posters, many using the umbrella image. From July 2019, not only was this wall recreated, but others sprung up seemingly everywhere. Without any form of central organisation, citizens got together and started claiming spaces for Lennon Walls, usually adjacent to the crowded Mass Transit Railway stations. When pro-China groups arrived to try and tear down the walls, scuffles often erupted, and what had been torn down was rapidly replaced by new posts.

This outburst of creativity on the walls was matched by a flurry of videos posted online. Some were cartoons, others a reworking of protest images with a musical background, while others spliced together the words of government officials and Chinese leaders, often to considerable comic effect. One image that appears to have hit a very tender spot in Beijing was the portrayal of the portly Chinese President, Xi Jinping, as Winnie the Pooh. On the Mainland, the hapless Winnie was suddenly declared to be persona non grata, and his image was rapidly removed from social media sites.

As the Lennon Walls spread throughout Hong Kong, so did the street protests. Some were small-scale and linked to specific local concerns, while others mushroomed from a modest size almost in direct proportion to the level of police response.

I have a vivid memory of travelling around various protest sites in August as a reporter keen to convey an impression of what was happening outside the main protest areas. I ended up in Tai Wai, a mixed area of public and private housing. Wearing a bright yellow vest with the word "PRESS" clearly inscribed on the back, I found, contrary to my usual experience of having to seek out people to interview, that passers-by were approaching me, pointing out used tear gas shells and other debris from a barrage of police action. Many said they had been going about their usual business when they'd got caught up in a flash protest. Often when this sort of thing happens, you hear people say things like "Why are they protesting here? It's usually such a quiet place." But that is not what I heard in the summer of 2019; angry citizens were furious over the police violence, and expressed admiration for the young protestors. The so-called "silent majority" evoked by pro-China spokespeople were not much in evidence on that night, nor were they easily unearthed in other localities I visited.

There was also an outbreak of "link hands" demonstrations, where protestors formed human chains. The first of these, on 23 August, resulted in a chain snaking some 30 miles around Hong Kong, emulating the famous 1989 "Baltic Way" anti-Soviet demonstrations in Estonia, Latvia and Lithuania. Again, here was innovation demonstrating an awareness of global protest. Many smaller "link hands" protests were held by school pupils, linking together all the schools in their localities.

The summer saw escalation on both sides: by an establishment swinging into gear to fight back, and by an increasingly defiant protest movement, with some members using fresh, unconventional tactics. Large-scale marches were still being organised, but a fair number of the movement's supporters no longer seemed convinced that this was the way forward. Things took a significant turn in this direction on 1 July, a key date in Hong Kong's political calendar: the anniversary of Hong Kong's return to Chinese rule. The Civil Human Rights Front, who in June had mobilised rallies of both 1 and 2 million people, had marked this day for many years by holding rallies, which had become an annual protest platform for a wide range of issues. But in 2019 the police banned the march.

This did not stop angry demonstrators, who ignored the police advice in great numbers and followed the planned route of the march. It was a bit chaotic, as the police were nowhere to be seen before the march reached its destination. At the outset, this looked as though this would be another mass rally, largely unhindered by law enforcement. Although the organisers were no longer marshalling the marchers, it began as a peaceful affair. However, it became clear that peaceful protest was not in the minds of the so-called frontline protestors, who were characteristically very young and uniformly clad in tight-fitting black garments, with masks obscuring their faces. They departed from the march and headed towards the Legislative Council. The mood within the march had been relatively relaxed given the absence of police officers but, as the march neared its end, word spread among the crowd and through online messaging that there would be an attempt to break into the building. The police, who had hitherto kept a low profile, were present in large numbers behind the government complex of which the legislature is part. Then, at around 4pm, we suddenly saw all these forces being withdrawn. This was unprecedented.

A large part of the crowd surged forward towards the Legco main entrance. Frontliners armed with makeshift tools began attempting to get through the doors, made of heavily reinforced glass. There was no move by the police to stop them, even though the battering went on for many hours. Finally, just before 9pm, these protestors broke into the building and made their way to the antechamber. Even then, the police were

135

nowhere to be seen. In fact, the only people trying to ask the demonstrators to think again about entering the building were a group of pro-democracy legislators, who were later lambasted by the pro-China camp for "encouraging violence". The reality was that they were doing their best to stop what they considered to be an ill-advised move.

Once inside, and much to their surprise, the protestors discovered that the police had also withdrawn from the interior of the building. Left entirely to their own devices, they embarked on something of a rampage, destroying a lot of furniture, pictures and equipment—but it was not quite as random as it first appeared to be. Signs were put up telling the protestors not to damage books of historic value, and a drinks fridge bore a hastily attached notice telling them not to take anything without paying: "We are not thieves, we don't steal," it said. There was much debate as to what to do, ending with a consensus (but not unanimous opinion) that there was no point in staying. Finally, around midnight, after protestors had evacuated the building, the police arrived in full riot gear, firing tear gas outside the building.

What on earth was going on? Despite changing explanations, police spokesmen never really explained why they had allowed this level of vandalism and unlawful entry to occur. Unbelievably, they proffered reasons such as it being too dark in the building and that they had concerns over safety; for a force that had spent the better part of the previous month showing very little concern for civilian safety and no qualms about operating in the dark, these explanations fell far short of credibility. The strong suspicion lingers that the police actually facilitated this occupation, to provide grounds for painting the protest movement as nothing more than a riot. Indeed, from that day on, the attack on the Legco building was to become the central focus of an unfolding government narrative, in which emphasis was placed on denouncing violence and chaos, while the causes of the protests were ignored. Indeed, officials talked of little else besides violence and chaos.

The events of 1 July prompted Chinese officials, who had hardly been showing restraint in criticising the protests, into an escalation of rhetorical rage. They spoke of "atrocities" to describe what had happened and declared that the movement was beginning to show "signs of terrorism". And, although the protestors had been very careful not to associate their movement with demands for Hong Kong independence, China saw the attack on the legislature as a "blatant challenge" by "separatists"—the ultimate charge against opponents who have moved beyond the pale, wanting to split up the nation.

But the uprising was moving on in new directions: protests in the non-central localities now spread in earnest. Around 30,000 protestors joined a march in Sheung Shui, very close to the Mainland border, on 13 July. The following day, over 110,000 protestors assembled in Sha Tin, the first of Hong Kong's new towns. The tenor of these demonstrations was notably angrier, and the young frontliners were visibly itching for a confrontation with the police. They got it in spades.

What is remarkable about these self-identified frontliners, who made no apology for their use of violent tactics, is the level of popular support they enjoyed. In December 2019, the *South China Morning Post* commissioned an opinion poll. Most surprisingly, some 13 per cent of those questioned said they "somewhat supported" violent action such as throwing petrol bombs or damaging public facilities, while 5 per cent gave their "strong" support.[2] In other words, almost a fifth of respondents were giving the nod to violent protest. I have asked many people why this is so. A telling response was provided by Louisa, a 23-year-old healthcare professional and a firm supporter of the protests. I met her during one of the many quiet periods during a prolonged demonstration. She described herself as a "non-aggressive" protestor who would not herself take part in violent action. However, she said, "I worry about the more aggressive, more radical people, but we sort of need them, because peaceful protests don't move the government's position."

On Sunday 21 July a new form of violence made its debut. It came with a savage attack on protestors by Triad gang members, apparently with police complicity. The attack took place in Yuen Long, close to Sheung Shui mentioned above, widely considered to be a stronghold of the ultra-conservative Heung Yee Kuk, the body representing Hong Kong's "indigenous" residents. Yuen Long is also home to powerful Triad gangs, which are believed to be closely linked with the Kuk. An explicit link between gang members and their political allies became evident in a video recorded shortly after the attack. It showed Junius Ho—prominent in the Kuk, and one of the most rabid of the pro-China legislators—greeting individuals in uniform white t-shirts and calling them "my heroes". Ho, a wealthy lawyer, is a complex character who enjoys being the centre of controversy and courts publicity with enthusiasm. This was very much the case when he got involved in the 21 July incident.

Triad gang members made their appearance on Sunday evening, following demonstrations elsewhere in Hong Kong—most notably outside Beijing's Liaison Office, where the state emblem was defaced. This sent officials into a paroxysm of rage. Black-clad demonstrators returning home found themselves (alongside numerous other citizens who were not similarly attired) confronted at Yuen Long station by a large gang of thugs wearing those white t-shirts, wielding sticks and other weapons, which they used unsparingly on unarmed people at the station. Desperate calls for police assistance went unanswered and, although the police were usually quick to respond to all forms of violent protest action, on this occasion the few officers on the scene did not intervene, and reinforcements took almost 40 minutes to arrive. By this point, forty-five people had been injured, some severely. A year later, the police admitted that plain-clothes officers had been there from the beginning of the riot to "monitor" the situation, but failed to explain why they had not summoned back-up.[3]

The thugs were able to vacate the scene without being arrested. The official explanation for this unprecedented lack of response was that the police were tied up dealing with protests elsewhere. Later, the police would change their story even more fundamentally, after suddenly discovering that the Yuen Long attack was in fact a battle between two armed groups, and that police reinforcements had in fact arrived within 18 minutes of being alerted to the problem. In support of this new narrative, they then arrested legislator Lam Cheuk-ting and charged him with rioting. He was one of a number of people who had been recording the incident as it happened, and had been beaten up by the Triads. At the time of writing, this extraordinary charge, like others involving victims of the violence, has yet to be proven.

Many people both inside and outside the SAR were taken aback by this brazen attack, seemingly carried out with impunity by gangsters with powerful political connections.

To understand how criminal gangs got involved in Hong Kong politics is worth a short detour, as they have long occupied an important role in society, despite Hong Kong's deserved reputation as a law-abiding society.

Senior members of Triad societies and those close to them have a significant power base in the rural areas, and fill leading positions in Chinese state advisory bodies, in the Hong Kong legislature and on the Executive Council. Their prominence in politics is not new. Sun Yat Sen, the founding father of the Chinese Republic, was a Red Pole, otherwise known as a 426, in the Kwok On Wui Triad society—in gang terminology, this made him an enforcer. As such, he is the best-known Triad in history. Sun joined at a time when the Triads were in transition from secret patriotic societies confronting China's Manchurian rulers to fully fledged criminal gangs. Triads played a significant role in the foundation of the Chinese Republic in 1912, and were subsequently used to assert the authority of the new Kuomintang government.

Once established close to the heart of the system, they got a taste for politics, which found them siding with the KMT during the civil war, from which the Communists emerged victorious in 1949. Most of the Triad leaders then fled to Taiwan and Hong Kong. In Taiwan, they re-established links with the new Kuomintang dictatorship. And it didn't take long for Triad societies to burrow deep inside colonial Hong Kong, where a blind eye was often turned to their activities—in part because of a high level of corruption in the police force, in part because they had powerful allies, and because crime was often easier for the regime to control when Triads themselves made sure that "freelancers" were kept in check. There was considerable Triad infiltration of the police, and they established a strong political base in rural areas like Yuen Long.

The gangsters' de facto co-operation with the British juddered to a halt during the Japanese wartime occupation of Hong Kong, as they infamously transitioned to collaboration with the new imperial masters. After 1945, and with surprising ease, they managed to recover their previous bases. Some years later, when it became clear that China was to resume sovereignty over the colony, Triad leaders again changed course, to draw as close as possible to the incoming authorities. Their efforts were spectacularly rewarded in 1984, when China's paramount leader Deng Xiaoping told a Hong Kong business delegation that "Hong Kong black societies [the Chinese name for Triads] are very powerful ... Of course, not all black societies are dark. There are many good guys among them." His remarks were followed some years later in 1993 by China's public security minister, Tao Siju, saying that Triads could be "patriotic citizens" with a role to play in building the nation.[4]

Like the Mafia, Hong Kong Triads have also gone into legitimate business, and are infamous for their control over large swathes of the local film industry and other parts of the entertainment world. This being Hong Kong, where property is the business that really matters, Triad bosses have infiltrated this arena, too. But, armed with endorsements like Tao's, Triad gangs have also become among the most avid supporters of Beijing, and have been mobilised in the past to beat up anti-government protestors or provide support for pro-China political figures.

Below the Triad elite is a far larger base of gang members, commonly estimated to number more than 100,000. That's a hell of a lot of people in a population of 7.5 million. Most of their activity is focused on protection rackets, drug-dealing, running prostitution rings, loan-sharking and occasional spectacular kidnappings for ransom. Although the big bosses are well known, arrests of these top leaders, or "Dragon Heads", are rare. Instead the police regularly round up the small fry.

Triads have also targeted a number of prominent pro-democracy leaders during the uprising. On one infamous occasion, they paid a gang of thugs from South Asian backgrounds to attack and badly injure Jimmy Sham, the leader of the Civil Human Rights Front. The Yuen Long attack on 21 July was followed by the mobilisation of gang members originating from Fujian Province, who were based in North Point on Hong Kong Island. After the attack, there were, rather typically, some token arrests of gangsters from the lower rungs of the Triad ladder. No senior figures were arrested.

Widespread calls for an investigation into the Yuen Long attack were ignored, and not a single police officer has been disciplined. Junius Ho, who himself was subsequently beaten up, easily survived a call within Legco for sanctions over his seeming endorsement of the attack. The police also rejected permission for a march to protest the Yuen Long incident, but it went ahead. This spurred another round of violence, with riot police deploying sponge grenades for the first time.

More worrying in terms of public policy was that, while the police were pushed to the forefront and endlessly lauded by the government and its masters in Beijing, the Lam administration receded into the background. Since this period of mounting protest, Carrie Lam herself has avoided all possibility of casual contact with ordinary people, never venturing outside without heavy police protection. Effectively, as the summer progressed, she and her government left the police to dictate the SAR's response to the uprising. The power of the force over its supposed political masters was laid bare when Matthew Cheung, Lam's amiable and equally uncharismatic number two, had the temerity to mildly criticise the police response to the Yuen Long attacks. He was forced to make apology after apology. No other official has since dared to say anything even vaguely negative about the police force.

As the protests increasingly moved out of the central areas, violence was escalating, usually after dark. The cycle of aggression and counter-aggression that emerged had the characteristics of ritual. This is not to trivialise what was happening. People were getting seriously hurt. Reporters started being deliberately targeted by riot police, and on both sides there was deployment of more serious weaponry. Protestors started throwing petrol bombs and heavy objects towards police lines. The police, now rarely emerging in public without full riot gear, were armed copiously. Arrests were stepped up.

While leaders of the Hong Kong government stayed largely out of the way, officials in Beijing ramped up their own visibility, speaking in aggressive terms about their response to what was going in Hong Kong. At a 6 August press briefing, Yang Guang, the spokesman for the Hong Kong and Macau Affairs Office of the State Council, issued a blunt warning: "Those who play with fire will perish by it." And, in case the message was lost, he added, "don't ever misjudge the situation and mistake our restraint for weakness ... Don't ever underestimate the firm resolve and immense strength of the central government."[5]

Yang's words were backed up by state media showing 12,000 People's Armed Police officers taking part in an anti-riot drill across the border in Shenzhen. The exercise, with protestors dressed like those in Hong Kong, made its target crystal-clear. Although the impact on the uprising was zero, other menacing exercises were held in the full glare of publicity.

* * *

These threats, however, were not ignored, but Hong Kong protestors were still in a buoyant mood, and looking for new ways to make an impact. They had been given considerable comfort seeing how much attention and sympathy they were gaining overseas, and were looking for a dramatic way to capitalise on this support. On 9 August, they appeared to have found a new form of protest that was guaranteed to speak to the outside world. Protestors converged on Hong Kong's International Airport, one of the biggest in the world and a central showpiece for the SAR. Although the airport was built in the last years of British rule, China had insisted that it should not be allowed to open until the new regime had assumed power. The British had reluctantly agreed to this during the latter part of frenzied negotiations concerning the handover. This is mentioned to stress that, although a superb transportation hub, the airport has also always had an important political and symbolic role.

Passengers landing in the SAR were confronted by a sea of black-clad protestors and handed a cheeky leaflet headed "Dear Travelers—welcome to Hong Kong". It went on to say, "Please forgive us for the 'unexpected' Hong Kong," and to explain why the people were protesting. Although there was some aggression against Mainlanders, overall the mood was friendly, and most arriving travellers seemed more bemused than angry over the obstruction course they had to navigate to get out of the terminal. Cedric, a 17-year-old school student in full frontliner gear, told me he was there because he had a feeling that protesting at the airport would take matters to a new level: "I just want to push back ... it's my future, it affects my freedom."

The occupation succeeded beyond expectation. The Lam government, with its customary complacency, hadn't thought that many protestors would bother to travel out to the airport, which is located far from the centre of town. It also assumed, so I was told by an official, that the protestors would get such a poor reception from visitors that the whole exercise would backfire. As ever, the government was wrong. On the contrary, passengers arriving from overseas were happy to be interviewed by journalists, and expressed support for the movement. Most importantly, from the protestors' point of view, the tactic of occupying the airport caught the attention of a worldwide audience.

The airport got back to something resembling normal quite quickly, but installed a host of measures to prevent a resumption of protest action—not least wide-ranging court orders preventing further demonstrations. Many of these measures remain in force at the time of writing.

Meanwhile, the already febrile atmosphere in Hong Kong kept getting hotter. China's in-house attack dog newspaper, the *Global Times*, started referring to the pro-democracy activists as "mobsters", a description quickly adopted elsewhere in the official media. Protestors—controversially, and to the unease of many people in the community—denounced China's supporters as Nazis, or Chinazis.

Practically every day of the week in August, there was a protest somewhere or other. Members of all the professions—lawyers, doctors, teachers, civil servants and so on—would assemble together on the streets to hold rallies. Under threat of dismissal, tens of thousands of civil servants walked out of their departments and marched on 2 August, threatening strike action. A general strike on 5 August, involving hundreds of thousands of other employees, brought wide swathes of the transportation network to a halt, and had impacts elsewhere. Even inside hospitals, there were sit-ins by medical staff protesting against excessive police force.

What was happening threatened to become a subject of caricature, with, on one side, determined-looking youths intent on violence facing equally determined police, most of whom were also young, and giving every impression of itching for a fight. Having covered Hong Kong demonstrations over a great number of years, I used to find it possible to strike up a conversation with officers during periods of standoff and waiting around. This was no longer possible by the summer of 2019, as the police became intensely suspicious of journalists and tended even to demur from eye contact.

A great many protestors, however, have been keen to talk, although I've had to keep pinching myself when I realise how young many of them are—I'm talking early teens here. What I found was that, behind the extensive protective gear that had become their uniforms, these were thoughtful people, well aware of what was at stake and the many problems of having embarked on this path of constant demonstration.

At a road junction one night in Yuen Wo Road, just outside what had become the heavily vandalised centre of Sha Tin, a group of three young women were standing around waiting to see what would happen next. "Sasa", a 21-year-old student who was spending all her weekends on the streets, told me, "Most of us are not scared of this government anymore." Her friend Lexi, just 16 years old, said, "If we are scared, I don't think we can have freedom." The young women would not directly confirm whether or not they had got involved in the more violent activity of throwing rocks and other objects at the police, but they had no hesitation in supporting this kind of action. "If we give up," said Sasa, "those who have been hurt and arrested will never forgive us."

As we spoke, other protestors were busy tearing up pavements for ammunition. The call went out for a hammer. No one on the ground seemed to have one, so an appeal was made to residents watching from the walkways of the public housing blocks along the road. A hammer was quickly produced. The people on the walkways were older, and did not seem inclined to join a protest that was clearly going to erupt into violence as soon as the police got round to clearing this stretch of road—one of many thoroughfares occupied on that particular night.

Moving on by car to the rather grittier Wong Tai Sin neighbourhood involved dodging a lot of road blocks, broken traffic lights and passing squads of demonstrators heading somewhere or other; it was not clear where. In Wong Tai Sin itself, things had already kicked off. The police, standing guard outside a heavily fortified police station, were firing off round after round of tear gas. Traffic control was in the hands of protestors, who were also responsible for clearing a passage for the more heavily armed people advancing on the police station. I was offered bottled water and saline solution to clear my eyes, and strongly advised to leave. What were their objectives in this part of town? The answer was never clear, but it seemed to me that they were agitating here because they lived here, because they were mad as hell and because, to be frank, they could get away with it.

By the middle of August, things became even more tense. Arrests were stepped up around Hong Kong. A knife-wielding man descended on a group of people posting messages on a

Lennon Wall in Tseung Kwan O, a middle-class area hitherto untouched by violent protest.

Although Hong Kong gave every impression of being immersed in violent turmoil as the summer wore on, it is important to stress that this was only part of the story. Inevitably, footage of violent protests makes a more indelible impression than a nuanced account of what was going on. Like many other Hong Kong residents, I was bombarded by anxious messages from overseas enquiring how I was "surviving". But the truth was that, despite the fact that the protests had spread throughout the territory, life as more or less usual was perfectly possible for those who wanted no part of the demonstrations. I have observed this prosaic truth covering protests in many parts of the world, where proximity to events is often a lot less scary than the edited highlights on television. Of course there was inconvenience, especially when it came to transportation, and of course there were other forms of disruption. However, the picture painted by the Lam administration—its self-defeating characterisation of Hong Kong in 2019 as a city gripped by chaos and violence—fell far short of reality. On the contrary, for many people the solidarity of the uprising and the numerous examples of mutual aid between citizens became a source of great pride.

The government, however, was focusing on its narrative concerning the need to stop violence and prevent the splintering of the Chinese nation. Demonisation of the uprising became a major goal of the Party's propaganda machine, supported in a typically clumsy way by the Hong Kong government, including lashing out at entities that were not even clearly part of the democracy movement.

Seemingly out of nowhere, on 22 August the CCP mouthpiece, the *People's Daily* newspaper, suddenly launched a savage attack on the Mass Transit Railway Corporation (MTRC) for giving "nice treatment" to protestors. It went on to allege that the MTRC had "even arranged special trains for rioters to escape for free". It is hard to exaggerate how surprising this was. Although people had indeed travelled to demonstrations on the railway, they also travelled everywhere else on the superb MTR service, which has been the pride of Hong Kong for its efficiency and convenience. Now, as the *People's Daily* made clear, nothing could escape the politics of the day.

The people who run the MTRC were both shocked and horrified. Although it has been partially privatised, the corporation is still majority-owned by the SAR government, and its directors are drawn from the ranks of the Hong Kong establishment. Not one of them had shown a scintilla of support for the protests. An emergency board meeting was convened as the company scrambled to pacify the Chinese government. In short order, an announcement was made that stations would be closed down without prior notice if there were violent protests in the vicinity.

At a stroke, the business of getting to protests, and perhaps more importantly, getting away from them, became infinitely more difficult; all the more so after buses were also withdrawn. But, if the plan had been to thwart protest by closing the transportation network, it seriously misfired. Although considerable inconvenience ensued, as large swathes or the entirety of the network were periodically closed down, what was even more evident was public fury at the MTRC. This intensified in the long weeks when the MTRC effectively tried to impose a curfew on the whole city, shutting down the network "for repairs", sometimes as early as 8pm. As the level of private car ownership in Hong Kong is low, and the people have become accustomed to a speedy, reliable public transportation system, these frequent and often arbitrary railway shutdowns had a major impact on everyday life.

In a dangerous vicious cycle of MTRC condemnation of protests and growing backlash from protestors, stations and trains became a prime target for vandalism. Later on, damage was done to track, causing even more chaos. Young protestors declared that they would no longer pay to use the service and simply vaulted over the automatic ticket barriers. Some did so because they were fearful that the police could trace their movements by reading their Octopus payment cards, owned by everyone in Hong Kong, which can be used on all forms of transportation and a lot of other places besides.

On 4 September, after three months of turmoil, Chief Executive Carrie Lam was forced to concede that the controversial extradition bill would not merely be suspended, but withdrawn altogether. In a rare moment of self-awareness, yet almost comic understatement, she said: "I recognise that our response may not address all the grievances of people in society."[6] For once she was right, because although withdrawal of the legislation met one of the movement's five demands, Lam's insistence that no others would be met, and her constant repetition of the need to end violence, did absolutely nothing to lower the temperature.

It might be imagined that, as the uprising escalated, the government would try and reach out to leading members of the opposition—if not for formal negotiations, at the very least for some kind of dialogue. But Carrie Lam flatly refused to even meet opposition legislators, and made not a single overture to protest organisations. One half-hearted attempt to contact student unions was made in July, when some leaders of student unions from the Chinese University and the Hong Kong University of Science and Technology were invited to hold secret talks. The students made the invitation public and said they would not participate in a "publicity stunt". No further effort was made to contact student unions, or indeed any other body that might be described as representing protestors. A great many meetings were held, however, with members of the blue camp.

This reluctance to speak to people who were not toeing the party line did not stop Carrie Lam from frequently talking about how she was "humbly listening" to the public and her earnest desire for a dialogue. Finally, in late September, something described as a "community dialogue" was held. Under heavy police guard, 130 citizens selected by ballot were summoned to the Queen Elizabeth Stadium, where Lam and four of her ministers sat uncomfortably inside this vast hall, which clearly would have had space for many more participants. The event was little more than a farce, as most of those present bombarded the officials with criticism. Lam rarely responded to specific complaints, sticking to a pre-prepared script of explaining government policy. The much larger number of people outside the hall made it impossible for her to leave until the early hours of the morning. This was supposed to be the first of a number of dialogue sessions; unsurprisingly, no more materialised.

Whatever shred of credibility Lam had managed to retain through the summer was made even slimmer on 3 September, when Reuters revealed a recording of a meeting with business leaders. She told them that, given a choice, she would have quit her job, but that she had not been allowed to do so by the central government in Beijing. This was little commented upon at the time, but at the end of her remarks Lam revealed her almost unbelievable strategy for going forward, citing—bizarrely for someone so umbilically attached to the atheist Communist Party—her strong Christian thinking: "Hong Kong will have to go through several stages. The first is stamping out the violence, maybe doing other things in time to come which at the moment are not very available. Having gone through this stage, the next stage will be, in accordance with the bible, would be [sic] resurrection. We will need to come back to life, some life. So thereafter we want a reborn Hong Kong and a relaunching of this Hong Kong brand."[7]

While Lam was talking about a brand relaunch, her first priority of "stamping out violence" was being overshadowed by alarming rumours of police action at the Prince Edward MTR station, the scene of numerous violent protests. This marked an even darker period of relations between protestors and the authorities. On 31 August, a tactical squad had entered the station, clearing it of reporters who could be relied upon to record events and locking it down for two hours. Later on, severely beaten protestors had emerged, and there were stories of others having been killed. The rumours continued to spread without the backing of concrete evidence, and there was fury after the MTRC refused to release CCTV footage taken while the station was closed, subsequently relenting but releasing only edited versions. The police dismissed the accusation of fatalities out of hand, the station entrance was turned into a shrine for the dead, and distrust on both sides deepened. It is difficult to convey quite how febrile the atmosphere had become, with mounting arrests, daily demonstrations, considerable vandalism and ominous rumbling from over the border, threatening the deployment of armed police to put down the uprising.

On the streets, protestors were no longer chanting "*Heung Gong ga yau*", or Hong Kong Keeping Going, but "*Heung Gong yan fan gong*"—Hong Kong People, Resist! It did not take long before this slogan was also replaced. The new words were "*Heung Gong yan, bousauh*". Hong Kong People, Take Revenge.

7

REVENGE

At eight o'clock on the morning of 1 October 2019, the red flag of the People's Republic of China was solemnly raised in the courtyard of the Hong Kong Convention and Exhibition Centre, as the centrepiece of a ceremony to mark the PRC's seventieth anniversary. Normally, VIPs who attend ceremonies of this kind are expected to stand stiffly to attention besides the flag pole, but on this day they had to watch the flag being raised through a video feed from inside the convention centre. Security considerations were cited for this precaution. It had previously been claimed that the guests were being moved indoors because of inclement weather, one of a large number of credibility-challenged official statements made during the Hong Kong uprising.

While the authorities dared not allow those inside to venture out, elaborate precautions had been taken to ensure that the public could not come in. Indeed, ordinary Hongkongers were kept as far away as possible. Extensive road blocks and heavy police cordons were erected to ensure that ordinary members of the public were nowhere close. The precautions were deemed to be necessary because Hong Kong was entering its fifth month of extensive protests, and they were escalating in bitterness.

The authorities had unrealistically hoped that the keynote anniversary, a major event in the Chinese political calendar, would somehow be marked with positive energy in Hong Kong, much in the way that enthusiasm was being generated on the Mainland. Dictatorships have a habit of fetishising key dates marking the ascendancy of their power, and the Chinese Communist Party has proved itself to be no slouch in this regard. Lavish celebrations were laid on throughout the country, but the major events were held in Beijing, topped by an extensively rehearsed parade featuring impressive amounts of military hardware. The Mao-shaped Xi Jinping, who, like the Great Helmsman, rarely smiles, presided stolidly over proceedings, dominating the stage with no more than the occasional graceful wave of the hand.

Hong Kong was represented at the parade in China's capital by more than 240 carefully selected delegates, including the Chief Executive Carrie Lam, accompanied by other ministers, business leaders, heads of media companies, legislators and a significant police contingent, including Police Sergeant Lau Chak-kei, who had become a hero on the Mainland for brandishing a rifle in the face of protestors and subsequently taking to social media to post his thoughts on these "cockroaches", as he and his colleagues were calling them. In other words, on this most important day of the 2019 political calendar, the people who mattered in the SAR's establishment were safely installed in Beijing, far away from the citizens they were supposed to represent. This was telling. Left in their place at the flag-raising in Hong Kong was a B-team of government officials and other guests, stuck in the aggressively soulless exhibition centre, where they were required to plough through a turgid ceremony. As they shuffled their feet and sipped tepid champagne, their main concern was not the weather, but how they could exit the hall and get home safely.

They had reason to be worried, as Hong Kong was in lock-down: most major MTR stations were in the process of being closed, shopping centres were shuttered, and all police leave had been cancelled, as officers clad in heavy anti-riot gear flooded the centre of town.

The intensity of the atmosphere was heightened by mounting rumours that units of China's People's Armed Police were poised to enter Hong Kong as soon as the anniversary was out of the way. As we have seen, highly publicised riot control exercises had been staged in the border town of Shenzhen, designed to send a signal. There were also reports of plans to strengthen the size of the People's Liberation Army garrison already in Hong Kong, which had so far spent most of the uprising confined to barracks and engaged in training exercises in remote locations. In case anyone was missing the point, a police spokesman, Chief Superintendent John Tse, warned that any protest in Hong Kong on National Day would be "very, very dangerous".

But the protestors were undeterred. Early in the morning, a group of climbers had scaled the face of the Lion Rock, which stands majestically on the hills of Kowloon overlooking Hong Kong and has come to symbolise the SAR's plucky spirit. They left a banner reading "Oct 1, national day of mourning—liberate Hong Kong". Fire officers were hastily despatched to tear it down, but this would turn out to be one of the least significant events of the day. Later on, the city centre was filled with protests, but many other parts of Hong Kong were also alive with demonstrations. Police used live ammunition for the first time, and Tsang Chi-kin, an 18-year-old school student, was shot in the chest. He was subsequently arrested while recovering in hospital. According to the police, 269 arrests were made that day and 1,400 tear gas cannisters were fired—a record at the time, but one that was to be exceeded many times over in the weeks that followed.

A planned spectacular fireworks show in Victoria Harbour was cancelled, but Hong Kong citizens saw fireworks of another kind on 1 October, as tear gas and bean-bag bullets were unleashed throughout the territory. The violence that flared on the day that Hong Kong was supposed to be celebrating the triumph of the Communist Revolution was little different from what had a become a new norm: street protests met by a crackdown, and an almost daily repetition of this cycle of unrest.

Ever since the Yuen Long attack in late July, Hong Kong had seen a rapid deterioration in relations between the police and demonstrators, and an extraordinary slump in the general level of public trust in the police force. The visceral hatred between officers and protestors quickly became incorporated into the lexicon of the protests, with the police calling demonstrators "cockroaches" and the demonstrators calling them "black police", or Triad police. Anyone who is sceptical about opinion poll findings could look to what has long proved to be a reliable indicator of public sentiment in Hong Kong: the movie industry. For decades, the local film industry has punched well above its weight in the Chinese-speaking world. Since the 1970s, the backbone of success had come from crime thrillers, with cops at their centre. But, after the events of July 2019, enthusiasm for films portraying the police in a positive light sharply dwindled, as movies that once had a winning formula in the genre were shunned by the public.

Government officials had been turning a blind eye to police blatantly flouting the rules stipulating political neutrality for public servants, prohibited from commenting on public policy. Officers of all ranks have frequently been pictured in the company of pro-China political organisations and, through the medium of the Junior Police Officers' Association, by far the biggest body representing members of the force, directly engaged in the political debate. A new low was recorded as soon as Chris Tang was installed as the new Police Commissioner in November 2019. In an interview with the *South China Morning Post*, he characterised the uprising as a "mob". He also warned the government not to set up an independent inquiry into the policing of the protests and said that the protestors' "demands" were "just slogans".[1] This open comment on political matters went way beyond the remit of Hong Kong's most senior police officer, but no one in the Lam administration dared raise any objection.

Tang is a trusted pair of boots on the ground. He has been received and praised at the highest levels of government on the Mainland. He is also more popular with the rank and file of the police force than his predecessor Stephen Lo, and he has made it his business to lead from the front. Although he had been Lo's deputy, Tang is cut from a very different mould. From day one of assuming office, he made clear that he would be nothing like the last Commissioner, stressing that the police would be proactive in responding to protest, and making it a point to be seen with his men and women on the frontlines of demonstrations.

Lo, remarkably, had never once visited the frontlines of the protests, and had given every impression of being much happier behind a desk. His skills were very much those of an ambitious bureaucrat, which might have served him well during more placid times. It had become increasingly clear, and not just by virtue of opinion within the force, that he had to go. His short tenure as police chief had ended, unprecedentedly, without any form of ceremony. One of the legacies of Lo's weak leadership, however, was that permission for deployment of heavy weaponry and use of force, previously strictly controlled by senior officers at the centre, had been given to area commanders, who were allowed to use their discretion to do whatever they thought best. Most officers interpreted this as a green light to abandon the restraint which used to prevail. Young people found "guilty" of wearing black, even when not actually at a demonstration, could expect to be stopped and searched routinely, and to have their personal details taken. More aggressive officers favoured getting them to crouch with their hands behind their heads, or to stand splayed against a wall.

Before the uprising, the Hong Kong police had enjoyed high levels of respect and trust. In November 2019, the force decided to change its motto of "We Serve with Pride and Care" to "Serving Hong Kong with Honour, Duty and Loyalty". The meaning of this change is hard to explain, but it clearly reflects acute awareness within the force of its declining popularity. A survey conducted by the Chinese University of Hong Kong in September 2019 found that 48.3% of those questioned had zero trust in the police. On a scale of 1 to 10, with 10 points indicating "complete trust", the average score given was 2.89.[2]

This was a dismal result for a force that had taken public confidence for granted. Another survey conducted a little later, from 30 November to 2 December 2019, was, in some ways, even more damning. The research consultancy Blackbox Research found that 73% of respondents had had their trust in the police eroded by the street clashes. This figure includes 65% of respondents self-identifying as pro-establishment voters. Unlike the Chinese University survey, "only" 26% of those questioned said they had zero trust in the police. But a mere 7% had full trust in the force.[3]

It is hard to pinpoint when protestors stopped using the slogan "Hong Kong People, Keep Going" and adopted the more aggressive chant of "Hong Kong People, Resist"; but a crucial day was 6 October, when demonstrations resumed on both sides of Victoria Harbour and the "Resist" slogan was heard everywhere. It was a response to the increased violence of the time. The beatings of protest leaders by gang members had been stepped up. Some of those assaulted were only known locally, such as Stanley Ho, an unassuming activist who was later elected to the District Council in Sai Kung, where I live. Journalists were severely injured: Veby Indah, an Indonesian journalist, lost an eye, while other reporters alleged that police were now treating them as protestors, declining to recognise the job they were doing. The yellow camp made far fewer attacks on individuals, but the level of vandalism rose exponentially, with fire bombs and other incendiary devices making an appearance. Destruction of public property such as traffic lights and road barriers was becoming almost routine.

The police armoury was steadily expanded and ramped up. Pepper spray, which can be very painful and causes temporary blindness, was routinely deployed and often used at very close range. Pepper balls fired by guns were being used for the first time, with an effect similar to that of pepper spray. Bean-bag rounds, also shot from guns, had come into play too—these consist of a small fabric bag containing tiny lead pellets, not designed to be lethal, but capable of causing serious injury. Sponge grenades are, as the name suggests, bigger, and get their name from having a rubber head, backed by hard plastic. Rubber bullets, previously used with great restraint as they can be very dangerous, were now being fired, often at close range, as a matter of routine. These are made out of harder material than sponge grenades.

However, the favoured and most widely used police weapon remained tear gas, which is not gas at all, but a combination of chemicals causing extreme irritation to the eyes and rapidly impacting the throat, lungs and skin. It is nasty stuff with a lingering impact on the environment, especially when deployed in the wholesale quantities deployed during the uprising by the Hong Kong police, who purchased a particularly potent version of this weapon and refused to disclose its contents. The government also ordered two enormous, armoured vehicles with water cannons, which were only brought into play from late August. At the time, solemn assurances were given that, because of the size of these vehicles and their potential for collateral damage, they would only be deployed very selectively. From the first day of deployment, however, this assurance was abandoned, and it was decided to fill the water cannons with blue dye plus another mysterious irritant. Predictably, there was collateral damage, most notably when members of Hong Kong's largest mosque emerged from their prayers while a protest was underway in the vicinity, the worshippers finding themselves drenched in blue dye.

At the end of 2019, reporters at *The Washington Post* provided an impressively detailed account of how the police were using this arsenal of weapons in breach of their own guidelines and protocols. According to *The Post*, "The guidelines ... were often ignored by police, who have misused chemical agents and used excessive force against protesters not resisting, according to experts in policing who examined dozens of incidents in consultation with Post journalists and in comparison with the police protocols."[4] The police have always maintained that their use of force was proportionate and lawful.

* * *

On 16 October, Lam delivered her annual policy address, unveiling a batch of giveaways to the public and a blunt warning that there was to be no political change or concessions to the protestors. A second attempt at placating the public with offers of cash was made in January, with a HK$10 billion (US$1.28bn) package of welfare grants. The response to both these initiatives was underwhelming, and did nothing to lower the tension of the protests. Indeed, there was something surreal in this attempt to focus on economic matters while Hong Kong was almost literally burning. A slogan posted on a number of walls summed up the contempt for a government trying to divert attention from the uprising with offers of cash. It read: "And after all these abuses of power, you ask us to shut up for the economy."

By bizarre coincidence, on 23 October, the day that the extradition bill was formally withdrawn from Legco, Chan Tong-kai, the now self-confessed murderer whose case had provided the pretext for the legislation in the first place, was released from jail after serving a sentence for money-laundering. Previous protestations by the Lam government over the extreme urgency for his extradition to Taiwan, where he was wanted for the murder, now rapidly got lost amidst a barrage of political wrangling between Hong Kong and Taiwan following his release.

An arguably more significant reminder of the reasons behind opposition to the extradition bill had come in August, when Simon Cheng, a 29-year-old trade official working at the British Consulate with zero public profile at the time, was arrested at the high-speed terminus in Kowloon, where trains depart for the Mainland. He was then taken back across the border to Shenzhen. Cheng's arrest in Hong Kong confirmed the suspicions of those who had protested against designating the terminal as Mainland territory. At the time, their protests were dismissed as an overreaction, and assurances were given that Mainland jurisdiction in the heart of Hong Kong was no more than a technicality. Cheng's case showed that it was much more than that: it offered the Chinese authorities a way to nab Hong Kong residents even before the extradition law was introduced.

Cheng was held for fifteen days, accused of "soliciting prostitutes" in Shenzhen. It is commonplace for political arrests to be made under guise of other criminal charges, the more salacious the better. (This also explains the arrest in Guangzhou of Kwok Chun-fung, the founder of a first aid group helping protestors. Kwok was detained in January 2020 on the same charge, "soliciting prostitutes".) After Cheng's release and rapid exit to Britain via Taiwan, he told the BBC that he had been tortured and forced to sign a confession.[5] His interrogators had primarily been interested in Britain's role in the Hong Kong uprising, wanting him to confirm that support, money and equipment had been supplied by London. The UK government dismissed these allegations, but was curiously hesitant in giving initial support to Cheng, though he was eventually granted asylum in Britain. Beijing insisted that his detention had nothing to do with politics.

Fortunately, by the standards of the Chinese judicial system, Cheng's punishment was light and brief; but, against the backdrop of law enforcement cracking down on the uprising with increasingly free rein, and no end to the violent confrontation in sight, the manner of Cheng's arrest, the forced confession and the lack of any kind of due process confirmed what people in Hong Kong feared about an extradition law, which could expose anyone to this kind of treatment and worse.

As protests mounted, the police became even more assertive in demanding counter-measures. This came to a head when the government acceded to demands from the police and their supporters for something to be done over the widespread use of face masks by protestors, which had become widespread at demonstrations well before they were worn by everybody as a consequence of the coronavirus. The police wanted masks removed because they obscured the identity of protestors, who were wearing them for precisely that reason—and to deter the worst effects of tear gas.

On 4 October the Chief Executive, circumventing the legislature, invoked colonial-era emergency powers to introduce a ban on wearing face masks at protests. The last time these powers had been exercised in Hong Kong was more than half a century ago in 1967, to combat far more lethal rioting initiated by local supporters of China's Cultural Revolution. Yet Lam indicated that she might well use emergency regulations for other purposes. Pro-China forces were urging the imposition of a curfew and a crackdown on the media. Lam made it clear that she believed Hong Kong to be in a state of emergency, citing the urgency of acting against violence. Dennis Kwok, the legislator representing the legal sector, told me that "once they get the taste for emergency regulations, they will use them and add to the political crisis with a constitutional crisis. It's the first step to totalitarian government."[6]

The immediate consequence of this move was that, yet again, Lam demonstrated her uncanny ability to become a lightning conductor for the uprising. Incredibly, she did so at a time when the movement had been going through a lull. It took less than a day for the lull to evaporate. Protests flared up again, at one point causing the entire MTR system to be closed down for a full week. Nevertheless, something positive did emerge from this attempt to curb protest by use of emergency powers. Demonstrating that the independence of the judiciary was still alive and kicking, Hong Kong's High Court accepted an appeal against the face mask ban. On 18 November, the court ruled it unconstitutional, saying that the prohibition "[went] further than necessary" in restricting fundamental rights.

This verdict was greeted with a mixture of bewilderment and fury in Beijing, where courts of law are viewed as arms of the executive. Hu Xijin, editor of the *Global Times*, was quick to give his response: "Many people will see the ruling as the High Court's accommodation of everything committed by these masked rioters ... It will further confuse right and wrong in the Hong Kong society, and prompt more people to take a sympathetic view of the rioters instead of condemning their violence."[7] The Lam government quickly issued an appeal, and managed to obtain an injunction allowing the mask ban to remain in effect pending a final judgment. When this came, however, the court handed only a partial victory to the administration, heavily qualified by strictures over the use of these powers.

Whereas official concern over masks had descended to the level of farce, matters of life and death now came to the fore. There had been a number of suicides within the democracy movement—it is hard to estimate how many, but over the course of the uprising there were at least a dozen cases where those who died had left messages of protest. There had also been casualties on the pro-China side of the fence. Junius Ho, the legislator who had been consorting with Triad members attacking people at Yuen Long Station in July, was himself stabbed, though not critically. Luo Changqing, a 70-year-old man, died from head injuries sustained by being hit with a brick during a relatively small-scale demonstration.

Remarkably, no one appeared to have died as a result of direct action by the police, despite the level of violence deployed. However, on 8 November, Chow Tsz-lok, a 22-year-old University of Science and Technology student, became the first protestor to die during a demonstration. Chow, a computer science undergraduate, was known on campus as being keen on sports. He had not been a political activist before the uprising started. He succumbed to injuries incurred while trying to escape from the police in Tseung Kwan O. At worst, the police were accused of pushing him over a multi-storey car park wall, and at best of obstructing access to an ambulance that had arrived to help him. Both accusations were vigorously denied by the force.

The immediate response to Chow's death was shock and muted anger. A few days later, a general strike was called in his memory. It paralysed transport, and spontaneous demonstrations flared in numerous locations. In the space of no more than a few weeks, the "Resist" slogan had hardened again, into a call for *bousauh*, or revenge. Students at UST, where Chow studied, were relatively muted in their response, but other universities exploded in anger. Protestors occupied the campuses of the Chinese

University and the Polytechnic University. Hong Kong University, City University and the Baptist University were also taken over by students, for a more limited period that was nevertheless punctuated by ugly confrontations between police and protestors. The remaining three universities were also affected by the protests, but less so.

The Baptist University campus is situated next to one of the camps occupied the People's Liberation Army, and was therefore considered to be in a particularly sensitive location. When news emerged that members of the garrison were being mobilised, it was feared that the long-rumoured use of force by the Chinese military was about to begin. However, the Beijing authorities opted instead for a nuanced approach, sending out a large squad of "volunteers" marching in step to take part in a clean-up operation initiated by pro-China organisations. It was the first direct intervention into the protests by the PLA garrison, and while there was disquiet over the deployment of the troops, it was also recognised that the PRC was quite capable of being subtle.

It remains unclear how many of those involved in these protests were actually students. What is known is that the occupiers of the Chinese University campus completely trashed the university railway station and blocked a major arterial road that straddled the campus. Neither side held back, as protesters started using not just Molotov cocktails but also flaming arrows—and were met with hundreds of rounds of tear gas and rubber bullets. Even Rocky Tuan, the University's Vice-Chancellor, was injured by a tear gas cannister as he tried to negotiate an end to the occupation. At Polytechnic University, much closer to the centre of town, an even more intense siege was underway. The campus is adjacent to the road that feeds into the main tunnel which connects Mainland Hong Kong with Hong Kong Island; it is also opposite the city's main railway station. The protestors succeeded in blocking this tunnel and vandalised the toll booths, severely disrupting traffic throughout Hong Kong. Access to the station was also largely blocked, providing another major transportation headache.

The siege of Polytechnic University lasted from 17 to 29 November. Conditions inside became dire, as food supplies ran out, injured people could not get treatment and sanitary conditions deteriorated. The police turned tables on the demonstrators by ignoring their barriers at entrances to the campus and imposing their own checkpoints to control anyone coming in and, more importantly from their point of view, to arrest anyone coming out. The occupiers fought police with bricks and fire bombs, although many of those inside the university had no part in this violent activity. The police response was dramatic. On a single day, 18 November, as officers forced their way into the university, they fired off 1,458 cannisters of tear gas, as well as 1,391 rubber bullets, 325 bean-bag rounds and 265 sponge grenades.[8] The police warned that anyone on campus would be classified as a rioter. This meant that many first-aiders, journalists and some of those who had come to the university trying to negotiate an end to the occupation were injured and arrested. Stories emerged of dramatic escapes through drains or by abseiling from bridges.

Supporters gathered outside the campus, and at one point people at a nearby demonstration were crushed in a stampede. By the time the authorities gained full control of Poly U, some 1,100 arrests had been made inside or nearby the university. The police said they had found almost 4,000 petrol bombs, and about 600 bottles of corrosive liquid, plus other weapons.[9] The campus looked like a battlefield.

Following the end of the siege, all of Hong Kong's universities ceased to be public places. Access became carefully controlled, which suggested a radical change to the universities' role in the community. This is not least because, long after the violence on campuses had faded, some universities were locked down against public access, to prevent protestors from entering campus again.

* * *

Despite the growing violence surrounding the uprising through the autumn, a poll commissioned by Reuters at the end of December 2019 found that 59 per cent of Hongkongers were still supporting the movement; more than one third said they had attended an anti-government demonstration.[10] While the government made valiant attempts in 2019 to shrug off polling evidence of its unpopularity, it was faced with much harder-to-ignore evidence in November, when pro-democrats secured an unprecedented victory at the district elections. After more than half a year of protest, the poll was seen as a referendum on the Lam government and its masters in Beijing.

District councils in Hong Kong have few real powers, and had long been a stronghold for pro-government parties. Despite the government's long-standing pretence that it had the approval of a "silent majority", some of its closest supporters feared that the November election would not go well for them. In light of these fears, the Lam administration broadly hinted that emergency regulations might be brought into play to postpone the elections, using the excuse of difficulties posed by the unstable atmosphere. Talking to people involved in discussions between senior SAR officials and pro-China politicians, I found out that the government had come close to ordering a postponement, but had convinced itself at the last minute that a massive backlash against protestors' violence would be manifest. A conclusion was reached, no doubt with the dubious benefit of advice from the pro-China parties, that although the pro-China camp would lose a few seats, control over the councils could be maintained.

To be fair, it was hard to imagine any other outcome: the pro-China parties have traditionally been far better financed and far more disciplined, not least because their supporters readily take orders on the conduct of elections from the Liaison Office. Moreover, by working hand in hand with the government, their councillors are able to achieve material benefits for their constituents. In other words, the pro-China parties are formidable. What's more, they had convinced themselves that the protestors had alienated the wider public. So the polls went ahead.

Yet again, however, the disconnect between the government and the people became clear. As the results came in, showing an unprecedentedly high level of participation with an incredible turnout of 71.2%, the democrats succeeded beyond their wildest dreams. The pro-China vote share was reduced to around 40%. Not only was control seized from the pro-China camp in all but one council (the outlier being a district where almost half the seats are appointed by the government), but the tsunami of support for the democrats gave them 86% of all seats up for election.

The pro-democracy camp, infamous for infighting and focusing on minutiae while bigger battles are lost through of lack of attention, had finally got organised and ensured a clear-cut choice for the electorate. They ended up with around 57% of the vote, a figure that had been achieved before, but in elections where victory was still squandered by infighting and vote-splitting among competing democrats. This time around, there was a higher level of co-ordination, and a far more focused effort to win seats. And it had paid off.

In the decimation of the blue camp, every one of the best-known pro-China councillors was swept aside, including Junius Ho, who also serves in the legislature and was associated with the July Yuen Long attack. The incoming democrat councillors included similarly well-known figures such as Jimmy Sham, a key protest organiser, and Lester Shum, one of the leading figures in the Umbrella Movement. Even if Carrie Lam and her people had been oblivious to the fact, the democratic camp had realised that this election was in fact a referendum on the government and the protest movement, and that—since the district council elections are the nearest thing in Hong Kong to an election by universal suffrage—these polls needed to be taken seriously. On the other side, the pro-China parties' traditional strength at local level had led to complacency and overreliance on stressing economic issues, while the majority of the electorate went to the polls with bigger political considerations in mind.

The public could not have spoken more clearly, yet the first response of the Chief Executive was to invite defeated candidates to meet her. She then held a second meeting with the election losers, and more or less promised to find them jobs on the teeming plenitude of government advisory committees. Not only did Lam decline to meet the newly elected councillors, but once they got down to business, civil servants, who normally service the work of the district councils, were instructed to withdraw when controversial issues were placed on the agenda. Many new councillors were then arrested at demonstrations.

Lam had long complained that, even if she wished to negotiate with protestors, she had no way of contacting their leaders. Now a golden opportunity had presented itself for dialogue with elected figures, and yet again Lam had decided that her best option was to never miss a chance to miss a chance.

Even if the administration was bent on ignoring the result of the election, there were still lingering opportunities for some kind of reconciliation. The most obvious way of defusing the tension would have been to establish an independent inquiry into the policing of protests. This proposal had support from right across the political spectrum. Moreover, public support for such a move was overwhelming. The December poll cited above also found that 74 per cent of those questioned wanted an independent inquiry into police brutality during the uprising.

Another of the protestors' demands, the end to prosecutions of demonstrators, could at least be met halfway by taking account of public interest when making decisions over cases that involved neither violence nor extreme vandalism. This, at any rate was the suggestion advanced by Philip Dykes, the Chairman of the Bar Association.[11] There was a very substantial precedent for withdrawing prosecutions in terms of public interest. As staggering irony would have it, this public interest argument had last been raised in Hong Kong by the police themselves, in a 1970s revolt against the establishment of the Independent Commission Against Corruption, which was cracking down on wholesale corruption within the force. In the face of a siege of ICAC headquarters, the British government backed down and declared that the bulk of officers under investigation would not have their cases pursued. Indeed, they would be allowed to keep their ill-gotten gains, on condition that a line was drawn beyond which corrupt practices would not be ignored.[12]

By contrast, in 2019, the police were firmly opposed to any suggestion of an amnesty for protestors, and adamantly resisted an independent inquiry. Instead they stood behind a limited investigation that was being conducted by the Independent Police Complaints Council (IPCC). This body, composed entirely of government trustees with limited powers of investigation, attempted to shore up its credibility by appointing a panel of high-level overseas independent experts to assist in its work. However, in December 2019, the experts quit, citing a "crucial shortfall" in powers and capability of investigation.

After considerable delay, the IPCC finally delivered its report in May 2020.[13] As widely expected, it concluded that the police had generally acted within guidelines, though it noted some areas where there was room for improvement. The level of the IPCC's determination to produce a version of events acceptable to the authorities was underlined by Clement Chan, chairman of the

IPCC's Publishing and Survey Committee: in an interview, he told me that the infamous July attack on protestors by iron-bar-wielding, Triad-related thugs at Yuen Long had in fact been a case of both sides being armed. When pressed to say which weapons had been carried by the protestors and other train passengers, he said they had umbrellas.[14] As the IPCC had largely been discredited before its report was delivered, its conclusions were greeted with a marked lack of interest, and did nothing to assuage demands for a full and truly independent investigation.

Never anxious to learn the lessons of mistakes in governance, the Lam administration pushed aside the debacle of the IPCC's report and tried to establish another committee, one that would look at "deep-seated problems in society". However, the plan was abandoned when it became clear that the government was having great difficulty finding anyone with credibility to sit on this body. At the time of writing, it appears to have been stillborn.

As 2020 began with very little expectation of change, it was marked, as ever, by a mass demonstration, followed by an outbreak of violence. In addition a large demonstration held every year in the middle of town on 1 January, 400 arrests were made across Hong Kong, where smaller rallies were held in a number of localities. It was hard to tell what would happen next. What did the new year have in store for the Hong Kong uprising? Both the authorities and demonstrators appeared to be in a state of exhaustion, mixed with nervous anticipation.

As we now know, it appears that the Party was working hard behind the scenes on a plan to effectively bypass the hapless Lam administration to change by edict the entire basis of the "one country, two systems" concept. In other words, Beijing was moving to introduce a draconian national security law, furnishing the state with wide powers to stamp out opposition. At the time, however, all of this was kept under wraps, even to the extent of Lam and her officials remaining in the dark, until the plans were unveiled in June 2020.[15] In the meantime, the CCP regime did what it usually does in these circumstances: it found a hapless scapegoat on whom to shift the blame for the failings of its own policies. Dismissals of officials fall very much within the age-old Chinese tradition of punishing subordinates to save the Emperor. Today's Communist Party emperors never admit to fault and work on the principle of sacrificing underlings to preserve the Party. As they say, in a particularly vivid Cantonese expression, someone had to eat the dead cat.

The first person chosen to eat this particular cat was Wang Zhimin, the head of China's Central Liaison Office in Hong Kong, who was fired in January 2020. As is usual in these matters, it was not spelt out why he had to go, but the rumour mill was not constrained by a lack of official information. Wang, a Mainland bureaucrat straight from "faceless officials" central casting, was apparently being held responsible for failing to predict the disaster of November's district council elections. This explanation was later given credence as the official line emerged from Beijing, containing many mentions of the poor quality of information supplied to the centre.

Wang was immediately replaced by Luo Huining, a former Party chief in Shanxi Province. Much was made of Luo's close connections with the security services and his no-nonsense reputation for carrying out difficult assignments: as well as being famous as a disciplinarian in Shanxi, his track record includes imposing heavy restrictions on the Tibetan minority in Jiangxi Province. A more mundane explanation for his appointment, however, was that it had to be made fast and, by taking Luo out of retirement, there was no need for more extensive job-shuffling elsewhere.

By contrast, there could be no mundane explanation for the second round of firings in February, when Zhang Xiaoming was demoted from head of the Hong Kong and Macau Affairs Office

(HKMAO) in Beijing, becoming the deputy. He was replaced by Xia Baolong, a more senior figure and a vice-chairman of the Chinese People's Political Consultative Conference, which ranks below the National People's Congress and is supposed to be a nationwide consultative body. Xia has an ugly reputation for stamping out underground churches while he was the Communist Party Secretary of Zhejiang Province. His installation at the HKMAO was therefore interpreted by some as bringing a more hardline approach to handling Hong Kong affairs. This makes the challenging assumption that the deposed Zhang had been in any way a liberal. More significant was Xia's close personal connection to Xi Jinping, a connection shared, albeit at a lower level, by Luo. It seems more likely, therefore, that the minor bout of bloodletting at the start of 2020 was essentially designed to bring troublesome Hong Kong affairs more closely towards the ambit of presidential control.

These purges at the top of the Liaison Office and the HKMAO prompted an outbreak of speculation about Carrie Lam's departure. She had been assured of support by the central authorities, but it is their way to support officials right up to the moment before they are fired. In all events, neither Lam nor any members of her administration were, at this point, going to be held responsible for their dismal performance in 2019. It was not even certain that a clean-up within the Hong Kong government would have done much good, bearing in mind the uninspiring choice of alternatives to take up the jobs.

While Beijing was shuffling the desks of those in charge of Hong Kong affairs, it looked as though the protests were somewhat fading. There was much discussion in the democracy movement over what to do next. The major election victory in November had led some protestors to suggest that attention should now be focused on the Legco elections scheduled for September 2020. Others favoured a ramping up of the outreach to overseas people and governments to put pressure on the regime in Beijing. In as much as it is possible to define a consensus within this amorphous movement, which still mainly communicates through a variety of online means, it seems that the idea of ending demonstrations and indeed violent protest enjoyed no more than minority support. Those in favour of keeping up the pressure on the streets worried over a lack of momentum. Their argument was that a cessation of demonstrations would bring the movement to a juddering halt. Others pointed out that only violent action had succeeded in producing a government response. A retreat from the streets, it was argued, would mean a loss of initiative, and would be a betrayal of those who had made considerable sacrifices for the movement over the past year.

Just as the street protests were losing steam, the government decided that it needed to redouble efforts to frame the protest movement as little short of a terrorist-style insurgency. Between January and March, the police carried out a series of high-profile raids and arrests, accusing suspects of bomb-making and possession of weapons or ammunition. These raids were conducted in the full glare of law enforcement's publicity machine, resulting in a flurry of charges. Such arrests continued throughout the year. Among those detained was Andy Chan, the leader of the banned Hong Kong National Party. In August he was charged not with membership of an illegal organisation, but with possession of offensive weapons and explosives. At the time of writing, these charges have yet to be proved, but they served the purpose of depicting Hong Kong as being under a terrorist threat.

Considerable publicity was also given to acts of alleged terrorism, though there was scant evidence to substantiate such assertions. Instead one of the police actions unveiled a seat being damaged in a public toilet (this was the reality of what happened, but police propaganda suggested a far more serious event), while another focused on a fire-bomb attack at a police housing compound, causing no injuries or damage and consisting of little more than the throwing of flaming rags. In February, an alleged bomb was "partially detonated" at the Lo Wu railway station on the border with Shenzhen, and another was defused. In the wake of an alleged bombing of the Shenzhen border post, which caused no damage, the police said they had found a single message on Telegram describing this attack as "just a warning" and stating that "there will be more real bombs to come". Talking up the threat of violence, Chief Executive Carrie Lam went so far as to brief locally based diplomats on the growing terrorist threat. In March, the show continued with the launch of a highly publicised anti-terrorism exercise by the Inter-departmental Counter Terrorism Unit, involving 250 officers from various branches of the authorities.

It is undeniable that the level of violence had increased, but this frenzy of activity clearly fell short of a credible demonstration that Hong Kong stood on the brink of terrorism. In June 2020, of course, it became clear why this avalanche of terrorist allegations had been made, once the National Security Law was announced.

While activity on the streets had cooled as 2019 morphed into 2020, there was a great deal going on below the surface. Most important were Beijing's well-disguised preparations for introducing the NSL. In Hong Kong, the government was busying itself with finding ways of deflecting another shattering rebuff in the Legco elections scheduled for September. And within the yellow camp, as we have seen, there was much discussion of what to do next. What no one had taken into consideration was the gamechanger that arose from the pandemic brewing across the border. As we shall see in Chapters 9 and 10, the convergence of a political and a health crisis was little short of a perfect storm. Though Hong Kong didn't know it at the start of 2020, the combination of the pandemic and the NSL appears to have drawn something of a line under the uprising, at least in the short term.

8

REVOLUTION OF OUR TIMES

While Edward Leung remained in prison for the duration of the 2019–20 uprising, his slogan—"Liberate Hong Kong, Revolution of Our Times!"—was ubiquitous. It had been denounced by Carrie Lam, Hong Kong's Chief Executive, as calling for a revolution that would "challenge national sovereignty, threaten 'one country, two systems', and ... destroy the city's prosperity and stability".[1] Once the National Security Law was in force from 1 July 2020, the slogan was banned on grounds of inciting variously secession, treason or sedition. But the ban cannot alter the fact that the uprising has produced a deep change in the way Hongkongers think about things, as it has had a profound impact on their lives in a great many ways.

Leung's slogan emerged when he was prevented from running for election in 2016, because of his support for a "revolution of our times". In October 2019, Tommy Cheung, a former student leader who had also played a key role in the Umbrella Movement, offered his interpretation of Leung's slogan: "What I meant [by adopting this slogan] was to restore the old Hong Kong where citizens enjoy different kinds of freedoms ... with election [candidates] not being deprived of their rights because of their political views and returning officers resuming their professionalism without political interference." He added: "The word 'revolution' should not be interpreted as bloody acts which aim for overthrowing a regime but [as] referring to a mega change in structure and thinking, like the industrial revolution and technological revolution."[2]

Cheung's mention of "mega change in structure and thinking" is key, because what he was writing about was a vital aspect of the 2019–20 uprising, which had produced an enormous sense of empowerment that swept through Hong Kong: citizens had learned that they did not have to rely on leaders to make things happen, and discovered a new sense of community. Likeminded people could be mobilised to achieve commonly held objectives. This realisation of new possibilities resulted in change on many fronts. The question is whether these transformations are merely ephemeral, or will be long-lasting. My view is that, although much of the upheaval and excitement of the uprising will pass and give way to life as usual, there is now a new usual.

Most revolutions take as their starting point departure from the status quo. The great revolution of 1911 that created the Chinese Republic self-consciously sought to define itself by the new rulers' differences from the deposed Qing Dynasty. The Communist Revolution of 1949 went a step further and declared itself, in Mao's words, to be a perpetual movement for change. The phrase "New China" is routinely employed by the regime to stress a break from the past, in both names of organisations and descriptions of the modern era. Disdain for the old reached a peak with China's Cultural Revolution of the 1960s, which ordered the outlawing of the "four olds"—old things, old ideas, old custom and old habits.

But the Hong Kong protests of 2019–20 were different. Although there was most certainly a demand for change, this was also a movement calling for the restoration of the old; of a time in the past when freedoms had prevailed that were now being whittled away. Some of those involved in the protests were frankly nostalgic and waved the former colonial Hong Kong flag on marches, but they were in a distinct minority—not least because most of the demonstrators had no personal experience of British rule, which had ended more than two decades ago, before many of them were born. What protestors really wanted to preserve from the old era was the concept and reality of freedom. The colonial administration offered a high degree of freedom but never brought real democracy to Hong Kong. Despite this, especially in the later years of the colonial era, freedom of expression had flourished, and the rule of law had remained solid.

In July 2019, the Hong Kong Public Opinion Research Institute conducted a study on attitudes towards the protests; its conclusions were released on 2 August.[3] What is most striking is that the overwhelming majority of those questioned cited the pursuit of freedom and democracy as major reasons for supporting the uprising. However, distrust of the central government in Beijing ranked as the single greatest reason for the protests, accompanied by distrust of Hong Kong's Chief Executive. Unsurprisingly, the highest levels of support for these ideas of greater freedom and democracy came from the younger generation; but there was a shared concern for liberty across the age groups.

The widespread support for democracy in Hong Kong explains why the movement became so embedded in local society. Hongkongers responded by going further than just joining demonstrations or voting for pro-democracy candidates: a great many got involved with self-help and individual grassroots initiatives that gave the uprising an all-embracing significance way beyond the demonstrations on the streets. In addition to fundraising, the resources of expertise were also marshalled in support of the movement. For example, an ad-hoc committee of advertising professionals took time out to help devise pro-democracy campaigns. Other services were also provided, sometimes in an organised manner but often on an individual basis. A great many lawyers spent their nights going around police stations providing pro-bono legal assistance to arrested demonstrators.

Among the first to come forward to provide voluntary services were people with some degree of medical training. As demonstrations escalated and got more violent, they rushed from place to place with heavy bags bulging with medical supplies, providing on-site first aid and helping the more seriously injured go to hospital. However, once the police started entering hospitals in search of injured protestors, many became wary over seeking treatment. At this point doctors and nurses stepped in to form a network of underground hospitals, sometimes in hotel rooms, at other times in apartments. How did the patients get to these makeshift treatment centres? Again, volunteers stepped forward. Some were taxi drivers; others were delivery drivers; and some were just citizens with vehicles who had been alerted on social media to the need for transportation.

This ethos of mutual aid pervaded the movement. Anyone who went to a demonstration would discover plentiful supplies of water and face masks, both to lessen the impact of tear gas and obscure identity. Total strangers have offered me food, while others took it upon themselves to offer me ways of escaping once violence kicked in.

As the number of protest arrests went into the four and then five digits, many people lost their jobs, and here too help came to hand from fellow protestors. A 28-year-old social worker, who uses the nickname Pop, set up a "Find a Good Boss" channel on Telegram, with the idea of putting together protest-supporting bosses and employees. Such was the response that Pop resigned from his job to work full-time on this project, which was overwhelmed with applications from both sides. There are many other Telegram and Facebook groups offering their services to protestors, including professional counselling, accommodation and products for people suffering from the after-effects of tear gas and other chemical poisons.

Two major platforms were launched for collecting funds, mainly used to cover the legal costs of the thousands of protestors who were arrested. One of the most effective of these citizens' initiatives took the form of flash money-raising campaigns, with millions of dollars raised for a number of causes. Getting people to make donations online provided an instant and meaningful way for large numbers of Hongkongers to get involved in the pro-democracy movement, many of whom would not necessarily want to go out on the streets, but were keen to express support for the protests. For instance, a great deal of money was raised to place full-page advertisements in leading newspapers around the world, calling for the international community to support the uprising. The first of these newspaper campaigns, in June 2019, was timed to coincide with the G20 summit in Osaka. "Stand with Hong Kong at G20", ran the top line, and it seemed to have some effect, because Hong Kong was indeed discussed by the world leaders at the event.

The ease with which protestors were able to get donations from the public resulted in the government and pro-China organisations declaring that shady foreign forces, including states, were funnelling money into Hong Kong to fuel the uprising. At the time of writing, the only "evidence" they have been able to produce for these claims is an assertion that such large sums could not possibly have been collected from the public, and therefore must have come from abroad. In fact, Hong Kong has a long tradition of generous donations to both political and social causes. All that was different this time was the size of the sums involved, and the speed with which the money materialised.

In December 2019, the police closed down one of these funds, the Spark Alliance HK, which had collected over HK$70 million (about US$9m). This was on grounds of suspected money laundering, charges that have yet to be proved. HSBC, Hong Kong's largest bank, moved rapidly to close the account, effectively freezing the money. Although the bank's action was well received in official circles, it led to an immediate customer backlash, with people taking their business elsewhere, and vandalism of the bank's branches. In 2020, the police started targeting a variety of other pro-democracy organisations, also on grounds of money laundering, as they demanded to see lists of donors. The intention of suppressing the flow of financial support to the movement could not have been clearer.

In sum, Hongkongers didn't have to take part in demonstrations to be a part of the uprising. A mass expression of solidarity with the movement had developed, and it continues to this day despite the crackdown, which intensified with the introduction of the NSL.

* * *

At the extreme end of the protest movement were vandals destroying the property of political opponents, but those supporting the protests had far less extreme options for making their views known, and could even do so—to some considerable effect—from their own homes. A call on social media in August 2019 for a 10pm "shout-out" brought yet another form of localised protest. People were asked to simply open their windows at this time and yell out slogans of the uprising. "Liberate Hong Kong, Revolution of Our Times!" was the most popular, but you could also hear others such as "Five demands—not one less", and "Hong Kong people, *ga yau*"—literally meaning "add oil", but understood as "Hong Kong people, let's go". In the SAR, where most of the population lives in tightly packed high-rise buildings, often built around a central square, this cacophony of sound had an enormous impact. For some people it was a way of venting their frustration; for others it was a means of spreading the protests.

There was, inevitably, kickback, as residents less enamoured by the uprising also opened their windows, often to shout obscenities, which were returned in kind.

Like other Chinese languages, Cantonese is tonal, and slight tonal inflections can considerably change the meaning of words; as a result, there is a strong Cantonese tradition of pun-based fun-making. In Hong Kong, widespread use of English adds to this linguistic dexterity, producing a wide range of "Chinglish". Protestors have been quick to exploit the possibilities this offers, often using language that is euphemistically described as "colourful". Sometimes this outpouring got out of hand, but it served the purpose of bringing the movement right into people's homes.

The emergence of a chasm between the blue and yellow camps has also been reflected in the media, where mainstream outlets are dominated by pro-China owners. Thirst for an alternative led to an upsurge in new online media outlets: broadcasters, newspapers, commentators, bloggers and chat rooms either explicitly supporting the movement or at least providing some counterbalance to the narrative of events provided by the established media.

A pair of heavily tinted glasses would be required to pretend that Hong Kong has anything resembling a long history of independent media; on the contrary, from colonial times onwards, most of the media has been controlled by private interests with a distinct agenda, alongside a minority of openly political newspapers. However, in the later years of British rule, a more independently minded media came to the fore. These halcyon days of journalism came under intense pressure following the handover, not least because control of the media has always been an important part of the Communist Party's agenda.

The one part of the traditional media world that has remained stubbornly insistent on maintaining an independent stance is the public broadcaster Radio Television Hong Kong (RTHK). It is under almost constant pressure to serve the government's propaganda requirements, justified by the fact that RTHK's budget is derived from public funds. However, the station takes seriously its remit as an impartial public broadcaster, and has declined to become a mouthpiece controlled by the Mainland. As pressure mounted during the uprising, with the purse strings attached to RTHK pulled ever tighter, a new committee of government trustees was appointed in 2020 to supervise the station's activities. Under these conditions, it is questionable how long independence can be maintained. Otherwise, broadcast media has come increasingly under the control of pro-China owners. The largest television station, TVB, was taken over by Mainland interests prior to the uprising and has been widely dubbed CCTVB by protestors— a reference to CCTV, China's main state-run broadcaster.

Most newspapers, too, are controlled by Beijing's local cyphers. The only major paper to consistently oppose the government has been *Apple Daily*. Its founder is Jimmy Lai, an eternal thorn in Beijing's side, who was smuggled to Hong Kong at the age of 12 from his family home in Guangdong and worked his way up from penniless, poorly educated immigrant to leading pro-democracy businessman. If there is a single person who tops Beijing's "most hated personalities" list, it is Lai, who seems to get under the Party leaders' skin more than anyone else. In August 2020, he, his sons and *Apple Daily* senior managers were arrested, as police staged a massive high-profile raid on the paper's premises. In December, after a flurry of other police actions against him, Lai was remanded in connection with an alleged fraud offence and quickly thereafter charged under the NSL.

However, in Hong Kong, as is the case elsewhere in the world, the established media has become of less importance, particularly to a younger generation with no interest in watching live television and even less inclination to buy a physical newspaper. With varying degrees of success, the SAR's big traditional media players have tried to move themselves online, but have often been less successful than the poorly resourced new media organisations, which celebrated their relative poverty and became essential to the protest movement. Many journalists from the mainstream media abandoned their jobs during the protest movements of the 2010s and were joined by others in establishing new outlets online, usually with little hope of financial reward, but making an impressive impact.

Among the most prominent of these outlets are *Stand News*, FactWire, Initium Media, CitizenNews, inMedia, *HK01* and the *Hong Kong Free Press*, an English-language outlet. Online radio is also gaining an impressive listenership, with stations such as Citizens' Radio and Myradio. Not only have these new outlets continued to proliferate through the 2019–20 uprising, but in 2019 news from these internet-based media companies was rated as the most trustworthy, overtaking television for the first time, as all other parts of the establishment media saw a slump in their ratings for credibility.[4] It is highly likely that, even without the uprising, the trend away from the established media would have accelerated, but it might not have been so political, or resulted in such an acute drawing of battle lines.

The bifurcation of the media and the wider division of society into blue and yellow camps has produced deep divisions among families and friends, where individuals often find themselves on different sides of the political divide. The most acute and painful conflicts have arisen within families where the older and younger generations find themselves in bitter disagreement over the protest movement: the Hong Kong Federation of Youth Groups, a pro-government organisation, published a survey in December 2019 finding that some 42 per cent of young Hongkongers had been arguing with their parents in the preceding six months; 71 per cent of these said that their disagreements had been over current affairs.[5] Hong Kong's housing shortage and astronomical housing costs mean that many younger people, even after marriage, live with their parents and grandparents in very cramped accommodation. It is a recipe for tension at the best of times.

A study by scholars from the University of Hong Kong, published in *The Lancet* in January 2020, revealed an alarming state of mental health in the SAR, greatly exacerbated by the protests. This very widely based survey, following 18,000 respondents over ten years, found that probable depression among residents over the age of 18 was five times higher in 2019 than had been the norm before the 2014 Umbrella protests (11% compared with 2%). Even more alarmingly, post-traumatic stress disorder symptoms were estimated to be affecting 32% of the adult population, compared with 5% by the end of the Umbrella Movement.[6] As the uprising has given way to the emergence of the coronavirus pandemic, stress levels appear to have spiked again. A survey conducted between May and July 2020 found that 87% of respondents were suffering from medium to high levels of stress and 52% reported levels of anxiety.[7] A combination of health and economic concerns appears to have been layered on top of the unease brought about by the political turmoil.

Divisions on a personal level were reflected by the wider development of the blue and yellow economies, in which those on both sides of the fence have resolutely boycotted businesses associated with the rival camp, and offered active support to their own. This political identification in economic and financial decision-making is rapidly becoming an established way of life. Deciding what to buy and where are usually mundane choices, but in the SAR they have acquired a political dimension. The spirit of the evolving "yellow economy" is very much part of the spirit of this revolution of our times, in which Hongkongers seek to merge their everyday activities with those of the movement. The new yellow business groups or "yellow economic circles", as they are known, are better organised than the pro-China companies, creating apps for people to find and support their businesses—mostly small-scale retail enterprises. These apps also told people which blue companies to boycott.

The blue economy is, rather obviously, bigger than the yellow economy, and is most clearly seen in companies allied with Beijing or owned by state entities. As we saw in Chapter 3, Chinese state enterprises started playing a dominant role in the local economy some two decades ago—from banks and insurance firms to petrol stations, property developers and telephone companies. The protest movement fostered a sense of deeper awareness among Hongkongers of the way the SAR is increasingly being enveloped into the embrace of its big brother to the north, as the PRC's tentacles dig deeper into all aspects of society. Formal and informal boycotts of these "blue" companies were accompanied by the more radical action of vandalising their premises.

* * *

Beijing has not been shy in exerting its considerable economic power to bully overseas companies outside Hong Kong. The mighty Apple corporation meekly bowed to pressure to remove a mapping app that was used by protestors to track police activity. Nike faced a massive Mainland retailer boycott of its highly popular sports products after it was lambasted for carrying Houston Rockets-branded goods, because the basketball team's manager had expressed support for the movement. Other companies were also successfully pressured into making changes: airlines that had listed Taiwan as a country were forced to backtrack, while Marriott Hotels & Resorts had to make a shamefaced apology for a similar offence. The list of very big companies being humbled in this way during the uprising is impressive.

In other words, after the uprising began, it became clear—even if it was not so beforehand—that political neutrality was no longer an option for the business community. This applied to both local companies and international corporations. Following the example of the property developers, large Hong Kong businesses took out prominent newspaper advertisements effectively pledging loyalty to the Party and slamming the protest movement. Local business leaders were summoned to meetings with Chinese officials, who laid out clear warnings over what would happen if any of them dared cross the line of showing sympathy for the protests. As we have seen, one of the highest-profile examples of a company forced to toe the line was the airline Cathay Pacific.

Local businesses were caught between a rock and a hard place. On the one hand, they faced pressure from the Party to offer political support; on the other, a great many of their customers were repelled by their kowtowing. Some companies gave their support willingly, others pragmatically; but the net result was a deepening of the alienation between big business and the people. As a result, many of these corporations faced boycotts and vandalism. The alliance of Hong Kong business and the Chinese Communist Party was hardly new, but in the past this incongruous combination had been shrugged off as no more than a marriage of convenience. This indifference faded in 2019–20, and many people were no longer willing to be quite so understanding of companies that had decided to involve themselves in the political struggle. As we have seen, the MTR network was subject to boycotts and vandalism after it decided to thwart access to transportation during demonstrations. An even greater negative reaction was directed towards the bargain-basement retailer Best Mart 360: seventy-five of its 102 stores in Hong Kong were attacked at least once in the six months to November 2019, and these branches were attacked over 180 times in total.[8]

One of the main targets of the yellow camp's ire was one of Hong Kong's biggest catering conglomerates, Maxim's—famous for its large Chinese restaurants, fast-food outlets and ownership of major franchises in the local market, such as the Starbucks concession. A daughter of the founder's family, Annie Wu, single-handedly shook the company during the uprising in ways she most certainly had not anticipated. Although she carries the prominent family name, Wu plays no role in the group's management; nevertheless she liberally evokes her association with Maxim's. She is also a long-time pro-China advocate and member of various Mainland bodies. Before the uprising, she had attracted little attention, but she was thrust into the limelight after going to Geneva in September 2019 to speak at the United Nations Human Rights Council, which was debating its response to events in Hong Kong. In fluent Communist-Party-speak, she castigated the protestors and their objectives, while presenting herself as representative of the Hong Kong majority.

Wu's remarks produced an immediate response, which was then exacerbated as she started giving interviews to Mainland media organisations, ramping up her original criticism of the protests. What she never mentioned was the central irony of the company's ownership: Maxim's is half-owned by the British-controlled Jardine Matheson Group, a company that traces its fortune to the days of supplying opium to the Chinese masses. Its history is intertwined with that of the entire British colonial enterprise. Jardines is perhaps better known as its fictional incarnation in James Clavell's 1966 novel *Tai-Pan*. This rather crucial detail appears to have been lost on both Wu and the protest movement, but the net result of her intervention was that Maxim's branches became a prime target for customer boycotts and levels of vandalism that saw premises being comprehensively trashed. Michael Wu, Annie Wu's nephew who runs the company, was confronted with the exquisite dilemma of either publicly disassociating himself from his aunt so as to curb the reaction in Hong Kong, or keeping quiet in fear of pushback from the Chinese authorities, who regulate the company's retail outlets and production facilities on the Mainland. He chose silence.

The blue camp has powerful backers well placed to punish yellow businesses. Being identified as an open supporter of the protests could result in heavy losses, most clearly seen in what happened to the Next Digital Group, publisher of the *Apple Daily* newspaper. Not only was it subject to police action, but it also experienced a 40 per cent plunge in its advertising revenue in 2019; its auditor, Deloitte Touche Tohmatsu, walked away from the job, citing professional risks attached to involvement with the company.[9]

At the time of writing, the attacks on pro-China premises have died down, but the lingering public anger against them has not disappeared, and the boycott of their goods and services continues. What remains to be seen is whether the bitter political divisions in society will lead to lasting changes in business patronage. Once the smoke clears, will people still think in terms of blue and yellow businesses? Will an almost permanent state of boycotts linger? This is entirely possible, and reflects a level of discord in Hong Kong that will be hard to dispel.

* * *

The uprising also clawed its way deeply into the public consciousness by embracing local culture and adding distinctive elements. Most famously, protestors produced their own anthem for Hong Kong. The song *Glory to Hong Kong* spread like wildfire after first being posted on the social media discussion board LIHKG on 31 August 2019, by a composer known under the pseudonym Thomas dgx yhi. Before this, demonstrations had been making do with Cantonese versions of songs like *Do You Hear the People Sing?* from *Les Misérables*. The new anthem has a complex melody and starts with the words (translated from Cantonese) "In angst, tears are shed o'er this Land". It features the more upbeat:

We shall strike
This perilous night
Determined to fight
With hope, with song, with dignity!

Shortly after *Glory* was released by Thomas, a full orchestration was provided by an ad-hoc assembly of musicians turning up in the middle of a shopping centre. The "Black Blorchestra" subsequently uploaded a music video for the anthem to YouTube, and were rewarded with a viewership of 1.5 million within a week.[10] The performers were clad in what had now become the full frontline pro-democracy gear: hard hats for protection against baton charges, black scarves around the lower part of the face, wide goggles to deflect the noxious effects of tear gas, and the black clothing that all protestors had been wearing since June. Those not playing wind instruments also bore heavy-duty breathing devices, widely used at demonstrations. Many more have watched the video since, and the anthem has now been translated into a number of languages, with a particularly moving Japanese version. And, almost certainly to the horror of the authorities, the boos at football matches that Carrie Lam had tried to outlaw at the start of the year were now replaced by the rousing singing of *Glory to Hong Kong*.

Hong Kong's experience of incorporating culture into the uprising is far from unique: every substantial protest movement has recognised the importance of developing artistic credentials in support of the struggle. The "people's art" of China's Communist Revolution was largely an emulation of the type of art created to support the Russian Revolution, and played a crucial role in creating a common sense of identity and purpose among Mao's insurgents. That this was later turbo-charged to foster the cult of personality surrounding the Chairman is exceptional, but only in the matter of degree. The Umbrella Movement had been more modest in turning culture toward politics, but the role of culture was now being taken to new heights in the 2019–20 uprising. The division between so-called "high culture" and so-called "low" culture was bridged in the process. People who had never gone to a painting exhibition or, say, a musical performance, found these cultural expressions coming to them and realised that they could take part. Culture did not need to be the exclusive preserve of specialists.

And so artistic works of all kinds were also pressed into the service of the movement. This was expressed in a great many ways, from the *Glory to Hong Kong* anthem to the animated short video entitled *Say No To China Extradition*, viewed hundreds of thousands of times and translated into twenty languages. The newly formed Hong Kong Artists Union provided another platform for creativity, its members pouring out a small mountain of paintings, sculptures, photographic and other visual works. Much of what appeared on the Lennon Walls throughout the territory embraced a level of artistic and historic value sufficient to attract the interest of curators, who are working on a comprehensive collection. The power of these images means that they have appeared in all sorts of places, even as the background for a clock face. I have one of these clocks. It is an old vinyl disc painted with an iconic image of a black-clad protestor, defiantly shielding him- or herself against a tear gas attack with a yellow umbrella.

The new flourishing of protest culture built on what had previously been a politically neutral base of Cantopop and Canto movies. From the 1960s, this distinctively Cantonese genre began replacing the dominance of Mandarin and English in Hong Kong's popular arts. Cantopop and Hong Kong movies had also spread, becoming hugely influential throughout Asia. The genre had put the tiny British colony on the map for millions of people who had barely been aware of where it was. In Hong Kong itself, this development was crucial in the forging of a local identity. In many ways, that identity was encapsulated by a seminal TV series called *Below the Lion Rock*, produced by the public broadcaster RTHK and first aired in 1972. It depicted working-class people struggling to make a better life for themselves. Running until 2016 (with a revival in 2020), the show became a sort of metaphor for the can-do spirit of Hong Kong people and their refusal to give up in the face of adversity.

What is known as the "Lion Rock Spirit" continues to be evoked to this day. And, of course, the Lion Rock itself is still there. This large rock face looking out majestically over Hong Kong, which uncannily resembles a lion's head, regularly finds itself hosting large banners supporting the democracy movement. The first big slogan of the 2019 protests, *"Ga yau"*, was very much a reflection of the Lion Rock Spirit.

The process of making the personal political was also evident in the upsurge of marches and other protest actions connected, but somewhat tangential, to the main movement. People were getting used to the idea of seizing their destiny in their own hands by taking to the streets. The existence of relatively small demonstrations over issues of local concern was not new. But now these protests mushroomed and got a lot bigger. In the border town of Sheung Shui, for example, tens of thousands gathered to protest against Mainland visitors flooding local shops, which was pushing up prices and stripping them of daily necessities. In another part of town, there were repeated demonstrations about public parks being taken over by "dancing aunties" from the Mainland, blaring out loud music with the suggestion that they intended to receive money for something more than their dancing. This outbreak of local protests accelerated when the coronavirus started spreading early in 2020, as the Lam government reverted to its traditional practice of not consulting local residents over controversial matters. Given the more extreme health risks surrounding the virus, the government might have been cautious about setting up quarantine centres, often in working-class housing areas. Emboldened by the new spirit of dissent, these plans triggered violent protests.

The police, who by now were treating all manner of street protests in the same way, rapidly ensured that these local demonstrations would look exactly the same as the mainstream democracy protests: tear gas was belted out, pepper spray fired to subdue protestors, and large numbers of arrests made. However, people had got used to the police response over the months of the uprising, and were not deterred. Street protest became their first reflex response; the more laborious business of signing petitions or trying to arrange meetings with unresponsive officials seemed almost laughable. New precedents had been set and no one seemed to be in the mood to break them.

More substantive than sporadic street protests was an upsurge in the number of new community or civil society organisations. As we have seen, demonstrations were organised by various professional and trade groups, but now these groups wanted something more permanent. The result was the formation of new trade unions, both to represent employees in the traditional manner of labour unions but also as a way of weaving the protest movement into the fabric of society, giving people a voice within their workplaces.

The politicisation of trade unions is not new in Hong Kong. The largest such organisation, the Hong Kong Federation of Trade Unions, is part of the Communist "United Front" complex. In 1990, the dominance of this pro-China organisation was challenged by the formation of the Hong Kong Confederation of Trade Unions (CTU). Its founders, such as the indefatigable Lee Cheuk-yan, were democracy activists heavily involved in the 1989 upsurge of protest. The wave of union formation that accompanied the 2019 uprising saw the creation of more new unions than ever before. By the first quarter of 2020, 1,578 labour organisations had applied for registration as trade unions. The government responded to this upsurge by dragging its feet over the process of registration.[11]

Many of the new unions overlap with established labour organisations; this is notably the case in the new civil service union, operating in the most highly unionised area of the Hong Kong labour force. There have also been new unions for information technology employees, bank employees, people working in the construction and engineering sector, the advertising industry, the accountancy profession and within large companies. One of the biggest of the new organisations is the Hospital Authority Employees Alliance, which mobilised 7,000 members to strike in February 2020 as part of a campaign to halt the spread of the coronavirus, by urging the government to close Hong Kong's borders to Mainland Chinese visitors. The union was also pressing for better protective medical equipment for hospital staff. The strike was controversial during a severe medical crisis, but it nonetheless attracted widespread popular support. It was also ultimately successful in seeing the administration reluctantly bow to its demands, despite initial government insistence that it should be ignored.

The new unions have not become part of the "old democrat" CTU, although it has been assisting them. Instead, they reflect the organisational sprit of the wider 2019–20 uprising, which is to be devoid of a hierarchy and to rely on spontaneous communication between members to make decisions.

* * *

Changes to deeply entrenched attitudes are often seen at times of social and political turmoil. The Hong Kong protests are no exception. During the Umbrella Movement, many young people had found themselves camping out in the streets for the first time, without parental or other forms of supervision. It was liberating in many ways, and did much to enhance the self-confidence of those who took part in these protests. Many of the protestors I spoke to then are now in their twenties, and refer back to that time as being pivotal in changing their views on all manner of things, from sexual orientation to the breaking down of class barriers—but, most especially, it changed their view of authority. Some time after the 2014 protests ended, I was talking to a man who had been involved. As it happens, he was somewhat older than most of those who had spent night after night sleeping on the streets. He told me that the protests had "made me feel alive for the first time in my life". I must have given him a doubtful look, as he added, "It really was life changing, I thought I was contributing to history."

In a January 2020 Facebook post, the pro-democracy legislator Eddie Chu Hoi-dick estimated that 69 per cent of those arrested during the 2019–20 uprising were in the 19–30 age group, equivalent to four out of every thousand young people in Hong Kong. Young people were also more likely to be stopped and searched, and tended to be more wary of the police even when they were simply out on the streets going about their normal business.

This profound fracture in relations between the police and the young is something quite new. For decades, the Hong Kong police have maintained good relations with younger members of society, going into schools and youth organisations to promote their work and foster co-operation. That kind of activity yielded high levels of support for the force, which was largely viewed as being relatively benign and uncontroversial. There is an authoritarian tradition in Hong Kong schools, which are very highly disciplined and foster a culture of deference to authority among the young. In general, there is a culture of respecting older people, who are not supposed to be questioned by younger family members. So, the police were accustomed to a positive attitude from the public. And policing was effective, reflected in low crime rates, with very little of the arbitrary street violence seen in other societies. This comfortable state of affairs was combined with a fully functioning independent judiciary, ensuring that those who got in trouble with the law were assured of being treated fairly.

As we have seen, this picture of harmony between the police and the public has now been shattered by the clashes of 2019–20, and it is very hard to see how amicable relations can be restored. The Lam government does not dare to suggest any kind of reform and, as we have seen, would not tolerate an independent investigation into police behaviour during the protests. Moreover, there have been numerous allegations of police brutality by both domestic and international bodies.[12] Most worrying is the high level of injuries among people arrested during demonstrations, coupled with allegations of beatings and assaults during periods of remand.[13] In May 2020, the Hong Kong Civil Rights Observer submitted a report to the United Nations Human Rights Committee suggesting that this abuse of power was both systematic and institutional.[14] Not only have allegations been made, but they are widely supported by video recordings of individual officers acting unlawfully: beating protestors, in one case driving a motorbike into a group of demonstrators, in another firing live shots at an activist already sprawled on the ground. There was also widespread flouting of rules stipulating that officers need to wear identification or be able to produce warrant cards. A High Court ruling in November 2020 declared this failure to follow protocol illegal, but the first response of the police was to say that they would be studying the ruling's implications, rather than simply following the judgment.

Despite these mounting allegations, not a single officer has been held to account, besides one policeman who was put under investigation for allegedly leaking details of an operation to protestors. In the face of all allegations, police spokesmen always insist that officers use reasonable force and act within the law. The rank and file see themselves as an embattled force. Officers have been assaulted when off-duty, claims have been made that their children are bullied at school, and there have been reports of family members being "doxed", in other words subject to online bullying, with their personal details placed online. I had imagined that police claims of harassment might be somewhat overblown, but was taken aback when a friend, who works as a part-time assistant in an international primary school, told me about being hit by some very small children during playtime. An apologetic teacher explained to him that someone had told them he used to be a policeman.

It can well be argued that the police have brought this on themselves, and that so many people have come to hate them because of officers' resolutely hostile attitude towards protestors, journalists, first-aiders and indeed anyone they view as being in the "cockroach" class. Like other services in uniform, the police have a strong sense of collective identity. In Hong Kong, not only do they tend to socialise amongst themselves, but they live together in housing exclusively allocated for their use. In the wake of the protests, members of the force started talking about sending their children across the border for schooling. A property developer has been talking to the Junior Police Officers' Association about creating retirement homes for former officers in the Mainland township of Zhaoqing. In other words, since 2019 there has been a move towards removing police families even further away from the rest of society.

There are far-reaching and troubling long-term consequences of having frontline law enforcers who are not merely distrusted, but actively despised by a large section of the community. This has been counterbalanced by fervent support for the police among those in the blue camp. The net result is a high level of politicisation in a force that is supposed to stand above politics.

Turning this around is going to be difficult, even more so than when the colonial government took decisive action to restore the reputation of the police in the 1970s, amidst a rising sea of complaints over corruption and dishonesty. If nothing else results from the uprising, the future of law enforcement has been thrown into question in ways that no one expected.

For many people, the most decisive attitude shift resulting from the uprising has been that the unrest and uncertainty over Hong Kong's future has prompted so many people to think of leaving. As the protests developed, there was no end of talk about emigration. This was akin to the great exodus that occurred after the 1989 Tiananmen Square massacre, amid fears of what would happen in 1997 when China resumed sovereignty over Hong Kong.

Precisely because this is largely an immigrant community, people's willingness to contemplate moving is greater than in societies where emigration has never been part of the community's personal experience. However, pinning down emigration figures is very difficult, both because many people who leave Hong Kong retain their resident's status and because the government does not compile emigration statistics. The only form of official figures is for "certificates of no criminal conviction", which are generally required by countries receiving emigrants from Hong Kong. In 2019, there was a 66 per cent surge in the number of certificates issued, bringing the annual total to 33,252.[15] However, acquisition of a certificate does not necessarily equate with emigration; nor, in a single year, does it take account of people acting on certificates previously issued. Moreover, as was seen in the aftermath of the 1990s exodus, many of those who left were doing little more than establishing a bolthole overseas, particularly in places such as Canada, Australia and Britain. Having done so, a great many have returned to Hong Kong.

Still, interest in emigration grew enormously in 2020 following the enactment of the National Security Law at the end of June, which prompted offers of refuge for Hong Kong people by a number of other countries, notably Britain, as we saw in Chapter 4. It seems that one of the unintended results of bringing in this draconian law was both to make protestors think of emigrating, while spurring foreign powers to give them the means to do so.

Moreover for the first time there was a surge of emigration to Taiwan. The Bloomberg news agency, using official Taiwanese data, estimated that, in the first seven months of 2019, immigration from Hong Kong rose by 28 per cent, and Hongkongers made up almost 10 per cent of all new residents.[16] A number of those going to the island state were explicitly political refugees, escaping possible arrest in Hong Kong; but most were not.

In October 2020, another, more general survey from: the Hong Kong Institute of Asia-Pacific Studies for the Chinese University of Hong Kong recorded that 43.9 per cent of the 737 individuals interviewed in the previous month said they would emigrate if they could, and 35 per cent were actively planning for this eventuality. The UK and Australia were the most popular destinations, followed by Taiwan.[17]

Leaving for another country is a big decision, but middle-class Hongkongers tend to have money and transferable skills; so the option is there, and appears to have become increasingly attractive. It is highly unlikely that anything approaching 40 per cent of the population will actually leave, but nowadays it is hard to avoid people discussing this possibility. Another poll, conducted by the Hong Kong Institute of Public Opinion in September 2020, found 20 per cent of respondents saying they were intending to emigrate, about half of them within two years.[18]

As in the 1990s, many of those who go may well be attracted back—but often when returning, they do so leaving their sons and daughters behind. This would add to the pressure of an ageing population and involve some of the brightest and best departing, with longer-term implications for how Hong Kong will look in generations to come.

PART THREE

THE UNEXPECTED AND THE FUTURE

9

VIRUS AND CRISIS

At the beginning of 2020, protests in Hong Kong were ongoing, just with less ferocity—but they were soon overshadowed by another development which spread rapidly far beyond the SAR: the outbreak of Covid-19 in the central Mainland city of Wuhan. The uprising and the virus were coincidental, but linked by the blow they have delivered to the Chinese regime. Had Beijing "simply" been coping with international fallout from the crackdown in Hong Kong, the diplomatic nightmare on its hands would have been quite serious enough; but the fallout from the pandemic turned the nightmare into a full-scale crisis of credibility. At home, the crisis had the effect of sowing doubt over the invincibility of the regime, as citizens slowly became aware that the pandemic was being covered up, and then started suffering from its dire economic impact.

What the virus exposed, or maybe confirmed, was that China could not be trusted or relied upon when it came to confronting crucial events that brought the interests of the ruling party into conflict with other, public interests. As we saw in Chapter 3, it is precisely this logic that always places Party before profits.

And to preserve the interests of the rulers the instinctive response of all authoritarian systems is to cover up bad news, as anything other than good news detracts from their preferred image of success. This is why China lost valuable time curbing the coronavirus and compounded the tardiness of its response by focusing on suppressing news of the outbreak, in preference to getting it under control.

In a series of social media posts, now deleted, Xin Meng—a researcher at China's National Institute for Viral Disease Control and Prevention—wrote that, when fighting a virus, "Politics comes first, security the second, science the third".[1] This means that, even when a deadly public health threat emerges and there is a compelling need for those in charge to be notified, the risks of delivering bad news tend to outweigh the benefits of behaving responsibly. The reality of how the system works is known throughout China. Wei Peng, a doctor at a fever clinic in a Wuhan community hospital at the epicentre of the outbreak, explained why, despite knowing about the new virus, he had not dreamt of bringing it to the attention of his superiors: "There is no gain for you if you report. No one would blame you if you didn't." On the other hand, the process of reporting things that the authorities do not want to hear only invites "tedious trouble".[2]

When the news eventually got out, however, there was no place to hide. The leadership in Beijing then came up with the proposition that its way of handling the pandemic was infinitely superior to the response of elected governments overseas, because only authoritarian governments have what it takes to deal with emergencies on this scale. In September 2020, President Xi put it this way: "The major strategic achievement gained from China's fight against COVID-19 fully demonstrated the remarkable advantages of the leadership of the Chinese Communist Party and socialism." He also said, "We have passed an extraordinary and historic test."[3]

Yet the pandemic quickly began causing serious political problems, both within China and for China's relations with the outside world. The outbreak of the coronavirus was the second major pandemic of the twenty-first century to have emanated not just from the PRC but, as it turned out, from the nation's notoriously dubious fresh food markets. The Severe Acute Respiratory Syndrome (SARS) epidemic of 2002–4 spread from a remarkably similar source. It mainly impacted Asian nations, albeit to a far less deadly degree than Covid-19, whereas the pandemic of 2020 was truly global. Stemming from this new outbreak was a much wider questioning of China's global objectives and methods of achieving them. This in turn emboldened even some of its closest overseas allies and hitherto reluctant critics to start challenging Beijing in ways that it had never been challenged since the opening up of the country some four decades earlier.

First up was the whole question of the extent to which Beijing had been transparent about the spread of the virus and its dangers. China had form here, as in 2003 there had been a four-month delay in coming clean over the SARS outbreak, which ended up killing 774 and infecting some 8,000 people, on the Mainland and elsewhere in the world.

Despite still unproven conspiracy theories, mainly emanating from the United States, about Covid-19 being a manmade disaster—allegedly, a leak from a shadowy research facility in Wuhan, the capital of Hubei Province—the overwhelming bulk of the evidence points to the outbreak originating at a food market selling wildlife for human consumption. American conspiracy theories on this point have been matched by equally unsubstantiated nuttiness coming out of China itself. In March 2020, Zhao Lijian, one of China's most senior foreign affairs spokesmen, used Twitter to promote the conspiracy theory that the US Army had brought the virus to China during visits to the nation.[4]

Zhao's allegations were left to simmer, leaving the more profound question of the precise moment when the seriousness of this virus was identified in China. This remains a matter of controversy, as does the moment when Chinese medical researchers realised that the virus was capable of human-to-human transmission. However, a clearer picture has started to emerge. A story first appearing in the *Wall Street Journal* on 8 January 2020, subsequently indirectly confirmed by Beijing, said that the Chinese leadership had been fully briefed about the dangers of this virus a day previously.[5] It is also entirely possible, however, that local authorities had known a great deal more about the disease before they finally mustered up the courage to report their findings to Beijing.

By 11 January, the first death from the virus in Wuhan was officially confirmed.[6] As the death toll rose and the spread of contamination accelerated, there was also considerable scepticism over China's willingness to provide accurate figures for rates of transmission or fatalities. In the PRC system, statistics are notoriously employed to serve political ends, and are also sensitive when it comes to natural disasters and pandemics. It is therefore highly likely that while Beijing was reporting success in curbing the virus, it was also underplaying the extent of its spread. A study by the California-based RAND Corporation, looking in detail at air travel data, was able to extrapolate that the number of cases reported in January 2020 was likely thirty-seven times lower than the real number of infections.[7] Following President Xi's visit to Wuhan in March, when he declared that the battle against the virus had been won at its epicentre, there was an immediate cessation of reports of new infections, although subsequently it became clear that the spread of the virus had not in fact ended.[8] Moreover, China kept changing the reporting goal posts, admitting that deaths in nursing homes had not initially been recorded and excluding all deaths outside hospitals.

This lack of transparency about the progress of the virus was reflected in how officials reacted in the early stages of the outbreak. Most alarming was that China's early warning system was only activated after the coronavirus had already started spreading at a worrying rate.[9] Even more astonishing is that the Wuhan authorities went ahead with a Lunar New Year mass banquet, involving 40,000 households, on 18 January.[10] This was well after evidence of the disease and its capacity to spread with alacrity were widely known. But people in Wuhan were becoming increasingly aware of the dangers. Most famously, Dr Li Wenliang, who had shared his concerns with fellow medical practitioners at the end of 2019, was hauled in by local state security officials on 3 January and accused of spreading rumours, requiring him to sign a confession to this effect. A month later, he died in hospital from the effects of the virus.[11]

Li's death released an unprecedented outbreak of fury on Chinese social media, which is notoriously tightly controlled. On the day of his demise, the censors found it hard to keep up with citizens' outrage: according to the Weiboscope project, which monitors Weibo, China's main social media platform, the authorities managed to censor around 117 of the 40,232 posts related to his death. But users of both Weibo and WeChat, China's most heavily used messaging app, continued to express their misgivings as the government struggled to get control of the Covid-19 narrative. When hundreds of WeChat accounts were shut down, either for critical comment on the government's handling of the crisis or for spreading news that was censored by state media, the shutdown itself became a topic, attracting some 3 million viewers before it, too, was shut down on Weibo. By 15 February, the WeChat censors had come up with 516 keyword combinations to thwart unwanted discussion of the coronavirus crisis. According to Citizen Lab, based at the University of Toronto, references to Dr Li were a big red flag for shutting down chats.[12] However, China's intensely tech-savvy internet users found ways around this censorship, mainly by using VPN networks that are much harder to control, and which are themselves the target for the Mainland's ever-vigilant internet police.

The unrest on social media sparked by the Covid-19 outbreak was probably greater than anything seen before, and it claimed some very high-profile web users. The most notable was Cui Yongyuan, a former state television host who has almost 20 million social media followers. He is far from being any kind of dissident, but had his WeChat account suspended and his Weibo posts blocked for the way he wrote about the pandemic.[13] A far more outspoken critic was Ren Zhiqiang, a Communist Party member and former property tycoon, who fearlessly took to social media in February 2020 to write about a "crisis of governance" arising from the handling of the outbreak. Seven months later, he emerged from the black hole of the Chinese judicial system to be given an eighteen-year jail sentence for corruption offences.[14]

Xu Zhangrun, a law professor, disappeared from sight in Beijing after writing, "The coronavirus epidemic has revealed the rotten core of Chinese governance; the fragile and vacuous heart of the jittering edifice of state has thereby been revealed as never before."[15] Xu Zhiyong, a better-known dissident, published an open letter to Xi Jinping calling on him to take responsibility for the crisis and step down. He wrote, "Where do you really think you are taking China? Do you have any clue yourself? You talk up the Reform and Opening-Up policy at the same time that you are trying to resuscitate the corpse of Marxism-Leninism." After going on the run, Xu was arrested in the southern city of Guangzhou.[16] Citizen journalists reporting from Wuhan, who attracted a very large following, were rounded up. Zhang Zhan, a Shanghai-based citizen journalist, was arrested in May for the crime of "picking quarrels and provoking trouble". She had travelled to Wuhan to report what was happening there. At least three others reporting from the city had been detained in February.[17]

Outspoken criticism of this kind is not new, but the attention being paid by normally passive Chinese citizens was; so too was the volume of criticism managing to find a way around the Great Firewall of China.

In March 2020, the dissident artist Ai Weiwei summed up what had happened: "The communist system, with its tight control of information and its accountability of officials only to their bureaucratic superiors, not to the people below, has been undermining social trust for decades. Citizens do not expect a volteface in trust just because a deadly virus appears. But without trust, people's immune system against lies breaks down. In the public sphere, all belief becomes ungrounded belief."[18]

Ai's crucial point about trust explains why the Xi regime was so worried about this outpouring of questioning, because one of its core lines of self-congratulation focuses on the extent to which the Party has earned the people's confidence. In the struggle to prevent further erosion of public trust, the regime was forced into a rare backdown, acknowledging that Dr Li's treatment had been unreasonable, followed by a desperate attempt in official media to portray him as a Party member loyal to the regime. In other moves, officials were fired in Wuhan, and some limited criticism of the way health authorities had handled the pandemic was permitted in state media.

A shutdown on further criticism was indirectly signalled with President Xi's arrival in Wuhan in March, as he declared victory in the "People's War" against the virus and lauded the Party's ability to turn the tide. The newly installed Party Secretary for Wuhan, Wang Zhonglin, issued a typically fawning statement declaring that the city's residents should be grateful to Xi and be sure to "listen to the Party and follow the Party". What happened next, however, marked a clear departure from the script, as citizens again took to social media, mocking and scolding Wang. His statement was quickly

removed—another concession, made at a time when concessions were no longer supposed to be made.

* * *

As the virus took hold on the Mainland, the Hong Kong government's will to act decisively had disappeared, and this paralysis
at the top was only compounded by the fear of making a single
move that might anger the already very angry Beijing leadership.
The first report of a virus infection reached Hong Kong in the
third week of January 2020. Though the spread thereafter was
slow, it was alarming to a population with the memory of the
SARS outbreak very much in mind.

What has never been admitted is the tremor of relief that pul-
sated through the Hong Kong government complex in Tamar, as
officials came to see the coronavirus crisis as an opportunity to
deflect attention from the political crisis, even to bring it to some
kind of conclusion. Based on my conversations with people who
attended meetings at the most senior level during this period, it
has been possible to put together a clear picture of their mood.
One of the participants was so incensed by the cynicism of officials
as to have encouraged me to ensure that it was more widely known.

In February, the opposition-supporting *Apple Daily* newspaper
claimed to have obtained a copy of a secret report to the central
government, in which Carrie Lam, the Chief Executive,
described the outbreak of the coronavirus as a "rare opportunity
to reverse the situation", after having been "attacked on all
fronts" during the protests. She reportedly urged Beijing to give
her the fullest support in tackling the pandemic to provide an
"opportunity to reverse the situation".[19] It is customary for the
Hong Kong government to respond to media reports of this
kind. In this instance it refused to comment, which can be taken
as a tacit admission of the story's veracity.

The virus outbreak may well have put paid to mass street protests, but it did nothing to assuage criticism of the government.

On the contrary, the Lam administration's handling of the crisis added to discontent. An opinion poll conducted in March 2020 revealed overwhelming anger at the official response. Over half of those questioned declared that the Lam government should not be credited for success in handling the outbreak, while more than 70 per cent took the view that credit for the low rate of infections should instead be given to the community, whose awareness of what to do had been greatly influenced by their experience of the 2003–4 SARS crisis.[20] Indeed, this is what has helped Hong Kong achieve a notably small number of infections and, at the time of writing in late 2020, a remarkably small number of deaths: the incredible self-discipline of the people, who were early adopters of face masks, who make lavish use of sanitising products, and who have kept their distance, all without needing officials to tell them what to do. The government may have learned nothing from SARS, but the people learned a lot.

Lam, whose deaf ear to public opinion is notorious, seemed as oblivious as ever to public criticism once the pandemic was underway. In early February, she went as far as to say, "I don't want to particularly describe how well my Government has been doing, but certainly we are acting in accordance with a strategy which is to protect the safety and the health of Hong Kong."[21]

The reality was that the government was very slow to act, waiting for Beijing to acknowledge the seriousness of the crisis before moving. Lam even tried to stop officials wearing face masks, as Hong Kong people started scouring the world for supplies. Even worse, despite it being clear that the main source of infection came from across the border, the government initially refused to close the crossings, or even impede cross-border traffic. While the administration dithered, hospital staff from the newly formed medical workers' unions went on strike to put pressure on the SAR to act. Eventually it did so, saving a slither of face by declaring that the border was not closed, merely partially shuttered. Strikers, whose demands for border closures were later vindicated, were threatened with jail and dismissal. (There was some backtracking in November 2020, when the authorities said they would only be docking strikers' pay—at a time when staff were working flat out to combat a fourth wave of the pandemic.)

The Lam administration finally managed to acquire a stock of face masks, but only months after private initiatives had already secured sufficient supplies. And, just in case any lingering illusions remained as to the competence of officials, in July 2020 it was revealed that 6 million masks purchased by the government had turned out to be fakes.[22] Although an official post-mortem on the SARS crisis had strongly recommended drawing up contingency plans for quarantine centres, nothing had been done in the intervening fifteen years; with the arrival of coronavirus, the grand officials who live in splendid style now rushed into a number of cack-handed schemes to locate these centres next to public housing estates. More protests ensued, and a number of these schemes had to be scrapped.

The Hong Kong government certainly did not have an exclusive franchise on bungled handling of the epidemic—other administrations around the world performed even worse—but for foreign governments the virus had not come hard on the heels of a prolonged period of civil unrest. What's more, the specific politics of Hong Kong and its status in relation to the Mainland exacerbated the government's failure to act. As citizens from other places were airlifted out of Wuhan, the Hong Kong administration, fearful of accusations that it was acting as an independent state, stood firmly on the sidelines, leaving literally thousands of Hongkongers stranded in Wuhan waiting to be taken out. Hong Kong residents were finally rescued weeks after other large-scale evacuations had been completed.

Another example of Beijing's shadow looming over the Lam government's strategy to stop the spread was its campaign in the courts for a ban on face masks, which had been worn by protestors long before the virus struck. Within weeks of Covid reaching Hong Kong, everyone was donning face masks in an attempt to avoid contracting the virus. Yet, as panic spread, the Lam administration doggedly pursued its appeal against mask-wearing, while even its own ministers began putting them on. The government's refusal to accept reality was rapidly descending towards farce. The battle came to a head at a court hearing in April 2020, in the midst of the coronavirus crisis, when officials were even more frantically urging everyone to wear face masks as a key measure to prevent the spread of infection. As we saw in Chapter 7, the resulting judgment in effect said that masks could be worn at legal protests, but were not allowed during illegal assemblies.

In July 2020, a new wave of the virus swelled the number of deaths and infections. Again the government seemed more anxious to politicise this upsurge than to tackle it. On the one hand, the virus was used as an excuse to ban all public demonstrations and postpone the September Legco election; on the other, great play was made over the help given to Hong Kong by the Mainland in terms of personnel and equipment. As some of the testing equipment turned out to be controversial, and the arrival of "experts" had all the hallmarks of a propaganda offensive rather than a medical boost, the Lam administration, yet again, floundered. In August, there was yet another upsurge of infections and the government decided to implement a universal testing programme, which again turned political, as fears spread that DNA collected by the testing companies, all of whom were Mainland-based, would be used to build up a wider database of Hong Kong citizens. And Carrie Lam did not seem to notice that testing was being undertaken in centres just like the polling stations that would have been used for the September election, had it not been postponed. The whole exercise, designed to restore confidence and control the pandemic, instead resulted in criticism from many quarters, which was ignored by officials on grounds that it was "political".

What could not be ignored was the brutal impact of the pandemic on Hong Kong's economy. Gross domestic product plunged by 9.1 per cent in the first quarter of 2020, and another 9 per cent in the second. The third quarter showed only an anaemic improvement, with a smaller decline of 3.5 per cent.[23] However, the real brunt of the crisis was borne by Hong Kong's poorest people, who either lost their jobs, were forced to take unpaid leave or had their working hours severely cut. Overall, the economic outlook in the SAR remains grim.

In the face of this hardship, government alleviation plans were slow to materialise. The worst of the measures had been the January offer of a "gift" of HK$10,000 (US$1,282) to every adult resident of Hong Kong, regardless of their circumstances— rewarding the very rich and the very poor equally. Payment was delayed until months after the scheme was announced, being timed to coincide with the start of campaigning for the (later cancelled) September election, in a clear effort to give a boost to the pro-China parties. A clutch of other measures were unveiled in February, with handouts to Hongkongers costing in total HK$71 billion, or seven times more than the January package.[24] Soliciting goodwill towards the government by handing out cash to citizens has failed as a strategy before; unsurprisingly, in the wake of the coronavirus, it failed again.

* * *

Unfortunately for Beijing, the pandemic has spread a message to the rest of the world that the Chinese regime was not to be trusted. The message the Party had been hoping to convey, both to its citizens and to the rest of the world, was that China had managed to conquer the coronavirus owing to the superiority of the Mainland's system, able to handle problems quickly and effectively under the guidance of dedicated leaders unhampered by the obstacles of democracy, under which decisions were delayed and obstructed by cumbersome and unnecessary processes.

The mobilisation of China's armed forces and the large-scale deployment of medical staff and auxiliary workers to crisis centres was indeed impressive. Moreover, Beijing's power to enforce lockdowns at short notice proved to be as brutal as it was effective. And China made much of its ability to construct a 645,000-square-foot emergency hospital in Wuhan in the space of ten days.[25] However, two months later, much the same feat was accomplished in London in nine days, despite Britain's less-than-stellar reputation for efficiency—and despite the "encumbrance" of an elected government.[26]

An even more telling rebuff to the narrative of China's superior ways of handling the crisis came from Taiwan, where a democratic government, supposedly riddled with all the labyrinthine obstacles that prevent decisive action, managed not only to keep the level of coronavirus infections and deaths remarkably low, but did so with the enthusiastic support of a population that did not need to be coerced into applauding its leaders.

Taiwan demonstrated its abilities as a first mover in effectively responding to the then unknown disease. On 31 December 2019, the island state quarantined all direct flights from Wuhan and quickly ramped up its programme of screening passengers arriving from other parts of the Mainland. It also rapidly ensured that the public had face masks, and introduced social distancing measures. Further measures were put in place in February to avoid the panic-buying of essential supplies seen elsewhere, not least in Hong Kong. The administration also moved expeditiously to give out subsidies to businesses and citizens.

Taiwan's leader, Tsai Ing-wen's popularity soared. In February 2020, local television network TVBS reported that approval of her government's handling of the crisis had reached 82 per cent.[27]

Taiwan was also the first country to draw the World Health Organization's attention to the virus, in December. However, its warnings were ignored. The WHO's leadership had effectively fallen under China's control, and Beijing had even succeeded in removing Taiwan from membership of the organisation's governing body, the World Health Assembly. The subject of Taiwan's participation in the WHO was so sensitive that, as I personally discovered, it sent senior WHO officials into meltdown when Taiwan was even mentioned. On *The Pulse*, a television news programme which I host, a colleague of mine raised the subject in a recorded interview with Bruce Aylward, Senior Advisor on Organizational Change to the WHO Director-General. At first, Aylward pretended not to hear the question; then he simply refused to discuss Taiwan, and put the phone down.[28] The interview went viral and resulted in both the programme and the broadcaster, Radio Television Hong Kong, being castigated by the government for even mentioning Taiwan. Calls were made for the programme to be taken off the air and criticism from officials went on for months after the broadcast. At the time of writing, the fallout continues.

Even as the coronavirus crisis deepened, Beijing was unflinching in its determination to exclude Taiwan from participation in international efforts to combat Covid-19. There could be no mistaking the level of politics involved in this situation, so much so that it contributed to the standoff between the United States and China, with the Trump administration deciding to cut off all funds and quit the organisation, despite the United States being the single largest contributor to its budget. American discontent centred on the WHO's handling of the pandemic, while largely ignoring all the other work undertaken by the organisation. US fury over the WHO fed into a chaotic background of souring trade relations, security concerns and a rapid deterioration in diplomatic relations. The incoming Biden administration announced rapidly after the November presidential election result was confirmed that it was reversing the decision to leave the WHO, but continued membership does not mean that Washington is happy about the way the organisation is being run, nor will it forget that the WHO is led by China's hand-picked nominee, who has showered slavish public praise on Beijing's handling of the crisis.

Tedros Adhanom Ghebreysus, the Director-General, has been a consistent Beijing supporter. He is customarily described as Dr Tedros, implying that he is a medical doctor. In fact, his background is as a public health researcher, making him the first non-physician to head the organisation. More importantly, Tedros served as Ethiopia's foreign minister at a time when China was drawing very close to Addis Ababa (2012–16). He took over at the WHO from another Chinese nominee, Margaret Chan from Hong Kong, who is known for controversial decisions in every post she has occupied during her career in public health bureaucracy. Chan was a stalwart Beijing supporter at the WHO, and has continued in this vein as a member of Hong Kong's Executive Council.

China's interest in the WHO is much the same as its motives for gaining a seat on the UN Human Rights Council in October 2020. In both places, it has someone on board to deflect criticism of the kind that greatly displeases Beijing. Opprobrium abroad over its handling of the SARS crisis in 2002–4 did much to focus minds in China on the need to ensure that the WHO was favourably disposed towards Beijing—Chan took up the leadership two years later. At the time of writing, Chinese nominees head four of the UN's fifteen specialist agencies, compared with just one headed by an American national.[29] As the PRC's influence over the Human Rights Council grew in April, Mitt Romney, the prominent US senator, wrote: "In recent years, China has succeeded in disproportionately positioning its citizens and proxies with loyalties to the Chinese Communist Party in key international governing bodies, allowing it to expand its geopolitical influence."[30] Romney argued that Covid-19 had "exposed China's dishonesty", and called for America to seize the moment and step up to international leadership. He did so while being well aware of the Trump administration's resolutely isolationist outlook and intense disinterest in multilateral institutions.

It was this vacuum in international leadership since 2017 that had emboldened Beijing to do precisely what Romney was urging America to do, and China could not have been more delighted by the behaviour of the WHO under the stewardship of Tedros, who took over from Margaret Chan that year. Yet the cost to the PRC of keeping the WHO onside and punishing Taiwan has proven to be high. Other nations have started looking more closely at Chinese nominees for UN bodies. In March 2020, China had expected its candidate to be installed as head of the UN World Intellectual Property Organization, but in the event the post went to the US-backed Daren Tang Heng-Shim from Singapore.

Back at WHO, a great many questions need to be answered. The organisation made its first public statement pointing to a cluster of cases in Wuhan on 4 January 2020, but drew no wider conclusions. Advised by the Chinese government, the WHO assured the global public that there was no need for travel or trade restrictions. On 14 January, the WHO finally admitted that this danger was present, only to tweet later that day that there was "no clear evidence" of human-to-human transmission of the virus. It is unclear whether the organisation was aware that the Chinese Centre for Disease Control had sequenced the virus more than a week earlier, and that two days later the Chinese Academy of Medical Sciences had managed to decode the virus.[31] Days really matter in a crisis of this kind.

While the PRC did not disclose these developments, the WHO was bending over backwards to praise the Chinese government for its efforts to supress the virus. It stated that Beijing's commitment to transparency was "very impressive, and beyond words". It now transpires that, behind the scenes, WHO employees on the frontlines of tackling the virus had far less confidence in China's behaviour than their Director-General. At a news conference in April, Tedros had implied that the information about the outbreak came from the PRC; only in July did the organisation finally admit that the first alert to the outbreak in Wuhan had come from its own office in China, not the Chinese authorities.[32] In fact, for most of January WHO officials had had enormous difficulty extracting information from Beijing. A combination of incomplete information and political considerations led to the organisation's much-criticised decision to wait until 30 January before declaring a global public emergency.[33]

Following a resolution from the WHO's governing body, a team was despatched to investigate the origins of the virus. WHO officials spent three weeks in China in August 2020 on what was described as a mission to lay the groundwork for a full international mission. Astonishingly, the team did not visit Wuhan.[34]

Beijing was, understandably, sensitive to allegations of cover-up and lack of transparency, which were giving the PRC a bad reputation in the rest of the world. In June 2020, the government issued a 37,000-word white paper detailing the extent to which China had been transparent in handling the Covid-19 crisis. All suggestions that information had been concealed were described as a "baseless accusation". The document, aimed at an international audience, stated: "China has always acted with openness, transparency and responsibility, and informed the international community of developments of the epidemic in a timely manner." Launching the white paper, Ma Zhaoxu, a vice-minister of foreign affairs, was in typically belligerent mood. He flatly denied that China's reputation had suffered and stated: "A very few countries have gone against the tide of history and insanely launched a smear campaign against China, fabricating rumours and spreading the political virus with every possible means. China has no other choice but to fight back against this kind of blame-shifting."[35]

Beijing has mainly opted for a heavy-handed approach to the international criticism over both its response to the virus and handling of the Hong Kong crisis. One very damaging example has been the mobilisation of Mainland students in places such as Canada and Australia to attack and abuse fellow students supporting the ongoing Hong Kong protests.

Whereas Beijing has, in the past, toyed with offering a conciliatory, smiling face to the world, since the start of the uprising and particularly the pandemic something very different has been on show.

In November 2019, China's foreign ministry mobilised its emissaries to step up their speaking engagements and to pen editorial commentaries setting out Beijing's stance. This followed President Xi Jinping's call for diplomats to assume a "fighting spirit". A signal from above like this quickly spurs action, and diplomats doubled their efforts. The most effective of these is Liu Xiaoming, the suave multilingual ambassador to Britain, who has become a frequent guest on various international talk shows.

This new trend, which emerged with force in the wake of the coronavirus crisis, has become known as "Wolf Warrior" diplomacy, favouring a much more aggressive assertion of the Chinese point of view. Named after the heroes of a popular action movie, Beijing's Wolf Warrior diplomats see themselves as fearlessly doing battle with all manner of foreign foes. Their stance comes with considerable risks, most notably as they gave every appearance of gloating during the coronavirus crisis over the devastation of economies in the West and high rates of infection compared with China. Beijing's embassy in Paris went so far as to allege that the situation in the country was so bad that French nursing home workers were abandoning their jobs. This provoked a furious response from the Macron government.

It was not just the French who took offence; a whole host of other countries were responding to Beijing's bluster in 2020 with a combination of exasperation and anger. In June, politicians from a dozen countries and the European Parliament established the Inter-Parliamentary Alliance on China. This body, founded pointedly on the anniversary of the Tiananmen massacre (4 June), was essentially a talking shop, but also a base for mobilising the international response to the Xi regime's increasing assertiveness. In the same month, the European Union announced that it was planning to introduce curbs on investments by state-owned foreign companies, ostensibly universal in application but clearly targeted at China.

It looked as though the Wolf Warrior offensive was cooling in the later part of 2020, since it was proving counterproductive—but, in an extraordinary statement delivered in October, Cong Peiwu, China's ambassador to Canada, threatened the "good health and safety" of Canadian citizens in Hong Kong, were Ottawa to put in place a scheme to offer political asylum to Hong Kong dissidents. There are some 300,000 Canadian passport-holders in Hong Kong.[36]

* * *

The Wolf Warriors' public displays of bravado were at odds with an internal report delivered to the Chinese leadership in April, where a very different picture was painted. Its contents, drawn up by a Ministry of State Security-linked think tank, the China Institutes of Contemporary International Relations, were leaked to Reuters. The report bluntly stated that global anti-China sentiment had risen to levels unseen since the 1989 Tiananmen Square crackdown. Focusing on the American response, it concluded that, in the wake of the Covid-19 crisis, Washington was viewing China as "an economic and national security threat and a challenge to Western democracies". It also expressed concern over how the fallout would impact Beijing's relations with other Asian states.[37]

These conclusions were based on considerable evidence. As we'll see in more detail in the next chapter, it was not just the US government that was falling seriously out of love with China, but also members of the Western public. There is little doubt that China's handling of the pandemic heavily contributed to the PRC's fast-declining popularity among Americans. A new low was recorded in a nationwide Harris Poll, conducted between 3 and 5 April 2020, which found that 90 per cent of Republicans and 67 per cent of Democrats surveyed believed the Chinese government to be responsible for the spread of the coronavirus. There were also high levels of bipartisan support for the US taking a hard line on trade with the PRC.[38] This is why Joe Biden's presidency is unlikely to produce any significant change in China policy.

This spirit of widespread political support for a hard line against Beijing was not confined to the United States in 2020, and it was fuelled by the impression the Xi regime was giving: that China was going out of its way to fuel suspicion and generate anger. The Party leadership first imagined that international criticism could simply be ignored; then it appears to have thought that it might be possible to nip it in the bud with an impressive display of co-operation around the world. But as the virus spread elsewhere with venom, and with the death toll rising exponentially around the world, Beijing became less and less sure-footed in calibrating its response to both the growing lack of trust and the clamour of condemnation.

To counter the diplomatic damage done by the Wolf Warriors' own goals early in the year, China sought to win friends by distributing medical aid and supplies abroad. Beijing ramped up commercial production of personal protective equipment (PPE), exporting some 70.6 billion masks in the period from March to May.[39] Over 120 countries had received surgical masks and other equipment by mid-April,[40] and medical personnel were widely despatched. However, the PPE offensive also turned out to be problematic, as recipient countries found that many of the test kits forming part of this aid did not work and that face masks were unsuitable. In the Netherlands, which had welcomed the supplies from China, pleasure turned to anger when it was discovered that 600,000 face masks designated for use by medical staff were unfit for purpose. In Spain, 58,000 coronavirus test kits were found not to work.[41] Chinese supplies to Europe also provoked a wider backlash as it was noted that distribution was carefully following Beijing's political priorities. Thus Italy, the European nation diplomatically closest to the PRC, received supplies first and in the greatest quantity. Even Rome ended up angry with China over what it had believed were gifts of supplies when Beijing retroactively demanded payment.[42]

Elsewhere in Europe, there were reports of Chinese cyberattacks on EU computing systems and even hospitals. Then, in May, it became clear that Beijing was not going to contribute to a European Union initiative to raise funds for vaccine development. Beijing's ambassador to the EU, Zhang Ming, explained this reluctance by urging the world to stop dabbling in "blame games", saying that China had already been a generous contributor in global initiatives to fight Covid-19, "despite daunting tasks of outbreak response at home". While forty-three nations had sent very senior representatives to the meeting that launched this initiative, China had ended up sending the more junior Zhang. This low level of representation and China's aggressive rebuff were both carefully noted.[43]

In October Beijing reversed its earlier reservations about international co-operation by joining the WHO global initiative to distribute vaccines. This followed earlier indications of the PRC's disinterest in such schemes, preferring to take a unilateral approach and to place itself at the centre of the action. Beijing's previous isolationism on this question had been seen over the summer, when Chinese researchers reached out to some of the biggest nations on its list of allies, notably Indonesia and Brazil, involving them in human testing of antiviral medication, with a promise of sharing the results and supplying vaccines when they became available. At the time, it had been made clear that this was China's initiative to help the rest of the world without getting muddled up in international co-ordination. Now, it seems, the PRC has realised that it needs a seat at the table.

Before the outbreak of Covid-19, 2020 had been designated as EU–China Year. This was seen as a major opportunity to enhance trading and diplomatic relations, against the backdrop of broad Western assumptions that China would become, or was becoming, increasingly reformist as its economy grew. But, as the pandemic developed, this illusion was dimming fast. European leaders were no longer looking for ways of enhancing ties with Beijing. Instead they began asking about broken pledges on access for their goods and conditions for EU companies operating in China. The EU was also unusually assertive in condemning Beijing's actions in Hong Kong, and was edging closer to the US position of seeing China as a strategic threat. In March, the EU Commission described the PRC as a "systematic rival" for the first time. In June, Ursula von der Leyen, President of the European Commission, described the relationship with China as "not an easy one". She was speaking at the end of an online summit between Chinese and European leaders, which had originally been designed to take relations to a new level. President Xi Jinping had been at pains to assure the Europeans that "China wants peace instead of hegemony". There was little sign in von der Leyen's statement that he had convinced anyone during his long video call with the EU leaders.[44]

Other European leaders were no less outspoken. Beijing's unforthcoming approach only seemed to confirm fears that had been growing before the start of the pandemic. The French President, Emmanuel Macron, had declared back in March 2019 that "the period of European naivety" in hoping for a reformist China, "is over." Speaking after an EU leaders' summit, he had added: "The relationship between EU and China must not be first and foremost a trading one, but a geopolitical and strategic relationship." Now, he was complaining that the PRC had not been transparent in divulging all it knew about Covid-19 at a time when the rest of the world had needed to be kept informed. Chancellor Angela Merkel, the only G7 leader to have been brought up under Communist rule and the most cautious in her dealings with the Chinese, had said at the same 2019 meeting that Europe should consider China as much a competitor as a partner.[45] Germany, traditionally reluctant to confront China, has also been critical in 2020 over Beijing's tendency to use the pandemic as a way of stepping into political vacuums. This was bad enough, but China's response to criticism of this kind was to tell foreign powers not to politicise the problem.

Britain had been keener than other European countries to keep Beijing onside, not least so it could achieve a good trade deal following the UK's departure from the EU. Under the premiership of David Cameron (2010–16), there had been much talk of cultivating a "golden age" of relations with China, but London had little to show for its efforts, and in 2020 the coronavirus outbreak brought these hopes juddering to a halt. In April that year, Dominic Raab, the Foreign Secretary, declared that Britain could no longer be doing "business as usual" with China in the wake of the pandemic: "We'll have to ask the hard questions about how it came about and how it could have been stopped earlier."[46] Relations deteriorated considerably the following month, when China first raised the prospect of imposing a draconian national security law on Hong Kong, which Britain alleged broke the understandings contained in the Sino-British Joint Declaration governing the handover of the former colony. As the world entered the 2020s, trade and economics were no longer to be the sole determinants of London's relationship with Beijing.

It was not only in the West that relations with Beijing were souring. Even in the Philippines, where the government had announced a firm pivot towards China, there was a sharp change in mood after the virus broke out, amid a realisation that many of the ambitious projects promised with Chinese aid were not going to materialise; rightly or wrongly, there was also a feeling that the influx of Chinese visitors and workers had brought the virus to the country. This was followed by outrage in June 2020 over Chinese military exercises in parts of the South China Sea where ownership is disputed. Relations with Australia, the PRC's biggest trading partner, plummeted over demands in Canberra for an independent international inquiry into the spread of the coronavirus, and sharp condemnation of Hong Kong's National Security Law. Even in Israel, which has worked very hard to maintain good relations with China, there was a sharp intake of breath in Beijing when the Netanyahu government indicated that it was bowing to American pressure to review its extensive co-operation with Chinese telecommunications companies, notably Huawei, in light of security considerations.

What is most surprising is the extent to which this re-evaluation of relations with China was taking place among countries Beijing had previously placed either in the firm ally camp or, at least, in the uncritical camp. In Asia, that included South Korea. In Africa, both Ghana and Nigeria were seen as inching away, while Brazil in South America, previously a big and reliable China supporter, showed itself ready to criticise and condemn Beijing, with President Bolsonaro's son launching a vitriolic attack on China for spreading the virus.

The coronavirus also delivered a sudden and unexpected blow to the extensive network of supply chain connections between China and the rest of the world, focusing attention both on the level of dependence on Chinese supplies and the dangers of partnership with a country that responds in such a prickly manner to criticism, combined with threatening behaviour. According to former US National Security Advisor John Bolton in July 2020, economic decoupling between America and China was "not only possible but is happening". He claimed this was due to exasperation with the kind of "state espionage that would boggle the mind of a US or European" company.[47] This decoupling is not confined to Western countries: Japan, for example, has initiated a US$2.2 billion fund to encourage Japanese manufacturers to quit China and come back home, or even to relocate to other South East Asian countries, to lessen dependence on Beijing.[48]

* * *

China can almost certainly weather verbal criticism, but the leaders in Beijing must be less sanguine over this threat posed to their export-driven economic model, which has underpinned the spectacular growth of the PRC's economy since it went into hyperdrive from the late 1980s.

The crucial message that the Communist Party delivers to its citizens is that it, and it alone, can deliver prosperity. China's share of global GDP at market prices had risen from 2% in 1995 to over 17% in 2019.[49] This is a herculean achievement that has lifted millions of people out of poverty, created an enormous middle class and built the world's second-largest economy. 2020 had been designated as a landmark year in which the goal of producing a "moderately prosperous society" (*xiaokang shehui*) was to be achieved. The hurdles to achieving this goal are considerable: according to the *2020 China Statistical Yearbook*, in 2019, over 40% of the population was still earning on average just RMB1,000 (US$141) per month. Nevertheless, 2020 was to have marked the point where, in the space of just ten years, GDP would have doubled to the equivalent of US$10,000 per person, per year.

After four decades of unbroken economic growth, the pre-virus plan was to maintain this growth for 2020, with a projected rise in GDP to above 6%. Instead, the economy shrank by 6.8% in the first quarter of the year, and 460,000 companies went out of business.[50] The Chinese leadership did the unthinkable by admitting in May that it would not be setting a target for the year as a whole. By the end of 2020, officials were proudly pro-claiming that the PRC had become the first major economy to emerge from the coronavirus with positive economic growth, fuelled by heavy state stimulus and an export surge releasing pent-up demand from earlier in the year. Nonetheless, economic growth was still the lowest it had been in four decades, at some 2 per cent. Indeed, a closer examination of official figures issued separately suggests that Beijing's narrative was stronger on wish-ful thinking than fact.

A good example is retail sales, the real engine of growth for China's economy, which fell by over 11% in the first half. Fixed asset investment was down by over 3%, a figure distorted by a rise in investment by state-owned enterprises and a fall in the private sector. When it came to industrial production, the gov-ernment claimed that this had only fallen by 1.3% in the first half of the year, although other figures revealed that some two thirds of industrial enterprises were operating at 20% below nor-mal production levels in May; other companies were in an even worse situation. Many economic analysts concluded that China's claims of revived growth were too good to be true.[51]

Economic growth figures are often disputed, but what mat-tered here was a growing feeling that the Chinese government that had misled the world in the early months of the pandemic was now doing so again, by proclaiming its unique achievement in coming through the crisis with economic growth intact.

The unease over Beijing's claims grew as Chinese commentators taunted other countries over their economic woes, which were contrasted with China's success and booming stock market. "China's economy, the first to succumb to the coronavirus, is proving to be the fastest to recover," proclaimed the *China Daily* newspaper in August 2020, explaining that success had been achieved because the "populace [was] willing to accept and implement strict virus control measures [due] to the fact that the world still needs its exports".[52]

There is room for considerable debate over both the extent of the pandemic's economic impact and China's claims of economic recovery. It is more than likely that, while most other economies have slumped into negative territory as a result of the coronavirus, China, by whatever means, will be able to register growth in 2020. However, this does not mean a return to the high levels of growth seen in previous years. The combination of the short-term pain caused by the virus and the broader ramping up of overseas efforts to lessen dependence on Chinese manufacturing suggests difficulties lying ahead.

Meanwhile, Chinese people will see the reality of an economic slowdown with their own eyes. Officially, as of April 2020, 6 per cent of the workforce was said to be unemployed;[53] but this does not account for vast swathes of rural unemployment, which are not measured, nor China's 290 million-strong army of migrant workers, who are either ignored by the statistics or, at best, not counted in full. The regime's credibility is being severely undermined by the gap between what it claims to be the employment situation and what people are experiencing in their daily lives. The same goes for poverty alleviation measures. The Party has always given priority to the urban areas, where it sees the biggest potential for political unrest and where it is easiest to organise state-directed economic boosters. Implementation of anti-poverty measures in the rural areas has always been patchy. The leadership can hail a victory over poverty, but this will ring hollow in homes where food is not on the table and where long-promised improvements, such as electrification, have failed to materialise.

The fate of small and medium businesses, which have accounted for 60 per cent of China's GDP for the last decade, is also problematic. Many of them are dependent on the dubious shadow banking system to survive, and most will not get the kind of government bailouts that only go to big businesses. The line between survival and failure is thinly drawn, and this stark reality faces many of the people the Party proudly points to as having prospered under its leadership.

At the end of 2020, it is not possible to observe major cracks in the system leading to unrest. However, there are some straws in the wind. Bank runs were reported in June in Baoding city, Hebei Province, and the town of Yangquan in Shanxi Province.[54] In both places, customers had got wind of what they believed to be the threat of banks disappearing under a weight of bad debt. These fears were not unreasonable, given the very high percentage of non-performing loans in the Chinese banking system. Public and private debt has rapidly risen since 2008 and by 2019 was equivalent to 300 per cent of GDP.[55] As the economy slows, pressure on the banking system can only increase. And, in a nation where the Party openly proclaims a trade-off between liberty and economic growth, it is hard to overstate the consequences of an economic slowdown.

Maybe the lasting damage will not be seen in the economic fallout, but in the damage to trust in the system engendered during the pandemic, as it became clear that not only was the outbreak concealed, but its spread downplayed with fatal consequences. Nevertheless, it rather looks as though although the coronavirus of itself has not shattered the Communist Party's credibility—but it might well have laid the grounds for a change of course in China. And, in the wider world, the combination of the fallout from the Hong Kong uprising and the pandemic has become a catalyst for changing attitudes towards the PRC—perhaps fundamentally, as we shall see in the following chapter.

10

HONG KONG IS NOT ALONE

THE WORLD IS WATCHING

As we have seen in the previous chapter, China's handling of the coronavirus had an enormous impact on its relations with the rest of the world. Arguably more lingering, however, will be the impression made on the international community as Beijing ramps up its crackdown on dissent on Hong Kong. Indeed, it is possible to say that the SAR is in the global spotlight in ways that it has never been before.

It's not that Hong Kong previously lacked an international profile, despite its small size; it has a habit of being in the news— but for all the wrong reasons. At times it has been in the headlines as a result of an epidemic or a financial crisis, at others as a quirky example of what happens when fantastic wealth is starkly contrasted with abject poverty. Hong Kong most definitely made headlines when China resumed sovereignty in 1997, but the overwhelming emphasis was on the leaders who were part of this process. Only in 2014, during the Umbrella Movement, and again in 2019–20 with the eruption of a new democracy movement, did the people of Hong Kong themselves become the focus of international attention. Their struggle for freedom has often been depicted as a David versus Goliath struggle, as the people dare to defy the world's largest dictatorship.

For obvious reasons, the Chinese leadership greatly dislikes this portrayal, and, more importantly, fears the impact it may have on the PRC's global aspirations. As a result, the Hong Kong uprising, and Beijing's response to it, have become a battle-field over China's image in the eyes of the world.

* * *

In considering the international response to Beijing's handling of Hong Kong, it is worth pointing out that the leaders in Beijing led the way in framing the Hong Kong question as a global one. From an early stage, the Party formed a conviction that the pro-test movement was in fact a product of foreign intervention. When tangible foreign intervention did appear, in the form of diplomatic protests and threats of sanctions, Beijing spared no efforts in saying that its suspicions had now been vindicated. This line of propaganda is mainly directed towards the home audience, but had some resonance amongst China's allies over-seas, particularly those such as Russia that make the same kind of accusations in the face of human rights criticism. The Chinese public is fed a constant diet of nationalistic propaganda, empha-sising the strength of the new China on the one hand, and, on the other, the hostility of other nations who are said to be jeal-ous of its growth.

Because the leaders in Beijing had limited reliable information about what was going on in Hong Kong, the Xi regime came to believe what paranoid dictatorships always believe: that the people had risen up because they were being manipulated by hostile foreign powers. After all, how could people the Party had never heard of mobilise protests of millions? How could they have developed a sophisticated propaganda machine and the organisational capability to sustain the movement over many months? The obvious answer to these questions, from a Beijing perspective, was that mysterious black hands were co-ordinating the movement from abroad. This paranoia of the Party leaders was readily echoed by their cyphers in Hong Kong. They will never do anything without being told to act by their masters in Beijing, and so they assume that this is how all politics works— there is always someone higher up telling people what to do.

It is interesting to note just how quickly China and its surrogates in Hong Kong raised the spectre of foreign meddling to explain the demonstrations. On 10 June 2019, a day after 1 million people took to the streets to protest against the extradition bill, the *China Daily* ran an editorial saying, "Unfortunately, some Hong Kong residents have been hoodwinked by the opposition camp and their foreign allies into supporting the anti-extradition campaign."[1]

As the movement developed into an entrenched uprising, the accusations of foreign interference, and indeed foreign financial support for the protests, were ramped up. In November, the *Liaowang Weekly*, a state-owned current affairs magazine, took to social media to report that the United States was sending agents to Hong Kong to stir up trouble and pay protestors. According to this lurid version of events, the average payment for turning up at a rally was HK$5,000 (US$641) per person, raised to HK$15,000 for those luring others to join in the demonstrations. At its most excitable, the magazine stated that HK$20 million would be paid to anyone who could "pass as a constable and kill a protestor, preferably in front of cameras, so as to incriminate police officers. A smaller sum was also offered for carrying out arson attacks across the city."[2]

These fantastic allegations were made without one scrap of solid evidence. However, this did not prevent Hong Kong government from latching, albeit more cautiously, on to the narrative that foreigners were manipulating the protests. Carrie Lam, Hong Kong's Chief Executive, told the American broadcaster CNBC in January 2020: "I do feel that perhaps there is something at work, although I said there hasn't been any conclusive evidence, so there is a bigger picture other than the domestic situation."[3]

Lam also followed the script used by other Chinese officials in citing a report by the US-based FAIR organisation, a media advocacy group, which compared CNN's and *The New York Times'* coverage of the Hong Kong protests with coverage of protests in Ecuador, Chile and Haiti. It concluded that the Hong Kong coverage had vastly overwhelmed that of all the other movements combined.

FAIR observed that the prominence given to Hong Kong was related to an impression of "worthy vs. unworthy victims", treated differently depending on whether they are fighting "against corporate power or corruption in a US-client state", or protesting these issues in a country outside America's sphere of influence and alliance, such as China.[4] I'd offer a more mundane explanation of media bias in these matters, derived from many years of experience as a foreign correspondent: coverage focuses on news that is relatable to overseas audiences. News coverage is rarely "fair", in the sense that, for example, thousands dying in parts of Africa are accorded less attention than a dozen people being killed in a place familiar to those watching or reading the news. So it is rather unsurprising that protests in Ecuador, Chile and Haiti received less attention than those in Hong Kong. Moreover, Hong Kong's democratic movement has attracted particular interest because of the marked youth of many of the participants, and their ability to keep coming up with innovative forms of protest.

Although FAIR is highly critical of US policy and an enemy of mainstream media bias, its report did not try to suggest that media coverage could be equated with foreign material support for the protestors. However, the organisation's work has been adopted by the Party as prima facie evidence of foreign meddling in Hong Kong. This is not a new view: Lam's predecessor, Leung Chun-ying, frequently declared that he was in possession of "irrefutable evidence" that foreign forces were behind the Umbrella Movement, claiming he would release this evidence when the time was right. Four years on, Leung has still failed to reveal anything of the sort.

The finger of suspicion over foreign intervention in Hong Kong's protests has most often been pointed at the US-based National Endowment for Democracy (NED). An August 2019 report by the China-leaning *Dimsum Daily* bluntly stated: "The National Endowment for Democracy (NED) has funded the 2014 Occupy Central in the past but many have begun to wonder if the Americans did indeed have a hand in the latest anti-extradition protests in Hong Kong. Numerous meetings between pro-democracy political activists, representatives from NED and top government officials have left us wondered [sic] if NED has funded the frontline protesters." Following this assertion was a litany of innuendo and circumstantial evidence, purporting to uncover a conspiracy linking together prominent pro-democracy leaders, the publisher Jimmy Lai (always a favourite target), and named and unnamed top US officials. The report was accompanied by photographs showing these actors with Hong Kong activists, and made dark suggestions of the Central Intelligence Agency's black hand guiding events.[5]

The NED is indeed a controversial organisation—it is supported by US government funds and it has expressed support for the Hong Kong uprising. But these facts are not sufficient to validate the allegation that it has been initiating or masterminding protests. In a statement published in December 2019, the NED's president said: "Repeated assertions by the Chinese government and state media outlets that NED is in any way orchestrating or financing the ongoing protests in Hong Kong are categorically false and are a sad attempt to distract from the reality of a genuine grassroots movement among the people of Hong Kong, who expect Beijing to uphold their end of the 1984 joint declaration that guarantees respect for the fundamental freedoms of the Hong Kong people under the 'one country, two systems' formula."[6]

The fact that the organisation denies orchestrating the protests is not definitive, of course, but its denial is at least supported by a degree of transparency not to be found among the pro-China organisations working against the democracy movement. The NED's annual report for 2019 details the material support given to various organisations in Hong Kong involved in human rights protection, defence of the rule of law, workers' rights and the promotion of what the organisation calls "evidence-based dialogue and policy-making". The sum total of funds provided in all these areas, says NED, amounted to US$642,943. But most of this money, $325,000, was channelled through the National Democratic Institute for International Affairs, a body that has held meetings with pro-China politicians in Hong Kong and maintained a high level of contact with both sides of the political divide.[7] Also, to put these matters in perspective, the money spent in Hong Kong by the NED is a small fraction of the funds raised by citizens contributing to a variety of pro-democracy organisations. A good example of this is the US$1.97 million raised in a matter of hours in August 2019, as 22,500 individuals donated after a call on the LIHKG forum to fund pro-uprising advertisements in international newspapers.[8]

* * *

Despite the lack of evidence that the protests have been orchestrated by black hands overseas, there is no doubt that international interest in Hong Kong's democracy movement reached unprecedented levels in 2019–20. Overseas media reporting on the uprising was considerable; solidarity campaigns were launched in a great many countries; and foreign governments made their concern known in ways that had never been seen before. This was in no small part due to the efforts of protestors themselves to attract foreign attention and put diplomatic pressure on Beijing. The Hong Kong protestors sustained an intense effort to remain in the international spotlight, not least because they had seen what has happened in other parts of China where very few outsiders were watching—notably Xinjiang, where hundreds of thousands of Uyghurs have been quietly hauled off to concentration camps ominously described as "re-education centres". The movement's international dimension therefore became crucial, with consequences that few predicted. This sparked frustration and cold anger in Beijing.

The Hong Kong protestors are well aware of Beijing's high aspirations for global leadership, and wanted to be sure that the world knew what happened in places where the PRC had control. At the protests themselves, it was hard to avoid people carrying both American and British flags, which were waved as a call for foreign countries to keep up the pressure on the Hong Kong and Chinese governments, as well as to keep up the pressure on Beijing in international forums. It is also noteworthy that the Hong Kong activists consciously linked their protests with those taking place elsewhere in the world, notably in Catalonia, where the streets were filled with people demanding autonomy, from Madrid. The Catalan demonstrators have been seen offering expressions of support for the people of Hong Kong, and this was reciprocated in October 2019 with a demonstration in the SAR supporting Catalan independence. Catalonia flags also had a very visible presence at the National Day rallies at the start of that month.

To put this in some context, 2019 was a notable year for protests around the world: besides Catalonia, there were very large demonstrations in Chile, Lebanon, Iraq and Russia. The British political theorist Maurice Glasman noted: "The common language of the protestors centres on the idea of democratic sovereignty; of political rights, dignity, freedom and democracy."[9] This description most certainly fits what was happening in Hong Kong. By the end of 2020, with the surge of protests in Thailand, this common thread was formalised with the formation of the so-called Milk Tea Alliance, linking together pro-democracy activists initially in Hong Kong, Thailand and Taiwan. It's a clever name that reflects a strong liking for various milk tea concoctions in all these places, with the important qualification that they are similar but different.

Well before this alliance came into being, Hong Kong protestors had been calling for the rights of people in Xinjiang and Tibet, a novelty of the 2019–20 movement. This is a very big red button matter for China. Hongkongers have usually shied away from this issue precisely because it is so sensitive; but, as the protests mounted, an awareness emerged of some commonality between the fates of Hong Kong and these other two supposedly autonomous regions. Seeing the colourful flag of Tibet waving at the demonstrations and hearing slogans in support of Xinjiang's Uyghur people must have confirmed Beijing's worst fears of the direction in which Hong Kong was heading.

The renewed interest in human rights in China, sparked by the Hong Kong uprising, has refocused international attention on both rights and environmental protection in Tibet, and has stimulated calls for sanctions in response to the internment of Muslim Uyghurs in Xinjiang.[10] In June 2020, US President Donald Trump signed into law the Uyghur Human Rights Policy Act; this opened the way for sanctions on individuals accused of human rights violations and, rather unusually, requires the FBI to report on harassment of Uyghurs and Chinese nationals living in the United States.

However, the spotlight remained on Hong Kong during the uprising, and led the US to introduce a spate of legislation targeted at China's crackdown there. The first significant move was the enactment of the US Hong Kong Human Rights and Democracy Act in November 2019. This act was first introduced in 2014, the year of the Umbrella Movement, and had stalled; but the 2019 protests prompted its rapid passage through the legislative process. The Trump administration moved quickly to fulfil the law's requirements and pass further legislation, declaring that the SAR's autonomy had been eroded to a degree that justified ending Hong Kong's special treatment: a range of commercial, legal and immigration benefits not accorded to the rest of China.

In July 2020, the pressure was stepped up with the enactment of the Hong Kong Autonomy Act, which specifically targets individuals deemed to be responsible for violating China's commitments to Hong Kong under the Sino-British Joint Declaration and the Basic Law. The Act allows for imposing travel bans on such individuals, and preventing both foreign and domestic American financial institutions from making substantial transactions in the US on behalf of banned individuals or organisations. This is most worrying for Hong Kong officials, many of whom have close family, investments and other ties in the United States. The law threatens them with exclusion from America, with the possibility of asset freezes for those identified as complicit in a range of actions judged to undermine internationally recognised rights.

There was wall-to-wall bipartisan support for this pair of bills, and there was more besides: a ban on exports of US defence equipment to Hong Kong and the end of licence-free export of so-called dual-use technologies that could be used for civilian or military purposes. This has brought the SAR into line with America's licensing requirements for the rest of China. The reality is that these laws are of greater symbolic importance than of substantive impact on Hong Kong's operations or economy; but it has been amusing to observe some of the Lam government's top officials, who publicly disdain any association with the United States, bitterly complaining of having to shift bank accounts and assets in the US over fears of sanctions.

At the end of June 2020, yet another piece of legislation was tabled before Congress: the Hong Kong Safe Harbor Act, which proposed to offer special refugee status to Hongkongers. Similar action has been taken in other countries, notably Canada and Australia, both of which were already attracting high numbers of Hong Kong immigrants before the uprising began.

As we have seen, the British National (Overseas) passport, still issued to people who were permanent residents in Hong Kong prior to 1997, was little more than a travel document without conferring any right to citizenship. However, there was a dramatic change on 1 July 2020, the twenty-third anniversary of Hong Kong's return to Chinese rule, when the UK announced that it would be giving BNO passport-holders and their dependants the right to settle in Britain, as a direct response to the imposition of the National Security Law. In February 2020, 2.9 million Hongkongers were eligible for BNO status, and some 350,000 of them held a BNO passport.[11]

In parallel with this foreign welcome of Hongkongers, a number of states, including the US, Britain, France and Germany, have terminated extradition agreements with Hong Kong, because they lack confidence in the rule of law now that the National Security Law is in force. These countries have also put Hong Kong on a blacklist for supply of military or policing equipment, or goods that could be used for surveillance purposes.

As the former colonial ruler of Hong Kong, Britain has stronger ties with the SAR than other Western powers, and has a residual monitoring role derived from the Sino-British Joint

Declaration, an international treaty lodged with the United Nations. There have long been calls by Hongkongers for the UK to be more assertive in defending the terms of this agreement. The PRC disagrees that London has such an obligation: at the end of June 2017, China announced that the treaty was nothing more than a historical document with no practical significance, adding that "it is not at all binding for the central [Beijing] government's management over Hong Kong".[12] Britain, however, maintains that it has a legal responsibility to ensure that China complies with the undertakings made in the treaty, and issues biannual reports setting out the level of compliance. In previous years, these had tended to contain breezy assurances that all was well; but the report issued in October 2019 was considerably less sanguine, highlighting several areas of concern and including a statement from Dominic Raab, the Foreign Secretary, urging the Lam government to engage in a "meaningful dialogue" aimed at preserving "Hong Kong's rights and freedoms and high degree of autonomy".[13]

Raab went further in a subsequent statement, which explicitly linked the crackdown in Hong Kong to China's standing in the world more generally. He asserted that the decision to offer citizenship to BNO-holders had been taken because China had enacted legislation violating Hong Kong's autonomy and strangling its freedoms. A key sentence in Raab's statement signalled the wider ramifications, as he said that Beijing's move could only "undermine international trust in the Chinese Government's willingness to keep its word and live up to its promises".[14]

Britain has not been alone in changing its stance on Beijing's integrity: even Australia, which in the past could be counted among the most Beijing-friendly of Western states, has assumed a very different approach. It has joined the US, Canada, France, Germany, New Zealand and Britain in expressing concern over the treatment of protestors and support for their demands for greater democracy. Australian Prime Minister Scott Morrison, who was widely criticised for not standing up to Beijing after assuming office in 2018, changed his tune in June 2020. This was mainly in response to the imposition of the National Security Law, but also came in the wake of heightened trade tensions: China had retaliated sharply on the commercial side after Canberra called for an international inquiry into the origins of the coronavirus epidemic. Morrison was now saying that Australia would "never be intimidated by threats", nor surrender its values in response to "coercion", from Beijing or anywhere else.[15] Most surprisingly of all, Japan, which generally shies away from this kind of thing, has also raised its voice over the uprising and its suppression.

While China has rhetorically shrugged off this avalanche of policy measures and verbal condemnations, describing them as meaningless, the ferocity of Beijing's own response has belied this lack of concern. In December 2019, just days after the passing of America's Hong Kong Human Rights and Democracy Act, the PRC suspended the long-standing visit of US military vessels and aircraft to Hong Kong, and banned several US-based non-governmental organisations—notably the National Endowment for Democracy, which, as we have seen, was accused of orchestrating the uprising. In June 2020, China also placed visa restrictions on US politicians and officials who had "behaved extremely badly" over Hong Kong affairs, days after Washington announced the same move in relation to Chinese officials' actions in Hong Kong.

As anger with the United States trundled on throughout the uprising, American journalists from three newspapers based in Beijing were expelled in March 2020, and barred from working in Hong Kong. America, it should be stressed, had started this process the previous month, by designating Chinese state media operating in the US as foreign missions that needed to register as such, which would make them subject to additional restrictions. China also targeted Voice of America, the US government-financed broadcaster. Confusingly, the network was blasted the following month by the Trump White House for amplifying "Chinese propaganda" in its reporting on coronavirus. In Macau, whose government is always keen to go that extra mile in demonstrating loyalty to Beijing, the SAR administration even banned leaders of the American Chamber of Commerce in Hong Kong from entering the territory for a social event.

These tit-for-tat responses from Beijing were very much part of the wider, deteriorating picture of 2020: a trade war, and a breakdown in diplomatic relations.

* * *

Arguably, the most serious consequence for Beijing of the world's response to the Hong Kong crackdown has been the changed international status of Taiwan, where Chinese sensitivities are at the highest possible level. As we have seen, Beijing has done much to tighten the diplomatic screws on Taiwan since the independence advocate Tsai Ing-wen was first elected president in 2016: the PRC has succeeded in getting seven nations to sever diplomatic relations with Taipei, while deepening its exclusion from participation in international bodies such as the World Health Organization.

The biggest overseas street rallies in support of the Hong Kong uprising were held in Taiwan, and the island state's government has emerged as an unqualified beneficiary. Not only did Tsai storm to victory in her re-election campaign on the back of fears that China would do to Taiwan what it was doing to Hong Kong; events in the SAR have also served to bring Taiwan closer to the United States, a long-cherished policy aim in Taipei. The apex of this achievement was reached in March 2020, when President Trump signed the Taiwan Allies International Protection and Enhancement Initiative (TAIPEI) Act, a bipartisan bill uniting both sides of America's bitter political divide. The TAIPEI Act represents a considerable step up in US relations with Taiwan, which has not been recognised as a state since President Nixon established diplomatic relations with China. It opens the door for enhanced security and economic co-operation, and for diplomatic initiatives that will lessen Taiwan's global isolation.

This new Taiwan-friendly policy does not signify a resumption of full diplomatic relations between Taipei and Washington. But this is small comfort for Beijing, which has slammed the TAIPEI Act and now worries that Taiwan's emergence from its American deep freeze will embolden other nations to expand their relationships with the self-governing island. Significantly, both Japan and Canada have been quick to call for Taiwan's reinstatement as a WHO observer.

* * *

Not only were things headed in the wrong direction in 2020 for Beijing's international relations, but the government was arguably making things worse for itself by its overreaction to criticism. The regime's leaders, who oscillated between shrugging off the criticism and deploying so-called Wolf Warrior diplomacy, were also open to accusations of breaking promises, notably on trade policy. British Foreign Secretary Dominic Raab was not alone when he placed the issue of trust into the context of the Hong Kong situation, where the PRC had not just blatantly broken undertakings given in the Joint Declaration, but had declared an international treaty dead because it no longer liked its requirements.

When Beijing assumed control of Hong Kong in 1997, it made much of the pledges it had given and pointed to its willingness to have these pledges embedded in the Joint Declaration. It had invited the international community to witness its willingness to incorporate a fully functioning capitalist society within its borders, and to allow a level of autonomy that would guarantee freedoms denied to the rest of the nation. With the introduction of the National Security Law from July 2020, these freedoms were swept away in the full view of the rest of the world. This was when the level of international response clearly moved from mere rhetoric to tangible action.

Usually, matters of foreign policy lie low on the list of governments' priorities. Involvement in the affairs of other nations is rarely a vote-winner and tends to have little upside. However, China's actions in Hong Kong have impinged on the minds of both ordinary citizens and political leaders to an unusual extent. As we know, around the world—especially in countries with significant Chinese communities—protestors have taken to the streets in solidarity with the Hong Kong uprising; and there has been internal pressure on foreign powers to show similar support at the state level.

In Britain, for instance, opinion polling has shown considerable public approval of the announced offer of residency for BNO-holders—this is remarkable, given that taking in a potentially massive influx of immigrants is generally a highly unpopular proposal. A YouGov poll conducted at the end of June 2020 found that nearly two thirds of respondents supported offering permanent settlement to BNO-holders. A similar poll conducted in 1990 had found only a third of respondents agreeing with this proposition.[16] The same pattern of dwindling public support for Beijing is reflected in a study by the Washington-based Pew Research Center. Conducted between 18 May and 2 October 2019, this survey found that in six major Asia-Pacific nations—Australia, India, Indonesia, Japan, the Philippines and South Korea—views of the United States were more positive than those of China. This was despite respondents having less confidence in Trump to do the right thing than in his predecessor Obama.[17]

Although the PRC's efforts to improve its public image have, if anything, been counterproductive, it is not for want of trying. Beijing works ceaselessly to win the argument abroad, not least by mobilising its small army of cyberwarriors on platforms such as Twitter and Facebook that are banned in China. As the uprising wore on, the Party launched its offensive to control the social media narrative about Hong Kong. In 2019, researchers at Hong Kong University's Journalism and Media Studies Centre looked into reports by both Twitter and Facebook, which had discovered co-ordinated network activities designed to frame the protest movement as separatist. Here and elsewhere on social media, there was extensive use of bots sharing disinformation about what was going on in Hong Kong. The HKU researchers ran data analysis on 640,000 Twitter accounts, finding that 20 per cent of them were bots.[18] The social media platforms inside China's Great Firewall, principally Weibo and WeChat, are even more vociferous in establishing a "correct" narrative for understanding events in the SAR.

Aside from all this cyberactivity, China is also heavily focused on telling the world its side of the story through the more traditional media. Intriguingly, the Party has found that the Hong Kong media, allegedly free and independent, has a useful role to play here, especially when it comes to addressing overseas Chinese audiences that have long looked to the former colony for both entertainment and news. TVB, Hong Kong's biggest broadcaster, is highly influential among overseas Chinese. It has proved to be a perfect vehicle for echoing the Beijing line, and retains a lingering credibility that China's state-controlled television channels lack.

Similarly, the *Sing Tao Daily*, an enthusiastic pro-Beijing outlet, often acts as a semi-official leaker of information, or floater of official lines that can be denied if they fail to take hold. Although it has a fading readership in Hong Kong, the paper has long been the most prominent in overseas Chinese communities, where its satellite editions are printed. The problem here is that *Sing Tao* mainly reaches an older generation: younger readers are put off by both its pro-China stance and the fact that their fluency in English makes it possible to read a vast array of other publications.

More intriguing and complex is the English-language *South China Morning Post*, owned by Jack Ma—China's richest man and, of course, a Communist Party member. The paper retains a degree of independence and often provides good, solid reporting of events both on the Mainland and in Hong Kong. This makes it an ideal vehicle for classic Communist United Front tactics—using a credible front to promote the Party's aims, while maintaining a distance from the Party itself. The propaganda bosses in Beijing have long sought a more presentable voice in the English-language media. The precise reason why Ma was persuaded to buy the paper at the end of 2015 is not known, but he cannot have been motivated by commercial considerations. The *SCMP* haemorrhages cash, even more so since the new owner has poured additional resources into the publication.

During the uprising, the already pro-government *South China Morning Post* became increasingly identified with the blue camp, and was given an additional role. It describes this as a "mission to lead the global conversation about China". The paper's news coverage has subtly shifted, and it has introduced a slew of pro-Beijing commentators to fill its comment slots. Meanwhile, it is also hosting conferences that promote Beijing's objectives. Most grotesquely, the *SCMP* is used for the messy business of providing credibility for political detainees' forced confessions on the Mainland, supposedly a free admission of their sins.

In an ideal world, the Party would probably not bother with using Hong Kong media for its overseas outreach, but even die-hard Party propagandists have come to accept that the regime's own stodgy, almost laughable fare does not come off well in societies with a free media. Nevertheless, great efforts have also been made to reinvigorate official media outlets. At the end of 2016, the greatly unwatched international arm of China Central Television was replaced by a far slicker operation branded as China Global Television News, which relies heavily on foreign experts with international experience.

The state-run *China Daily*, the Party's main international print newspaper, has also undergone a revamp in the Xi era. Armed with a shovelful of cash, it had persuaded at least thirty foreign newspapers to carry inserts of its content in supplements branded *China Watch*. Astonishingly, some of the world's most prominent publications took the money and ran these supplements, including *The Wall Street Journal The Washington Post* and *The New York Times* in the US; *Le Figaro* in France, *El País* in Spain, *Handelsblatt* in Germany, the *Mainichi Shimbun* in Japan and *The Sydney Morning Herald* in Australia.[19] Britain's *Daily Telegraph*, which ran *China Watch* supplements for over a decade, suspended its participation in the scheme in April 2020 as a result of alarm over articles connected to the coronavirus pandemic. It is unclear whether other participants in this scheme have also withdrawn, but from 2020 there was a decline in the frequency with which these supplements appeared.[20]

The purpose of this expenditure and the ramping up of state-controlled broadcasts overseas is both to directly furnish foreign audiences with China's version of the news and to give legitimacy to these stories back home, where it can be said without mentioning the sponsorship deals that an article, in fact originating from *China Daily*, has appeared in *The Washington Post*. This looks very much like Beijing talking to itself, and it is part of this curious process of seeking validity from overseas, while simultaneously disdaining the foreign and accusing it of peddling false news.

The Hong Kong government has also played its role in spreading the message overseas, splashing out to the tune of millions of dollars on full-page advertisements in leading German, British, French, American, Canadian and Japanese newspapers. The results of this mini-propaganda offensive can only be described as minimal; and when, in September 2019, eight global public relations companies were asked to work on a campaign to enhance the Lam administration's reputation, they all declined, and the government gave up.[21] Instead it used its own resources to launch this global newspaper campaign, focusing on the strength of the Hong Kong economy and the safety of investments in the SAR despite the unrest. This was largely a response to the far more successful series of pro-democracy, citizen-funded newspaper advertisements.

Despite these enormous efforts to win over global public opinion, officials in Beijing are both infuriated and puzzled by the fact that the apparently powerless people of this tiny part of China are able to swan around the world and be enthusiastically received abroad. Hong Kong democracy advocates are regularly feted in Washington, including during the uprising. Joshua Wong and other young activists have found themselves addressing large gatherings of the Washington elite, and have given testimony to the US Congress. Denise Ho, the pop star, scored a telling victory at a United Nations human rights meeting in Geneva, where the Chinese representative tried to stop her speaking, but she succeeded in delivering a short address that was shared and avidly watched on social media. Older democracy leaders too were received at the highest levels of the Trump administration, including Martin Lee and Albert Ho, founders of the Democratic Party; Anson Chan, the former number two in the Hong Kong government; and media publisher Jimmy Lai, the founder of *Apple Daily*.

In its rage over this high level of access in Washington, Beijing's official media took to describing these democrats as "The Gang of Four", a rather surprising echo of the name given to the coterie of leading cadres around Mao Zedong at the time of the Cultural Revolution. A report in the *China Daily* said: "Besides coordinating strategy for the so-called 'pro-democracy movement', they have been accused of becoming pawns in the hands of anti-China forces in the West to meddle in Hong Kong affairs."[22] In December 2020, Lai became the first member of this group to be charged under the NSL for "collusion with a foreign country or with external elements to endanger national security". This offence carries the possibility of a life sentence.

While Hong Kong's democrats are feted in the West, China's own surrogates overseas often get short shrift when trying to explain Beijing's actions in Hong Kong. Thus it seems as though the enormous time, energy and resources poured into improving China's international reputation in the wake of the Hong Kong crackdown has borne little fruit. The question is, does it matter? Will Beijing have suffered, or could it yet suffer, permanent damage to its global strategy as a result of the uprising?

* * *

The Xi regime makes a point of feigning disinterest over what other countries say partly because its Wolf Warrior diplomacy plays well with the home audience, and partly because it is confident that—despite a certain amount of sound and fury from foreign powers—none of them, in the last analysis, will really put themselves out for Hong Kong. That includes the United States. As Li Su, a prominent Mainland academic who heads the Modern Think-Tank Forum, bluntly put it: "America doesn't even qualify to be China's opponent ... What are they going to do, fight a war over Hong Kong?"[23]

Moreover, despite the fact that the United States has been the most vocal supporter of the 2019–20 uprising, the wily officials in Beijing were well aware of the erratic and often contradictory stance of the Trump administration. Sometimes this has descended into farce, as it did in November 2019, when President Trump made the extraordinary assertion that, if not for him personally, "Hong Kong would have been obliterated in 14 minutes." He added, "I'll tell you we have to stand with Hong Kong but I'm also standing with President Xi. He is a friend of mine; he is an incredible guy." According to Trump, 1 million Chinese soldiers had been on standby to invade the SAR when his intervention prevented them from moving in.[24] No one in Beijing even bothered to contradict this patently absurd statement, but it confirmed an impression among China's leaders that they were dealing with an easily distracted president not overly bothered by facts.

What both the rulers in Beijing and the protestors on the streets of Hong Kong had in common during the uprising was an exaggerated notion of international interest and willingness to get seriously involved in the struggle for democracy. At times, Hong Kong was no more than a convenient pawn in the wider objectives of US foreign policy; at other times, the protests genuinely fired the imagination of both governments and citizens overseas. But the mistake of the protestors was to believe that this overseas support would be consistently and meaningfully sustained, and that obtaining it would produce results in Beijing. Yet this relies on an assumption that the Chinese leadership fully understands the self-inflicted challenge to its international reputation and strategy that has resulted from the crackdown in Hong Kong.

There is another reason that the Xi regime shrugs off criticism from Western and other powers: in the hermetically sealed system of the Communist dictatorship, where bad news is kept from leaders, there often seems to be limited awareness of the damage being done overseas. But with Hong Kong in the international spotlight, Beijing has to think very carefully before taking any extreme form of action to suppress further protest. As the old slogan goes, the whole world is watching.

11

FOLLOW THE MONEY

Why did the government in Beijing not send in the tanks to crush the largest revolt seen on Chinese soil since 1989?

Part of the answer may be Beijing's wariness over further tarnishing its relations with the outside world. But another key lies in the sage advice famously proffered by Deep Throat in *All the President's Men*, the 1976 film about the Watergate affair. "Follow the money," the prized informant tells journalist Bob Woodward: that money trail would reveal what was really going on in the infamous White House cover-up.

What holds good for investigating murky doings in Washington very much applies to understanding a crucial aspect of the real relationship between China's leadership and Hong Kong. Here too it is necessary to follow the money, which reveals a compelling, yet rarely used, explanation for the way the Beijing dictatorship has handled its errant son in the south. In short, the PRC has shown restraint and avoided using brute force in Hong Kong because China's most influential people all have an impressive personal financial stake in the SAR, an interest that would be jeopardised if the whole system were to collapse in the wake of a violent military crackdown on protests. Or, to put it another way: who seriously thinks that China's leaders would want to burn down the bank holding their family's money?

It is somewhat surprising that there has been so little focus on Hong Kong's key position as the vessel that pilots this cash out of China, and on how this impacts the leadership's thinking about Hong Kong. Its role as the financial exit route is no small thing, because the Chinese elite is forever seeking forms of insurance to preserve at least a part of their wealth should a purge remove them from power. They know that, in a system ruled by a dictatorship, even the most powerful can see their fortunes transformed literally overnight. If and when that happens, they want to have made sure that their family's finances are still secured—this involves shifting money beyond the reach of the state.

Power struggles regularly convulse the PRC's political system. And there is a predictable pattern to what happens to those who lose out. First up, they are likely to be charged with corruption—because corruption, which permeates the regime, is always a convenient and plausible pretext for dealing with those who fall out of favour. The losers in these internal Party wars go to jail, and their assets are confiscated. However, because of the way the CCP system works, any assets that have already crossed the PRC's borders tend to be safe. Not only are funds abroad difficult to recover, but there is also scant evidence of serious government attempts to do so.

There are good reasons why China has problems seizing overseas assets, not least the difficulty of securing co-operation from foreign governments well aware of the lack of an internationally recognised judicial process within the PRC. Chinese officials do not wish to be embarrassed by going to foreign courts, where the case for asset seizure would be open to scrutiny by an independent judiciary. However, the more compelling reason for not recovering these assets lies in the awareness of those making the rules that they too might, at some stage, be vulnerable to such a seizure. Who knows when a change of fortune may strike? With this in mind, the people at the heart of the system have every incentive to leave alone safety nets that they themselves might end up using.

Safe in the knowledge that assets can be ferried abroad and are unlikely to be confiscated even after a purge, the elite's next consideration is to find ways of getting their money out. This is where Hong Kong comes in, as the supreme gateway for outgoing Mainland funds, which can then be delivered on to a secure international location. And here we start to see the conflict of interest at the heart of Beijing over what to do about Hong Kong. The SAR is in pole position to play this financial role for the Party elite precisely because it is not the same as the rest of China, especially since the establishment of the PRC in 1949. Hong Kong has, or had, freedoms, an independent legal system and the kind of financial infrastructure that is compatible with other parts of the world. Thus the SAR has become irreplaceable as the trusted middleman able to get the money cleaned up and out of the Chinese state's grasp.

Other jurisdictions are available for this purpose, but they lack Hong Kong's physical proximity to the Mainland. Moreover, they lack the unique distinction of being under the political control of the PRC while retaining a layer of internationally recognised legal protection. In addition, other territories do not have the experience and ease of doing business that is offered by Hong Kong's system. It might be imagined that another exit option is Macau, China's other SAR, but it is tainted by its reputation for money-laundering associated with the casino business. Macau can certainly handle some of this exit cash, but its financial system is simply too small to cope with the really massive outflows from the Mainland.

Hong Kong, on the other hand, is a great place to hide wealth from prying eyes. The SAR was ranked fourth in the 2020 Financial Secrecy Index compiled by the British-based Tax Justice Network, which campaigns for greater transparency in relation to taxation and financial globalisation.[1] Top of this list were the Cayman Islands, followed by the United States and Switzerland. Commenting on the history of Hong Kong as an offshore financial hub, the Network says: "The government's promise to uphold the principle of 'keeping intervention into the way in which the market operates to a minimum' is a classic see-no-evil approach to financial regulation, designed to attract offshore business, dirty and clean, with few questions asked ... Hong Kong was always intended to be a familiar, trusted, Chinese-speaking offshore centre for the Chinese leadership and élites—a place where business could be partly controlled but also significantly protected from mainland scrutiny."[2]

* * *

So, Hong Kong is the premier destination for these funds; and, thanks to the diligent work of a number of journalists penetrating a wall of secrecy, it has proved possible to identify a consistent and sophisticated pattern to these cash outflows. It is nevertheless impossible to estimate the precise level of the Chinese elite's financial, property and other holdings that are vested in Hong Kong or transiting through the territory to rest in offshore locations. However, all indications point to the sums being very large indeed.

The extent of Hong Kong connections to the murky world of companies registered in the British Virgin Islands (a notorious tax haven) was revealed by the International Consortium of Investigative Journalists (ICIJ), which exposed in 2016 the activities of Mossack Fonseca, a Panamanian law firm specialised in setting up offshore companies for the rich and powerful. The

ICIJ's work is better known as the Panama Papers. These reveal that some 16,300 shell companies have been set up through offices in Hong Kong and China, representing 29 per cent of Mossack Fonseca's active companies worldwide. The Panamanian company's busiest global office was also located in Hong Kong.[3]

Aside from the business conducted by just this one company, the ICIJ investigation found that 26,000 (or 10 per cent) of all the firms in its overseas shell company database were controlled from Hong Kong, with another 33,300 from the Mainland.[4] The papers also show that approximately US$1.4 trillion went into these offshore shell companies from China between 2004 and 2013. This money is derived from a number of sources, including corruption, money laundering and tax evasion.[5] Even more sensitive, from the Party's point of view, is the inclusion in the Panama Papers of so-called "clean" money that has left China, because even businesses who have acquired their cash legally are well aware of the dangers inherent in leaving their assets in a country controlled by a dictatorship.

Hong Kong was the most convenient place for businesses to set up companies, because the identity of their principal shareholders could be disguised. Another layer of anonymity was secured by having the companies controlled by offshore entities. In this framework, Mainlanders can place their stake in a business with an offshore company, funnel the money out of China, and then leave it overseas or bring it back to the SAR from these offshore havens. Between 2013 and 2015, funds from offshore locations accounted for the largest source of foreign investment in Hong Kong.[6] Most of this so-called foreign investment was in fact made by locally based individuals and corporations, making a pit stop in Hong Kong before wading offshore in order to come back as "overseas" investment. Thus taxation is avoided, bothersome questions over the origin of the cash can be ducked, and massive profits beckon.

The laxity of controls and the lack of transparency in the Hong Kong banking sector do not just attract hot money from the Mainland but from elsewhere too, as was seen in 2017, when a major scandal involving money laundering for Russian criminal gangs came to light. In view of this and other developments, the Hong Kong government was sufficiently embarrassed to make a tentative attempt to restore the SAR's reputation for probity. In that same year, laws were amended to compel all companies to keep a register of beneficial owners. Typically, the government, which has problems with transparency, could not bring itself to make this register public. Moreover, there is still scope for avoiding disclosure by simply moving the cash rapidly through Hong Kong before it lands in an offshore entity.

Although Hong Kong's reputation is undermined by this frenzy of hot money exiting the Mainland, it remains a sufficiently credible jurisdiction to be respectable in the world of financial institutions. This has given rise to the growth of a spectacularly large asset and wealth management industry in the SAR, with assets under management officially estimated to total US$23.95 billion as of July 2018. Of this total, US$4.33 billion is vested in trusts, a way of disguising the ultimate ownership of the cash. It is also possible to extrapolate from these figures that at least half of this amount came from Hong Kong and Chinese sources, but it is difficult to go further and strip out the Hong Kong element, because so much of it consists of money originating from the Mainland.[7] What's more, while it's possible to identify the significant piles of cash flowing to Hong Kong from the Mainland, it is much harder to quantify the amount of hot money derived from corruption within the PRC. For obvious reasons, there are no reliable figures on this subject; but all the circumstantial evidence points to a great deal of these ill-gotten gains making their way to Hong Kong.

All that is known for sure is that corruption in China is on a massive scale. President Xi Jinping has often referred to the problem of corruption as the biggest threat facing the Communist Party. Back in 2004, before he was even China's ruler, he famously told cadres: "Rein in your spouses, children, relatives, friends and staff, and vow not to use power for personal gain." Between 2013 and 2016, almost 1 million officials were convicted for corruption offences.[8] Many of those caught up in the net were Xi's political opponents, who have been pushed aside under the banner of fighting corruption. This vast nationwide campaign has also swept up and jailed many local officials, minor functionaries and other small cogs in the state machine. But Xi's main focus has been on the people he described as the "tigers" at the top of the list, embezzling eyewatering sums of money.

The money allegedly stolen by these tigers runs into billions of dollars. A leaked People's Bank of China report dated 2008 estimated that, since the mid-1990s, corrupt public officials had managed to get US$123 billion out of China.[9] Other estimates of the total untraced assets leaving the country are much higher. Another leaked report, this time from China's anti-corruption unit, the Central Commission for Discipline Inspection, stated that by 2012, US$1 trillion of corruptly acquired cash had left the country.[10]

To get an idea what big-league Party malfeasance looks like in China, consider the case of the famously iron-faced Zhou Yongkang, jailed for life in 2015, the highest-ranking Party member to be convicted of corruption.[11] The Chinese authorities seized US$14.5 billion from Zhou's family and associates, among the 300-odd people who were rounded up in the wake of his arrest. The authorities confiscated some 300 apartments and villas; antiques and contemporary paintings with a market value of RMB1 billion (approx. US$162m); more than sixty vehicles; expensive liquor; and gold, silver and cash in both local and foreign currencies.[12] Besides getting on the wrong side of President Xi, Zhou's greatest error seems to have been his remarkable complacency in keeping so much of his money on the Mainland, which explains why so much was confiscated.

The same fate appears to have afflicted Zhao Zhengyong, CCP chief of the relatively poor Shaanxi Province in north-western China, who never enjoyed Zhou's prominence in the Party but went on trial in 2020 for a massive corruption spree that yielded cash and assets totalling over US$89 million.[13] The authorities were able to confiscate this horde because, like Zhou, he had failed to ship it overseas. Most big-league corrupt officials, however, are not so lax; they recognise the pressing need to get their money out of the PRC, and to clean it up.

One dramatic illustration of the flight of hot money from a prominent family relates to the overseas assets of Bo Xilai, the former Politburo member and powerful Party boss of Chongqing, who was jailed for life on charges of corruption and abuse of power in 2013. His example shows that money that has left the country will remain untouched by the authorities. Bo and his wife Gu Kailai were involved in a most extraordinary scandal, which led Gu to receive a life sentence for poisoning the British businessman Neil Heywood. Thanks to an unusually public trial, it became clear that the heart of the scandal lay in a dispute over a luxury villa in France, valued at €7 million. Ownership was hidden behind the creation of a company registered in the British Virgin Islands, allegedly controlled by Heywood and his associate. As revealed by the Panama Papers, however, Gu was the real owner. And according to her testimony at trial, she had suspected that the frontmen might be trying to get hold of the property for themselves.[14]

It is widely assumed that Heywood acted as a middleman for much of the couple's financial affairs, but Gu also had two sisters who were active in Hong Kong business, and Bo's brother Bo Xiyong was the vice-chairman of the Hong Kong-based China Everbright International.[15] The murdered Neil Heywood was also involved in two luxury London properties for which Gu Wangjiang, Gu Kailai's sister, was registered as the acting authority in transfer of their ownership to and from a BVI company. Gu Wangjiang also appeared to have personal shareholdings worth US$79 million and was listed as a director of companies in Hong Kong, Panama and China.[16] Given the closeness of these family ties, and a record of business transacted between the sisters, it is reasonable to assume that Hong Kong was used as a transit point for Bo/Gu family money leaving China. This was certainly the view of the Mainland authorities, who sent a team to Hong Kong in 2012 as part of their corruption investigation into Bo and made some middling effort to get its hands on the overseas family assets. Both Bo Xilai and his wife remain in jail.

It should be stressed that by no means all of this hot Mainland money is directly derived from overtly criminal activities. A very large amount comes from influence-peddling: family members of senior Party officials are able to use their connections and offer implicit, or indeed explicit, promises of access to decision-makers, in return for involvement in legitimate businesses and the opportunity to work alongside blue-chip financial institutions.

There is no better illustration of how this works than by looking at the family of President Xi Jinping himself. In a groundbreaking investigation, the Bloomberg news agency found that relatives of the President had investments in companies with total assets of US$376 million; including an 18 per cent indirect stake in a rare-earths company with $1.73 billion in assets, and a $20.2 million holding in a publicly-traded technology company.[17]

The main player here is the President's elder sister, Qi Qiaoqiao. At the time of publication, her ultimate property portfolio in Hong Kong amounted to US$50 million, including a US$31.5 million home in one of the city's most prestigious waterside districts. The share price of a technology company partly owned by her daughter Zhang Yannan rose forty-fold over the three years after Zhang acquired her stake.[18] Other family members own the Yuenwei Group, a property developer and telecommunications company. It has also been reported that, in the aftermath of the 2012 Bloomberg report, Qi, her husband Deng Jiagui and their daughter Zhang sold or liquidated investments worth hundreds of millions of dollars, although they retained a sprawling business empire through Yuanwei, a company based in the Hong Kong border town of Shenzhen.[19]

As Bloomberg noted, "No assets were traced to Xi ... his wife Peng Liyuan ... or their daughter, the documents show. There is no indication Xi intervened to advance his relatives' business transactions, or of any wrongdoing by Xi or his extended family."[20] Nor are there any accessible records suggesting that either the President or Peng have direct control over the assets belonging to his wider family. However, there is a recognisable pattern in Chinese finances of family members' assets not being directly linked to the person of influence who has been the rainmaker for the family's good fortune. Xi's annual salary amounts to US$22,000, which is staggeringly low for the head of the world's largest state. All senior Chinese officials are paid extremely low salaries, but have a lifestyle suggesting access to considerably greater wealth than could be derived from what they are officially said to earn.

Indeed, the Xi family is hardly first in line when it comes to benefiting from connections to the Party elite. The list of China's new rich can be closely correlated with these families. In another groundbreaking report, Bloomberg News (which has since stopped reporting on these matters) traced the fortunes of 103 people closely related to the Party's founders and most prominent leaders since the 1949 Revolution.[21]

These so-called "immortals" of the CCP are now ageing, but their families have been shameless in using their revered status to make fortunes for themselves. General Wang Zhen's offspring are particularly famous for their impressive business holdings. The general rose to fame by demonstrating how the People's Liberation Army could achieve self-sufficiency by living off the land, so it is ironically fitting that his children have demonstrated a particular knack for lavish familial self-sufficiency. One son, Wang Jun, is a founder of the CITIC group, which was the pioneer among Mainland companies making their way to Hong Kong. He is also a major player in the China Poly Group, once famous as an arms trader and oil explorer in Africa, but better known in Hong Kong as an up-and-coming property developer; and "is considered the godfather of" China's burgeoning golf club industry, arguably its most powerful operator. His daughter, Jingjing, lives or lived in a Hong Kong luxury apartment partly owned by CITIC. Wang Zhi, the third son, moved in another direction, partnering with Bill Gates to develop a Chinese version of Windows.

Then there is the family circle of Deng Xiaoping, once paramount leader of the PRC. His son-in-law, He Ping, chaired the Hong Kong-listed Poly Group until 2010. His own son, Deng Pufang, runs a charity which is also known for its numerous business interests. The leader's daughter Deng Rong and his son Deng Zhifang both went into the property development business, with major developments in the Hong Kong border town of Shenzhen. Another Deng son-in-law, Wu Jianchang, has moved nimbly between government service and both state-owned and privately held companies listed in Hong Kong. Wu's son Zhuo Su, Deng Xiaoping's grandson, has also emerged as a businessman involved with Mainland, Hong Kong and overseas-based companies with interests focusing on metals.

To take another leader's family, Wang Xiaochao, son-in-law of former President Yang Shangkun (1988–93), is also connected to the Poly Group (a truly well-connected conglomerate). Yang's daughter, who served as honorary chairwoman of a

CITIC subsidiary, is also firmly immersed in the web of *guanxi*-based companies, in other words the businesses with the best political connections.

The descendants of the immortals are not alone in leveraging the political connections of their fathers and grandfathers. Among the big *guanxi* businesspeople are family members of the infamous former premier Li Peng, who presided over the Tiananmen Square massacre in 1989. His daughter Li Xiaolin and her husband Liu Zhiyuan figure prominently in the Panama Papers. Li became a Hong Kong resident and vice-president of the China Power Investment Corporation, a state-controlled entity with stock market listings in Hong Kong and Shanghai; she and Liu are also linked to British Virgin Islands-registered subsidiaries.[22] Wen Yunsong, son of former Premier Wen Jiabao (2003–13), also figures in the Panama Papers with a BVI-registered company, which was established with the help of the Hong Kong office of a Swiss bank.[23] Based on the ICIJ's treasure trove of documents, Hong Kong's *Apple Daily* newspaper has worked out that families of six current and former members of the Politburo (the Communist Party's ruling body) had control over offshore companies, with Hong Kong-based assets totalling some US$269 million in value.[24]

Once again, it needs to be stressed that all this money pouring out of the Mainland is not necessarily the product of corruption or even of *guanxi*-style business. China has many self-made rich people. Admittedly, they all need to find a way of accommodating the Party if they wish to retain their wealth, and many of them do so by going down the road of hiring the relatives of influential people. They also, probably without exception, seek the safety net of establishing offshore companies, both as a form of insurance and to keep prying eyes away from their businesses.

Prestigious international banks operating in Hong Kong pop up frequently in the Panama Papers as intermediaries helping

Mainland entities establish these offshore companies. Their creation is very big business for the Hong Kong offices of global financial corporations. UBS, via TrustNet, helped more than 1,000 clients from the Mainland, Hong Kong and Taiwan to set up offshore companies; TrustNet performed the same service for more than 400 PricewaterhouseCoopers clients. In total, between 2003 and 2007, TrustNet set up 4,800 companies for clients from these jurisdictions, according to the ICIJ files.[25] A 2018 survey by the accountancy firm Deloitte estimated that the SAR's wealth management industry expanded by 127 per cent between 2010 and 2017, beating all other jurisdictions studied in terms of growth.[26]

The golden thread running through all these disclosures is the role played by Hong Kong, either in ferreting the money out of the Mainland or as a base for putting the cash to work, often in the form of buying property assets. Many members of the Mainland's ruling families have acquired Hong Kong residence and live in the SAR, while flitting both overseas and back and forth to the Mainland.

The existence of Hong Kong as a gateway for the safety of Mainland assets is more than an insurance policy, because it does not just provide the means of recovery when things go wrong; it is also the means of making the cash grow.

* * *

The exquisite dilemma facing China's rulers is whether they are prepared to compromise their personal interests in Hong Kong for the sake of what might be described as the national interest or, more importantly, the Party's interests. In theory, there is no need to agonise over this problem, as Mao Zedong clearly laid out the duty of Party members in this regard: "At no time and in no circumstances should a Communist place his personal interests first; he should subordinate to the interests of the nation and of the masses. Hence, selfishness, slacking, corruption, seeking the limelight, and so on, are most contemptible, while selflessness, working with all one's energy, whole-hearted devotion to public duty, and quiet hard work will command respect."[27]

The words of Mao continue to be studied in China with Jesuit-like fervour, but also with the utmost cynicism. Party members certainly understand their duty but have developed an ability to interpret these duties in self-serving ways. Thus they have come to believe that serving the Party, the nation and the masses is best achieved by securing the position of the Party elite. This piece of sophistry involves some challenging contortions, nowhere more so than in Hong Kong, where the regime is desperate to exercise absolute control. In its efforts to do so since the start of the 2019–20 uprising, China's leaders are undermining the "one country, two systems" concept by the day and, by so doing, risk destroying the very system that preserves their wealth. Beijing appears to understand that a sharp military crackdown would have an immediate impact on the personal interests of the regime's elite, but appears to believe that the same is not true of cracking down on Hong Kong's open, internationally connected commercial system, which has always been underpinned by the rule of law and the freedoms required to create a truly international financial centre. In the bizarre, hermetically sealed world of a dictatorship perfectly capable of delusion, it is fondly imagined that absolute political control over Hong Kong and a clampdown on its freedoms are somehow compatible with the SAR's ability to continue functioning as a global financial hub.

This assertion is yet to be truly tested, and it has yet to be revealed whether the destruction of "one country, two systems", built up over more than twenty years, can in fact be destroyed in very short order. But the devastation of Shanghai's role in international business in the wake of the Communist Revolution might serve as an uncomfortable reminder of the speed at which an international centre can indeed be dismantled. Another example comes from the destruction of Lebanon's role as the commercial centre of the Arab world, in the wake of the civil war that began in 1975. Cosmopolitan Beirut collapsed with alacrity, even though there was no replacement for it as the Middle East's commercial and financial hub.

Perhaps some of those in the Chinese leadership scratching their heads over the need for a gateway to move out their great wealth might be thinking that a number of alternatives to Hong Kong exist. The problem (see Chapter 12) is that they do not, and at the time of writing there is a global trend toward greater business transparency, accountability and supervision of business. Finding a replacement for Hong Kong is therefore becoming infinitely more difficult. Havens are not two a penny.

Notwithstanding the dangers of destroying Hong Kong as an open society, members of the Chinese regime appear to believe the risks are worth taking. Some of them may even have already secured sufficient transfer of their wealth much further overseas so as not to worry too much about Hong Kong. The Tax Justice Network pointed this out in its 2020 report: "For added secrecy ... Hong Kong structures are often combined with structures in other jurisdictions outside the Chinese orbit. In particular, the British Virgin Islands became the secrecy jurisdiction of choice for Chinese and Hong Kong élites from the mid-1990s, amid fears of Chinese control."[28] But there is a staggering level of ignorance in Chinese ruling circles over how a free society works, and a lack of understanding of the interconnection between liberty and the functioning of commerce.

Many Party leaders may soon discover that, even though they did not send in the tanks in preference to a crackdown by other means, it is still not possible to maintain Hong Kong as an international business centre with Chinese characteristics.

12

ENDGAME?

In 1995, *Fortune* magazine carried a famous cover headed: "The Death of Hong Kong". The handover of power was just two years away, and the pundits in New York were confidently predicting that, once the British colony was handed back to China, the party would be over. The territory would be rapidly absorbed into the Mainland, depriving it of its distinctive character and freedoms.

After 1997, representatives of Hong Kong's new SAR frequently brandished this cover, smugly asserting how wrong it had been. They are no longer doing so. This in itself signals a degree of self-aware uncertainty about Hong Kong's place in the PRC, reinforced by the way that local officials have adopted fluent Beijing-speak when facing opposition both at home and abroad.

Fortune was not alone in busying itself with predictions of Hong Kong's fate under Chinese rule. The doomsters of the 1990s were matched by cheerleaders for the Mainland dictatorship, who faithfully followed the party line in predicting a "glorious future". It is tempting to declare that the truth of Hong Kong's status in the 2020s lies somewhere between these two extremes; but, and there is no need to hold the presses for this revelation, the future is hard to predict. The most that can be said is that, in the short term, the fragile edifice of liberty in Hong Kong has been shaken more than ever; yet has not entirely collapsed. It should also be stressed—because it is sometimes difficult to remember amidst the mounting crackdown—that as Hong Kong moves into 2021, it still clings to a degree of freedom that contrasts vividly with conditions on the Mainland. The question is: how long will this differentiation continue?

For a long-term view, it makes sense to draw lessons from the history of other autocratic and dictatorial regimes in the last century. This history shows that, however impregnable they appear to be, such regimes are, at end of the day, vulnerable. Beijing's insistence on the futility of revolt is taken from the standard despot's playbook: dictatorships never fail to stress their impregnability. Yet they retain a collective memory that says otherwise. The People's Republic of China is poised to surpass the longevity of other modern one-party states; it may therefore prove an exception to the rule. But it may equally follow the example of its mentor, the Soviet Union, and see its foundations shaken from the periphery. Indeed, the leaders of the Chinese Communist Party might be advised to look more carefully at how the Soviet regime collapsed.

The starting point for such an examination would have to be 1968, when the tanks from the Soviet Union and other Warsaw Pact states rolled in to crush the Czechoslovak democracy movement commonly known as the Prague Spring. As they did so, it most certainly looked as though the regime could not be shaken. One of the sternest foreign rebukes of Moscow's crackdown came from Zhou Enlai, then China's premier. His remarks at the time now make fine reading for lovers of irony. Zhou accused the Soviet Union of "fascist politics, great power chauvinism, national egoism and social imperialism", and compared the Soviet action to Hitler's invasion of Czechoslovakia in 1938.[1] His denunciation was part of widespread international criticism, but appeared to have little effect. The famous Prague Spring was suppressed, dissidents thrown into jail, order restored and, on the surface, the status quo resumed.

At the time, it was assumed that Soviet power had been enhanced, rather than weakened, by having confronted the Czechoslovak challenge. It certainly emboldened the Soviet Union to expand the global reach of its activities and to tighten its grip on its satellite states. International condemnation faded into a background of vague unease, and relations with Moscow got back on course. Yet, just two decades later, things looked very different, as it became evident that the Czechoslovak people had not forgotten what it was like to fight for liberty. In 1989 they were back on the streets, and the lumbering Soviet Union was no longer able to resist the people's demands. It lost power in Czechoslovakia not because foreign states had been helping the protestors, but because its own system was rotten and crumbling, and because a public that had tasted a moment of freedom during the Prague Spring had been prepared to seize an opportunity to do so again. Their spirit of defiance had not been extinguished by the tanks, and the activists who had been slung in jail back then were now emerging as the new leaders of the country. The play-wright Václav Havel, a prominent figure in the 1968 democracy movement, was installed as president. The Czechoslovaks were not alone: revolts flared in other Soviet satellite states in 1989, and these disturbances from the periphery ended up bringing the entire Soviet Union to its knees.

Totalitarian states meeting their downfall through unrest and revolt from the periphery is not a phenomenon confined to the Soviet Union. Throughout history, empires have crumbled and dictators who thought they would rule forever have been forced to flee, when their control has faded not at the centre of their domains, but far from the seat of power. In the twenty-first century, this has been seen in the Middle East, where revolts against entrenched dictatorships in places such as Sudan, Syria, Algeria and Tunisia all began stirring on the periphery before spreading to the centre. More pertinent to the subject of this book is China's own history, which bears eloquent testimony to this process of unrest from the periphery. It was seen during the Taiping Rebellion of the mid-nineteenth century and, decisively, in the downfall of the Qing Dynasty in 1911, a process initiated by uprisings in the south. And history may well end up recording that Hong Kong had its Prague Spring moment in 2019.

Chinese leaders are avid students of history and remain wary of any sign of rebellion, anywhere in the country. Yet the Communist Party is torn between fear of losing control and a conviction of its invincibility. The Xi regime, following the iron rule of dictatorships, believes that only the strictest discipline will ensure that it does not share the fate of the Qing Dynasty, or indeed the Soviet Union; but also that these controls will work. It is against this background that we should understand the hard line taken in Hong Kong.

The harsh crackdown on the Hong Kong uprising has been every bit as devastating as anything that could be achieved by sending in the tanks. In the modern era, repression works equally well when carried out by the men in grey suits, with their surveillance devices and their powers to implement laws that effectively create a police state, while maintaining the illusion of no change. And in Hong Kong, Beijing has a willing band of local Quislings who do enthusiastically as they are told.

* * *

Some people argue that a crackdown on Hong Kong was inevitable at some point, once Beijing's commitment to preserving the SAR's autonomy had shrivelled. However, that commitment may never have been as strong as it appeared. As we saw in Chapter

1, with his speech to the drafting committee of the Basic Law in 1987, Deng Xiaoping stressed that his vision for "one country, two systems" was to create a genuine difference between the Mainland and Hong Kong; but he also made clear that the concept of "two systems" was not designed for the political sphere. He warned of the dangers of free elections for Hong Kong and the need for Beijing to exercise ultimate control over its affairs. In other words, Deng's vision was of a freewheeling Hong Kong, dedicated to the business of business—but firmly under Beijing's political management.

The Hong Kong experiment was supposed to show China's tolerance of diversity and commitment to being a reliable member of the international community, by adhering to an international treaty granting considerable autonomy to the SAR: the 1984 Sino-British Joint Declaration on the Future of Hong Kong. But when the Joint Declaration was signed, China lacked the kind of influence and clout it has today. The PRC was, as Deng Xiaoping famously said, "keeping a low profile", and biding its time before displaying its strength. Today, China is home to the world's second largest economy and its envoys cross the world, dishing out cash here, advice there, and establishing alliances that underline Beijing's global clout. Tian Feilong, one of a group of Chinese academics regularly called upon to explain Chinese policies to overseas audiences, was uncharacteristically straightforward in explaining what it meant for the boot to be on the other foot today: "Back when I was weak, I had to totally play by your rules. Now I'm strong and have confidence, so why can't I lay down my own rules and values and ideas?"[2]

This is why the Joint Declaration is today regarded by Xi's China as a historical remnant of no practical significance. From the perspective of the Party leadership, the cost of shrugging off commitments made in a bilateral agreement is a small price to pay for decisive action to end continued defiance in Hong Kong. The international backlash cannot compare with the danger that the SAR's taste for liberty poses to the integrity of the PRC. Any concept that embodies a high degree of autonomy for a part of China was always going to come into conflict with the Party's obsessive concern over the need for control. The dissident artist Ai Weiwei is clearly of this view: in the wake of the NSL's introduction, he told the *Independent* in July 2020, "The Hong Kong situation has shown us that this authoritarian society will never give any space for discussion or negotiation. It is simply incapable of communicating with those with different ideas or ideologies."[3]

So, on the one hand, we have a dictatorship that has decided the experiment with autonomy has run its course; while, on the other, we have the people of Hong Kong, who took the offer of "one country, two systems" seriously, and who are desperately clinging on to the degree of liberty it entailed. In so doing, and it is astounding to say this, they have launched the biggest challenge to the Chinese dictatorship for at least four decades.

* * *

The idea that tiny Hong Kong could have a profound impact on the mighty Chinese Communist Party was in no one's mind at the time of the handover; but, equally, back then no one was expecting the emergence of a leader with a level of control not seen since the time of Mao Zedong. After Xi Jinping was installed in power in 2012, he began asserting his dominance; it later became apparent that this vice-like grip would spread to Hong Kong, shattering all hopes that the SAR could retain its promised high degree of autonomy.

What are the consequences of Xi's new iron fist for the Mainland? Cai Xia, a retired Central Party School professor, who used to believe in reform of the Party as opposed to an end to the dictatorship, made a startling address to an online private group; it then entered the public domain, in June 2020. She was subsequently expelled from the Party, lost her pension and had her savings confiscated. In exile in the US, Cai appeared to have abandoned her previous caution. Her blunt assessment, albeit carefully avoiding any mention of Xi by name, declared: "the Party itself is already a political zombie. And this one person, a central leader who has grasped the knife handle ... the gun barrel ... and faults within the system itself—that is: one, corruption among the officials; and two, the lack of human rights and legal protection for Party members and cadres. With these two grasped in his hands, he has turned 90 million Party members into slaves, tools to be used for his personal advantage. When he needs it, he uses the Party. When he doesn't need it, Party members are no longer treated as Party members."[6]

A huge ideological vacuum has opened up in a one-party state whose ruling body was founded on a now unwanted and unhelpfully cosmopolitan Marxist outlook: lip service is still paid, and there are many pictures of that old man with the big beard, but because the substance of Marxism is problematic, the regime has reverted to the comfort zone of every single dictatorship that has ruled in modern times—a form of hyper-nationalism mixing patriotic pride with xenophobia. Party veteran Cai still seems attached to Marxism, but also combines fatalism with a vague feeling that the present state of affairs cannot last for ever. She warned in her address that, "during the lifetime of our generation, within five years, we will witness China go through another period of major chaos. It is difficult to tell how this chaos will end. Chaos breeds ruthless characters. And then we'll walk that former path all over again. So much misfortune for the Chinese people. Maybe it's fate."

Fate only goes so far in changing society. It may spur developments but, at the end of the day, change only occurs when people make it happen. It has never been the case, even during the darkest days of the Cultural Revolution in the 1960s, that there was no diversity of opinion in China, no level of resistance to the government, nor indeed forces working within the system for a change of regime. Opposition to the Chinese Communist Party is not for the fainthearted but, then again, all dictatorships extract a heavy price for defiance; this was certainly the case during the 1989 Tiananmen protests. Yet dissent has not been extinguished.

Li Fan is the founder and director of the World and China Institute in Beijing, and an unusually outspoken reformist. He believes that the era of reform prior to 1989, and a tentative revival of reformism in the 1990s, left an indelible impression on Chinese people. In July 2020 he wrote in *Foreign Policy*: "China lacks a tradition of democracy, but during four decades of reform, relative openness, and foreign engagement, Chinese people learned about freedom, rule of law, human rights, and civil society ... even now, civil society is quietly growing. I continue to see people criticizing the government and promoting ideas of democracy, rule of law, and freedom on websites and social media. I have observed growing membership in house churches. Citizens are organizing at the local level and engaging in a wider range of activities. Farmers are organizing to protect their rights. Even more remarkable, environmental NGOs are still working to supervise conditions in their localities. Civic groups are still very active working at the community level."[7]

Maybe Li is overoptimistic about the impact of these developments, but it is important to bear in mind that, besides the big picture of an all-powerful dictatorship, there is a more nuanced picture of change taking place within Mainland society. There are also, as there have always been, indications of fracture and hints of challenge to the leadership within the Party's senior ranks—were it otherwise, the level of Xi's purges after taking power would have been unnecessary.

The regime's domestic troubles are clearly not over; and the unfinished business of events in Hong Kong could yet be the spark that lights the flame. The 2019–20 uprising gave some people on the Mainland (those who managed to leap over the Great Firewall of Chinese censorship) a glimpse of what defying the regime looked like. It's true that most people relied on state media, which portrayed events in Hong Kong as amounting to chaos, terrorist-style violence and general instability. In a nation that experienced considerable upheaval in the twentieth century, the fear of turmoil plays well to the home audience, whose members either have personal experience of it or at least are well-versed in the history. But the prominence given to the Hong Kong uprising by Chinese state media was risky, too: it provided documentary evidence that challenges to the dictatorship are possible.

Layered on top of this is the yet-to-be realised impact of declining economic growth. It was always inevitable that four decades of almost unrelenting expansion could not go on forever, but it was the shock of the coronavirus that has brought this process to a halt in an untimely fashion. Beijing aims to resume the economic momentum experienced before 2020, but this seems unlikely, not least because of the global impact of the coronavirus pandemic, and active efforts by many nations to decrease China's role in their supply chain.

* * *

Where do these developments leave Hong Kong's place within China? Before considering Beijing's intentions for the future of Hong Kong, it is worth recapping the elements of the SAR that it actually wishes to preserve—all of them in the sphere of finance and commerce. As we have seen, despite its diminished role in the Mainland economy, Hong Kong continues to play a vital role in China's financial system with its ability to raise funds from overseas as well as to channel Chinese funds abroad.

One of the biggest manifestations of this role is that Hong Kong remains by far the biggest offshore centre for Chinese corporate bond sales; crucially, these sales give Chinese corporates access to hard currency. Some US$177 billion of bonds for Chinese companies were in circulation in Hong Kong in 2019.[8] China's currency, the renminbi, is not freely convertible and remains subject to strict government controls, making it largely useless in international markets. However, by channelling funds through Hong Kong, a de-facto offshore renminbi business has been created under the control of the Hong Kong Monetary Authority, which allows certificates of deposit posted in the SAR to be used for trade overseas. The authority boasts that "Hong Kong is the global hub for trade settlement in renminbi, serving both local and overseas banks and companies".[9] Aside from this, since 2004 Hong Kong banks have been allowed to hold renminbi deposits. This facility has been widely used by corporate entities and is popular among individual bank customers. It provides another means of increasing the international tradability of the Chinese currency.

And crucially, as we have seen in the previous chapter, Hong Kong provides a vital role in safeguarding the personal financial interests of China's ruling elite. The SAR is under their control and provides a perfect base for looking after their families' wealth, shipping it overseas for safekeeping, all in a manner that cannot be undertaken within the Mainland itself. Destroying Hong Kong as a financial centre is therefore far from an attractive proposition.

The Party is in fact quite ambitious in believing that Hong Kong can continue to serve as an international business centre, and can somehow do so without the essential elements required to fulfil this role. The Beijing leadership assumes that the SAR can continue to function as an international hub despite measures that diminish the rule of law and curb freedom of expression and movement. It even believes that an international business hub can thrive despite the supervision of the dreaded secret police, now openly installed in the territory.

In many ways, as we have seen, the international business community operating both on the Mainland and in Hong Kong only has itself to blame for fostering this illusion. Beijing will have noted the supine attitude of leaders of some of the world's largest companies, who have made their way to the capital to assure their hosts they would do whatever it took to secure a slice of the Chinese market, potentially the largest in the world. CEOs have lined up to establish manufacturing bases in the PRC, where they don't need to worry about labour unrest, the workforce being as obedient as it is cheap. These corporate giants rejoiced in the fact that their hosts were welcoming, and not fussy about all those bothersome environmental and other regulations that cause headaches back home. What could possibly go wrong?

The Party leadership knows all this, and has good reason to privately snigger as it observes some of the biggest figures in the business world listening respectfully as they are lectured on their shortcomings and promised any number of rewards if they learn to play by China's rules. They must have especially enjoyed the persistent attempts by Mark Zuckerberg to get Facebook into China; he has even promised to make it Facebook-lite, to allow the social network to leap over the Great Firewall. When he tried addressing them in his faltering Mandarin, they snickered some more and shut the door in his face.

As China imposed the draconian National Security Law on Hong Kong from July 2020, Beijing made a point of ensuring that every single major company with business in the territory offered fulsome public support for the crackdown. When British-based HSBC was slow off the mark, official media taunted the bank until an impressive kowtow was made. Of course, this was not quite enough, because the Party just loves to see these major foreign companies squirm, particularly those such as HSBC whose profitability is heavily dependent on their Hong Kong operations. As we have seen, the British-controlled Cathay Pacific had to bow even lower and accept Mainland supervision of a wide swathe of its operations.

As for the major international corporations operating on the Mainland itself, they have been forced to permit Party officials to be embedded in their operations, by way of establishing Party branches which need to be consulted over business decisions. These companies even have to display the hammer and sickle, the Party's symbol, within their premises. Overseas carmakers were among the first to agree to this level of intervention, but now it can be seen among a diverse variety of firms, ranging from Disney to L'Oréal to Dow Chemicals.[10]

What the Communist Party has taken away from this collective corporate abasement, both before and during the uprising, is that it is perfectly possible to clamp down on Hong Kong's freedoms and impose laws directly from Beijing without serious repercussions from the business community. So it's unsurprising that the Chinese leadership believes that "one country, two systems" can be whittled down to the bare minimum necessary for Hong Kong to continue business as usual. The SAR will be allowed to have banking systems, investment houses and other forms of commerce that are distinct from those on the Mainland, but this is to be the sum total of the remnant of "two systems". Autonomy in political affairs and within civil society would be little more than one notch above what China allows in its other allegedly autonomous regions, where toleration of difference is reduced to harmless local customs, a façade of local leadership and very little else.

This is the plan—but what Beijing neither expected, nor has managed to get to grips with, is the enormous international fallout of its suppression of the Hong Kong democracy movement. This has had consequences not only for diplomatic relations, as we saw in Chapter 10, but is also starting to impact on economic and commercial relations. Like all authoritarians, China's leaders are profoundly cynical, and they are convinced that the rest of the world is ultimately just as cynical; that, when it comes to business, cynicism is what makes the wheels go around. At the end of the day, profit will lead, and the hapless countries that wallow in empty talk of democracy will not allow their fancy ideas to get in the way of making money.

The academic Minxin Pei has succinctly summed up this state of mind: "the [Party's] worldview is also colored by a cynical belief in the power of greed. Even before China became the world's second-largest economy, the party was convinced that Western governments were mere lackeys of capitalist interests. Although these countries might profess fealty to human rights and democracy, the [CCP] believed that they could not afford to lose access to the Chinese market—especially if their capitalist rivals stood to profit as a result."[11]

Until 2020, this calculation might have been accurate. But what is beyond reasonable dispute is that the combined impact of the Hong Kong uprising and China's handling of the coronavirus outbreak has changed the terrain for the PRC's standing with the rest of the world, as much as it has done within the nation itself.

This realisation is yet to dawn in Beijing. China's leaders, for all their avid study of what happens overseas, do not really understand the dynamics of elected governments. They have explained away the increasing foreign hostility as a product of jealousy. Even before the events of 2020, when Beijing started facing the kind of pressure from overseas that had not been seen in four decades, a commentary in the *Global Times* gave a flavour of official thinking. It said: "China needs willpower now more than ever to face all the challenges and has to keep developing through all the contemptuous looks and resentment stemming from jealousy."[12]

Defiance in the face of criticism abroad is understandable; but jealousy is hardly a sufficient explanation of why foreign governments and companies are concerned over the way that the PRC behaves. They have electorates, or customers, who see images of Chinese brutality on their television screens and lobby their politicians to respond. Moreover they have leaders who need to be seen defending their values. As we have seen, the PRC is more unpopular and more untrusted by Western public opinion than ever before. This reinforces the determination of Western governments to shift the China relationship further away from the old conceit of forming a partnership with a benign dictatorship.

More importantly, leaders of democratic nations are also expected to defend national interests. As Chinese goods flooded around the world, as foreign intellectual property disappeared down a black hole in the Mainland and re-emerged with a "Made in China" label, and as companies who had invested in the PRC encountered obstacles that Chinese companies were not facing when they went abroad, there was always going to be kickback. It came with some force in 2020, prompted by both the crude face of Chinese oppression revealed in Hong Kong and great unease over the way Beijing handled the pandemic.

President Trump was early getting in his criticism of China's behaviour and, in July 2020, FBI Director Christopher Wray laid out in the starkest terms the administration's view of the PRC. He said that China now represents "the greatest long-term threat" not only to national security, but to America's economic vitality.[13] A month later, Mike Pompeo, the US Secretary of State, doubled down on these remarks in a speech to Czech senators, where he said that the challenge from Beijing today was "in some ways much more difficult" than that posed by the Soviet Union during the Cold War. He linked this to the globalised nature of the economy, and China's large role in it: "The CCP is already enmeshed in our economies, in our politics, in our societies in ways the Soviet Union never was."[14]

America was soon joined by others who had previously been reluctant to confront China, particularly after the crackdown in Hong Kong. Much of this new backbone from the international community has been demonstrated in trade negotiations and bilateral attempts to secure a level playing field for doing business with China. It is the result of what Joerg Wuttke, President of the EU Chamber of Commerce in China, has engagingly described as "a build-up of promise fatigue".[15]

Beijing factored in an international backlash to its actions in Hong Kong, but the PRC tends to assume that Western hostility is a given—therefore it can hardly be a reason for constraint. Chinese leaders are like the infamous supporters of London's Millwall Football Club, very loyal and very aware of their unpopularity, who chant from the terraces: "No one likes us—we don't care!" Nevertheless, as we saw in Chapter 10, the Party is torn between caring and ignoring all criticism. Beijing has responded with Chinese officials mobilising the full dictionary of Cold War-style vocabulary, on the one hand denying that other nations have any right to meddle in the PRC's internal affairs, on the other hand decrying the arrogance and bullying of nations. This rhetoric disguises unease in Beijing, and a realisation that the regime is now threatened with a level of international pressure that it had assumed had been laid aside four decades ago, when Deng began opening up China to the rest of the world.

Were it just the case that a fiery war of words was underway, China could probably live with it and wait for it to go away. However, what has been happening goes beyond mere rhetoric, and has been reinforced by an intense effort to break Chinese supply chains that feed industrial companies around the world. A good example of this, and one largely overlooked in the flurry of activity in the United States, was the bipartisan initiative in February 2020 to introduce the US Pharmaceutical Supply Chain Review Act, in part in response to the coronavirus crisis, but in larger part to end reliance on China for the production of essential drugs. As suspicions and resentment have grown, countries in Asia—notably Vietnam, Myanmar and Thailand—have been delighted to welcome foreign companies who once relied on China for low-cost supplies. The PRC's biggest technology companies—not least the telecommunications giant Huawei—have gone from being accepted and welcomed as leaders in telecoms infrastructure, with a big retail presence, to being viewed as hostile parties using their presence overseas to spy on foreign countries.

Then there is the big question of intellectual property exchange, which has become acutely political, with overseas companies increasingly accusing China of stealing. Companies doing business in the PRC used to be reluctant to talk about this sort of thing, but in 2019 the CNBC Global CFO Council published a survey taken among some of the world's largest companies. The study found that a third of the twenty-three participating companies, whose collective market value totals almost US$5 trillion, said that they had suffered intellectual property theft by Chinese firms in the past decade.[16] China has always denied that such thefts were occurring, but in December 2018 it published a statement setting out thirty-eight punishments for intellectual property violators. This response shows that the issue has done much to lower trust in doing business with China, and that this is of concern to Beijing. Trust is a valuable commodity that is hard to regain once lost.

A great deal has flowed from these developments, markedly in terms of the American response starting with a trade war, bans on Chinese companies operating in the US, diplomatic relations being threatened by consulate closures, economic sanctions on individuals accused of undermining human rights in Hong Kong, curbs on media organisations by both China and the US, and even a hint of military confrontation in the South China Sea. It is quite a list.

The trend of turning away from friendship with Beijing, and specifically from collaboration with Chinese business, by no means amounts to the end of China's role as the world's manufacturer; but it almost certainly marks the end to the consistently expanding trajectory of China's economic reach.

This is well recognised in China itself, where the official media started pushing a new "dual circulation theory" in 2020—a typically cumbersome way of explaining that the PRC has to become more self-reliant. This new emphasis is a tacit admission that the kind of co-operation China has enjoyed with big companies overseas is likely to be considerably reduced, thus lowering access to overseas technology. Essentially, "dual circulation" means ramping up domestic consumption of Chinese goods to replace the shortfall in overseas demand, and aiming to create self-sufficiency in key components, notably semi-conductors. China's five-year plan for 2021–5, unveiled in November 2020, has enshrined this theory into the state's official programme. Yet it is far from certain whether domestic demand in a slowing economy can take up the slack. Around a third of the nation's non-farm jobs are tied up with the export industry—that equates to 180 million workers, a significant number of whom will need to be redeployed.[17] All in all, trade accounts for around 17 per cent of the PRC's gross domestic product.[18]

* * *

What's more, while Beijing has tacitly accepted that the fallout from the coronavirus and the clampdown in Hong Kong will have serious implications for the way that the Mainland economy develops, it has yet to face up to the even more profound economic implications for the SAR. Indeed, it is not an exaggeration to say that, since the introduction of the National Security Law in July 2020, a massive question mark now lurks over whether the SAR remains fit for purpose as the middleman for China's international commerce.

As we have seen, a number of Western states—including the US, Britain, France and Germany—have already terminated extradition agreements with Hong Kong because they lack confidence in the rule of law under the National Security Law, and blacklisted the SAR as a recipient of military, policing and surveillance equipment. This change in relations at government level has also been reflected in the stance of Western corporate giants, too. After the NSL came into force, the tech giants Facebook, Google, Twitter, Zoom and Microsoft all announced that they were pausing their policy of accommodating Hong Kong government requests for users' data. In August, the American Chamber of Commerce in Hong Kong surveyed its members and found that over a third of respondents were considering moving assets and operations overseas, in light of the US government's sanctions on the SAR following the imposition of the NSL, and in light of the law itself. Some 69 per cent declared themselves to be either somewhat or extremely concerned over the impact of the legislation. Only 21 per cent were not concerned.[19]

How this will play out in the long term for Hong Kong's economy very much depends on the extent to which Hong Kong comes to resemble a run-of-the-mill police state. Upping sticks and moving offices abroad is a big step, and organisations and people will only go this far under extreme pressure—most will wait and see. But there is always a breaking point.

If there really is an exodus of global business from the SAR, what will Beijing do?

Chinese officials have hinted that they see no problem in Shanghai taking over Hong Kong's role. These hints have been bolstered by support for Shanghai's stock exchange, the build-up of the Pudong area as a financial centre, and the focus on getting foreign financial firms to set up in the city. Modern Shanghai certainly has the appearance of a leading international business centre. The gleaming towers that puncture the skyline are filled with offices of some of the world's biggest companies. But the regime misunderstands the reality of what's going on in Shanghai. It sees a city that looks as if it is world-class (closer examination of some parts of the sprawling metropolis tell another story) and it concludes that it is only a matter of time before the rest of the world shares its vision.

What Beijing overlooks is that very few of the international companies who have set up shop in Shanghai want to have regional, let alone global, headquarters established there. They still need to sign contracts in a jurisdiction where they have confidence in the rule of law. They require open access and freedom to obtain information that is crucial in decision-making. Most of all, they only really feel comfortable operating in a location that can provide guarantees of consistency and predictability, whereas they know that, in a dictatorship, rules can change fast and there is no hope of redress.

International companies doing business in China are prepared to have offices in Shanghai, some of them quite extensive; but these are there for the sole purpose of conducting transactions in the Mainland market. If they can underpin these transactions by signing contracts elsewhere, they will do so; and if it is possible to conduct sensitive parts of their business elsewhere, they will certainly do this as well.

The stock exchanges of both Shanghai and Shenzhen have enjoyed phenomenal expansion, but still mainly cater for the local market. International investors keen to secure a stake in Chinese equities head to Hong Kong—essentially because they value the protection given to their investments by the local legal system. Moreover, currency transfers are easier, and the regulation of the SAR market is more transparent.

The argument used to be made that Hong Kong could command a premium price because it possessed freedoms and flexibilities that did not exist on the Mainland. But now, as the two systems move closer together, will the SAR still be able to attract international business at that price?

Here we come to the CCP's ultimate conundrum in Hong Kong, even if the Party itself doesn't quite grasp it. For its own purposes, in terms of both economic prosperity and personal financial interests, the leadership must preserve the "special" part of the Special Administrative Region; yet it cannot allow dissent and calls for reform to go unchecked, for fear of other parts of China taking inspiration. Hong Kong will be lost if the regime goes too far in imposing Mainland-style control, and yet the regime is obsessed over the dangers of loss of control if it does not go far enough. To stamp out the defiance, Beijing's toolbox has been reduced to little more than a single weapon: the hammer which cracks down on any sign of trouble. The more flexible means of control have been abandoned; the pretence that truly free elections are tolerated or that freedom of expression can survive is barely made. The Party appears to be confident that the blunderbuss has worked, and that the Hong Kong uprising has been definitively put down, as dissidents have learned the cost of resisting the inevitable.

The crackdown in the SAR has been so extensive that no sector of civil society is spared. Beijing is confident that Hong Kong's unruly people have been brought to heel and that the way has been opened for a bright, trouble-free future under the firm control of the Party leadership. The Xi regime now wants to see the full integration of Hong Kong into the People's Republic, most likely within the newly created Greater Bay Area that spans neighbouring Guangdong and Macau. This is despite the fact that Deng Xiaoping, the father of the "one country, two systems" concept, frequently said that the idea of full integration for Hong Kong was never in his mind.

Beijing's endgame in Hong Kong, therefore, is an improbable combination of the terrifying and the unrealistic, albeit never bluntly spelled out. The Party is keen to extinguish all remaining embers of liberty in the SAR, and to force its people into acceptance of the new order. China's leaders really believe that it is possible to have "Hong Kong without Hong Kong characteristics". But Hongkongers themselves may yet prove them wrong.

* * *

Hong Kong's battered and bruised opposition is clearly aware of the Party's thinking, and is braced for an acceleration of the clampdown. In the short term, the prospects for open defiance have probably become too risky for the millions of people who once thought it was safe to come onto the streets to protest. But this doesn't mean an end to the democracy movement. Far more likely in the current circumstances are new and highly inventive forms of passive protests.

Examples already abound. When the police invaded the *Apple Daily* offices on 10 August 2020, calls immediately went out on social media for people to buy shares in the paper's parent company, as a means of expressing solidarity. At one point that day, the share value rose by over 300 per cent. By midnight, when the first copies of the paper were hitting the streets, they were immediately sold out; the presses rolled again and again to keep up with demand. In the face of a boycott by most commercial advertisers, readers have flooded the newspaper's pages with small ads offering support. When it became clear that the slogan "Liberate Hong Kong, Revolution of Our Times!" had been banned, people started displaying blank sheets of paper; everyone quickly realised what they meant. The banning of the protest movement's anthem, *Glory to Hong Kong*, quickly led to the song's words being replaced by numbers. In September 2020 during the Hungry Ghost Festival—when Chinese people honour the dead and burn incense and various forms of papercraft symbolising things that the spirits may need, such as clothing and gold—protestors added new elements to the offerings, from ballot boxes to various pieces of demonstrators' paraphernalia.

Hongkongers are quick adapters. They have learnt the language and practice of resistance in a myriad of new ways. Like the citizens of the former Soviet Union and its satellite states, they will not let the spirit of defiance fade. They simply have to find new ways of keeping it alive. As Hong Kong buckles down to the reality of the white terror sweeping through the SAR, humour is going to be a formidable tool of defiance, and Hongkongers are learning to use it. Of course, it is not as dramatic as millions of people protesting on the streets; but the flame of resistance keeps burning until something happens to trigger the realisation that there is a chance for change.

So, how do the protestors see the endgame for Hong Kong? The immediate answer is that the opposition is divided; unanimity is, after all, a privilege reserved for dictatorships. Yet there are two broad objectives on which they all agree. The first is for Hong Kong to recover the high degree of autonomy it was originally promised; the second is that progress needs to be made towards achieving a democratically elected government. Since the crackdown, achievement of these objectives seems to have moved further and further away—yet Hong Kong's mini-constitution embraces both concepts.

Beyond these key aspirations, there are greatly differing views among the people who have poured onto the streets, who languish in prison in unprecedented numbers, and who face persecution on multiple levels. However, their greatest hope, at least for the time being, has been voiced by a young protestor quoted earlier in this book: that Beijing will at least leave them alone. This is hardly likely; but nor was Hong Kong's stubborn resistance to tyranny.

Well before the National Security Law was introduced, the protest leader Joshua Wong wrote that, "no matter how grim the future looks, I refuse to give in to the growing sense that there is nothing we can do and that Hong Kong is finished as the clock ticks down to 2047"—a reference to the year when the "high degree of autonomy" was originally supposed to end.[20] And, on the day before the NSL came into force, Lester Shum, another of the better-known young democracy leaders, wrote on Facebook that "twenty-three years have passed [since the handover] and Hong Kong people have not succumbed to tyranny. In the past few years, they have been at the forefront of fighting tyranny globally. I do not believe that a national security law can change this position, and I will never believe it ... The city is definitely not dead."[21]

Shum's view is supported by a Reuters-commissioned poll that was published in August 2020, after the National Security Law had been imposed and once the roundup of opposition figures was well underway. By comparison with the previous, pre-NSL survey in June, Reuters recorded a slump in support for the protest movement as such, but a greater level of support for its aims. For example, 70 per cent of respondents were now in favour of an independent inquiry into police activity during the uprising; support for an amnesty for arrested protestors had risen to almost 50 per cent; and demand for universal suffrage was steady at 63 per cent.[22]

The difference between supporters of the democracy movement and the leaders of the Communist Party is that the latter deeply distrust Hongkongers, while the former are convinced that the people will prevail. As we've seen throughout this book, the Xi and Lam governments are pathologically incapable of seeing themselves as part of the problem, instead viewing Hong Kong's protestors as the defect in need of correction. The regime is just as blind to the nature of its own people as it is to the nature of foreign democracies and corporations.

Many people in Hong Kong, probably too many, expect that pressure from outside will save the SAR from the worst excesses of the dictatorship. In reality, nations overseas are quickly distracted from what happens beyond their borders and will always put their own interests first. Ultimately, Hong Kong's fate can only be determined by its people. But, as this book has hopefully shown, there is every reason to believe that Hongkongers will continue demonstrating the same resilience and creativity that drove the 2019–20 uprising.

Maria Ressa, the impressively brave Filipino journalist and human rights activist, offered a powerful call to arms in a documentary about her: "Every generation gets the democracy it deserves, so fight for your rights. Fight for democracy."[23] No one has ever pretended that this fight is an easy one—on the contrary, as research by Richard Youngs has shown, only a third of pro-democracy protests since 2010 have yielded any kind of success.[24] It is also axiomatic that, in a fight against a dictatorship, the ruling power will possess superior force and access to superior resources. But all of that counts for nothing once the majority of people see that change is possible and lose their fear of their rulers.

Defying the dragon of the Chinese regime involves sacrifice and determination. Both are qualities that have characterised the Hong Kong spirit and its incredible history of overcoming adversity. As Lester Shum said: "The city is definitely not dead."

APPENDIX I

TIMELINE OF THE PROTESTS, THE VIRUS AND THE US–CHINA TRADE WAR (2019–21)

2019

Feb 15—Hong Kong government introduces amendment bill to allow extradition of Hong Kong residents to the Mainland.

March 31—First protest against the bill draws 12,000 marchers.

April 24—Long prison sentences handed out to leaders of 2014's civil disobedience "Umbrella Movement".

April 28—Second protest against the extradition bill joined by 130,000 people.

May 20—Government seeks to fast-track bill through legislature (Legco), bypassing normal procedures.

May 30—In response to concerns raised, primarily by business groups, government announces amendments to the bill.

June 1—As US–China trade war escalates after a year-long battle, China imposes tariffs on US$60 billion worth of US goods.

June 4—Annual commemoration of 1989 massacre of democracy protestors at Beijing's Tiananmen Square draws 180,000 people, far higher than attendance in previous years.

June 9—Record turnout of some 1 million protestors objecting to the extradition bill.

June 12—Legco surrounded by protestors, thwarting second reading of the bill. Police react with heavy riot gear and designate protestors as "rioters". More tear gas used on one day than during the entire Umbrella Movement.

June 15—Chief Executive Carrie Lam announces a "pause" in enacting the bill. First of a number of protestor deaths recorded when 35-year-old Marco Leung falls off a walkway near Legco (suicide suspected).

June 16—Largest march in Hong Kong's history sees some 2 million people protesting against the bill.

June 21—Some 30,000 protestors surround police headquarters as allegations of police brutality mount.

June 26—Protestors call on G20 countries to support Hong Kong protests. A small section of the 80,000-strong crowd at the march move on for a second siege of police HQ. Tentative truce in Sino-US trade war agreed, with US pausing 25 per cent tariffs on US$300 billion worth of Chinese goods.

July 1—Twenty-second anniversary of the Hong Kong handover marked by mass rally of some 500,000 people. Younger protestors break into Legco building, ransacking it and causing damage leading to shutdown of the council.

July 7—First sign that demonstrations are moving from the centre of town to the districts, with a 230,000-strong march in Kowloon.

July 9—A Lennon Wall "census" finds that 165 walls in almost every district have been established; citizens post comments and posters on these in support of the protests—a homage to the walls erected in memory of the late John Lennon during the 1968 Czechoslovak uprising against the Soviet Union.

July 21—Police order a partial ban on a march drawing 430,000 people, with a significant number ending up outside China's Liaison Office: state emblem is defaced, stirring an outpouring of rage from Beijing. Later in the day, an organised mob of thugs with Triad backgrounds attack protestors and others at a train station in Yuen Long, north Hong Kong. Police do not intervene for some 40 minutes, allowing serious injuries to occur.

July 26—First of several airport sit-ins, designed to focus international attention on the protests.

APPENDIX I

Aug 1—US Treasury designates China a currency manipulator; additional tariffs imposed on Chinese goods.

Aug 3–5—Protests break out in a number of localities, marked by increasing levels of violence and arrests.

Aug 6—Chinese government ramps up response to protests with warnings of Beijing's willingness to intervene, threatening that "Those who play with fire will perish by it" and that protestors should not underestimate the "firm resolve and immense strength of the central government". Mainland media broadcasts images showing 12,000 People's Armed Police in a riot control exercise across the border in Shenzhen. In following days, more exercises held and given wide coverage.

Aug 9–12—Sit-ins at airport lead to heavy flight disruption. Mainland hits out at Cathay Pacific Airways for allowing staff to participate, demands sackings of staff and firing of top management. Swire Pacific, Cathay's parent company, backs down, orders tight control on staff, fires two most senior officers; subsequently chairman also forced to resign.

Aug 18—Third million-plus rally held, despite partial police ban, and accompanied by solidarity protests in some thirty-seven cities around the world.

Aug 23—Another protest, designated the Hong Kong Way, emulating 1989's massive anti-Soviet human-chain demonstrations in the Baltic states (Estonia, Latvia and Lithuania).

Aug 24—Mass Transit Railway begins process of closing stations near where protests are planned in order to minimise attendance—this later escalates with closures of entire system and an effective curfew, with network shutting down at night.

Aug 25—Water cannon deployed for first time as police ramp up tactics to subdue protests. Despite pledge of selective use, water cannon henceforth routinely deployed and made more effective by adding blue dye with stinging agents.

Aug 31—Protests in working-class Mong Kok/Prince Edward areas culminate in incident at MTR station where police attack passengers on trains—unfounded rumours allege fatalities. This area establishes itself as centre of violent, late-night protests. First appearance on YouTube of *Glory to Hong*

Kong, becoming anthem of the protest movement, henceforth heard at all rallies.

Sept 2—China lodges case at World Trade Organization against allegedly unlawful US tariffs.

Sept 2–30—School students all over Hong Kong take part in human chains, stirring alarm and anger in official circles.

Sept 3—Carrie Lam announces withdrawal of extradition bill, a move castigated by protestors as "too little, too late".

Sept 5—US and China agree to thirteenth round of trade talks.

Sept 8–Dec 1—All marches now banned by police on grounds of preventing rioting.

Sept 19–20—Mid-level trade talks begin against background of China and US agreeing to exempt wide range of goods from additional tariffs.

Sept 26—Government launches "public dialogue" at a tightly policed meeting, giving citizens an opportunity to quiz Lam and other officials. Supposedly the first in a series of meetings, but no more held.

Sept 29—Escalating overseas support for Hong Kong uprising in seventy-two cities, marking Global Anti-Totalitarianism Day.

Oct 1—China marks seventieth anniversary of CCP rule with largest ever military parade in Beijing; official ceremony in Hong Kong confined to an indoor venue as protests flare over the entire territory. Unprecedented number of arrests and first police shooting of a protestor with live ammunition.

Oct 4—Carrie Lam evokes colonial-era emergency powers, starting with ban on face masks after agitation from police force seeking to identify protestors. Ban triggers new wave of protests. MTR network closed "until further notice".

Oct 11—After week-long shutdown of MTR system, limited service resumes. Legco sessions also resume for first time since July.

Oct 29—Joshua Wong, arguably Hong Kong's most famous protest leader, banned from standing in November district council elections.

Nov 1—China wins its unlawful tariffs case at WTO, giving it the right to retaliate.

APPENDIX I

Nov 4—Chow Tsz-lok, a 22-year-old student, seriously injured while escaping police during an anti-protest operation.

Nov 8—Chow dies, becoming the first fatal victim of a police operation. Vigils held in ten locations around Hong Kong. Protests mount with campuses at epicentre; classes cease in universities.

Nov 11—Call for citywide strike gets lukewarm response, but shooting of another protestor, again at point blank range, leads to intensification of protests. Remarkably protestor, aged 21, survives but is subsequently charged.

Nov 12–13—Protestors erect road blocks, occupy university campuses.

Nov 17–29—Centre of clash moves to Polytechnic University, which falls under siege for twelve days, resulting in mass arrests, daring escapes from campus and considerable vandalism. Leads to an unprecedented 213 people charged for rioting.

Nov 18—High Court rules that face mask ban is unconstitutional.

Nov 19—Beijing slams High Court ruling, saying all constitutional matters can only be determined by executive of the National People's Congress (China's rubber-stamp parliament).

Nov 24—Landslide win for democrats at district elections following record turnout and routing of pro-China parties, who have held control of district councils since they were established.

Nov 26—US issues new guidelines, clearly aimed at China, to protect telecom networks from importing equipment and technology capable of threatening national security.

Nov 27—US President Trump signs into law Hong Kong Human Rights and Democracy Act, which threatens sanctions against individuals deemed to have violated human rights in Hong Kong, and a bill banning munitions sales to Hong Kong police, both the result of bipartisan initiative.

Nov–Dec—Hard to pin down dates, but in this period first reports emerge of infectious disease in Hubei Province (capital Wuhan).

Dec 1—First authorised march since September draws 380,000 protestors but ends in violence after being banned while it is underway.

Dec 8—800,000 people march to mark both six-month anniversary of protest movement and International Human Rights Day (10 Dec).

Dec 13—Phase One of Sino-US trade deal concluded: US withdraws a number of threats to impose new tariffs on Chinese goods, China pledges to increase purchases of US goods and services by US$200bn within two years.

Dec 19—Police crackdown on Spark Alliance, one of two major organisations collecting funds to support protests. HK$70 million (US$9m) confiscated, four arrested for "money laundering".

Dec 24–9—Tests made at number of Mainland hospitals following admission of patients with unidentified form of pneumonia.

Dec 30—Wuhan medical authorities alert healthcare institutions in city to possibility of a new virus.

Dec 31—Wuhan authorities formally inform central authorities in Beijing of possible new viral infection; World Health Organization formally notified.

2020

Jan 1—Fourth protest of over 1 million marchers: begins peacefully, but ends in violence after police declare it unlawful and begin arresting participants. Authorities close down a seafood wholesale market in Wuhan City linked to cases of atypical pneumonia. Mainland security officials arrest eight people for spreading "rumours" about these cases.

Jan 3—Dr Li Wenliang, the whistleblower who spread news of virus to wider public, forced to sign confession of spreading a false statement. Forty-four people who worked at wholesale fish market have now been confirmed to have an illness linked to still-unknown virus.

Jan 4—WHO makes first public statement about cluster of cases in Wuhan. Hong Kong government announces "serious response level" to virus outbreak but does not institute border checks. Dissatisfied with performance of its top officials handling Hong Kong affairs, Beijing replaces head of Central Liaison Office.

Jan 8—*Wall Street Journal* breaks story about emergence of novel coronavirus in China.

Jan 9—Xinhua, China's official news agency, publishes interview implicitly confirming *WSJ* report. WHO also confirms the novel coronavirus, congratulating China on its rapid discovery and advising against imposition of travel restrictions; states that, according to Chinese authorities, virus does not transmit readily between humans.

Jan 11—Wuhan confirms first death of virus patient two days earlier, but says still no clear evidence of human-to-human transmission.

Jan 12—Dr Li Wenliang hospitalised with coronavirus symptoms.

Jan 13—First confirmed case of Covid-19 outside China identified, in Thailand.

Jan 14—WHO tweets that there is no clear evidence of human-to-human transmission of novel coronavirus.

Jan 15—US–China Phase One Trade deal signed.

Jan 17—US begins health screening of arrivals from Wuhan.

Jan 18—40,000 households in Wuhan City attend mass banquet to celebrate Lunar New Year, later identified as key moment in spread of the virus.

Jan 19—Spread of virus to Shenzhen (bordering Hong Kong) with first patient diagnosis.

Jan 21—Trump states at World Economic Forum that relations with China have never been better. First virus patient hospitalised in Hong Kong.

Jan 23—First protest against Hong Kong government's handling of coronavirus crisis, specifically its refusal to close border with Mainland; however, first quarantine centre opened. China closes transportation links to Wuhan. WHO Emergency Committee fails to reach agreement on declaring a global health emergency.

Jan 24—Cases mount in Wuhan; Hubei Province declares Level 1 emergency. US President Trump tweets, "China has been working very hard to contain the Coronavirus. The United States greatly appreciates their efforts and transparency."

Jan 25—Hong Kong declares health emergency, closes major entertainment venues.

Jan 26—Communist Party establishes central control body to fight virus, Premier Li Keqiang put in charge.

Jan 27—Wuhan mayor admits failure to disclose virus information in timely manner.

Jan 28—In response to rising and highly unusual expressions of anger on Chinese social media, China's Supreme Court criticises reprimand of Dr Li Wenliang and seven other Wuhan doctors accused of spreading rumours. Hong Kong begins closing border links with Mainland. President Xi meets WHO's Tedros in Beijing: they agree to send international experts to China, Tedros expresses appreciation of Chinese leader's commitment and transparency.

Jan 29—US begins evacuating citizens from Wuhan; flurry of evacuation flights organised by other countries.

Jan 30—WHO finally declares "Public Health Emergency of International Concern" but stresses confidence in China's ability to keep it under control. Trump states that China has been working very hard to combat the crisis.

Jan 31—Very high level of coronavirus cases in Hubei and 875 cases confirmed in other provinces. Trump suspends entry to US for most travellers from China.

Feb 2—WHO confirms first coronavirus fatality outside China, in Philippines on previous day.

Feb 3—Non-emergency public hospital workers in Hong Kong initiate five-day strike demanding border closure. Strikers castigated; Lam announces closure of ten border crossings out of thirteen, but says full border closure would be both "inappropriate and impractical", and "discriminatory" and "stigmatising" against Mainlanders (border finally largely closed in March).

Feb 7—Dr Li Wenliang dies as result of virus.

Feb 8—Death toll in China exceeds that of 2003 SARS epidemic, with 811 deaths recorded on the Mainland.

Feb 11—WHO decides to name the disease "COVID-19" and confirms its international spread, with Singapore worst affected outside China.

Feb 13—In second round of firings, Beijing replaces head of Hong Kong and Macau Affairs Office.

Feb 14—Hong Kong Court of Appeal overturns previous ruling on banning protests outside Legco.

Feb 16—WHO overseas expert team arrives in China.

APPENDIX I

Feb 29—China sends medical experts to Iran in first stage of overseas outreach to help tackle virus.

March 5—Edward Leung, leader widely held to have inspired the uprising and serving a six-year sentence for rioting, reported to have been transferred to a maximum-security jail. China fulfils trade deal commitments by halving tariffs on US$75 billion worth of US goods.

March 10—Xi visits Wuhan for first time in crisis; from now on China's narrative of events implies that virus has been conquered on Mainland.

March 11—WHO declares global pandemic. China donates US$20 million to WHO.

March 12—Chinese medical experts arrive in Italy, bringing supplies.

March 13—National emergency declared in US.

March 17—China begins shipping test kits to eleven countries. Trump begins long series of attacks on China's handling of pandemic, calling it "the China virus".

March 19—China reports no new local infections for first time.

March 26—China's total number of cases surpassed by US.

March 27—Hong Kong, with low infection rate, announces range of shutdowns and social distancing regulations, with emphasis on limiting public gatherings to four people.

April 9—Hong Kong Court of Appeal partially overturns ruling on mask ban; by now, however, entire population of Hong Kong wearing masks to prevent coronavirus contagion.

April 13—Chinese state bodies intervene for first time on conduct of Legco, castigating the opposition for filibustering.

April 15—Liaison Office chief Luo Huining declares China's "zero tolerance" for acts endangering national security in Hong Kong.

April 17—Beijing states that it has supervisory powers over Hong Kong government.

April 18—Fifteen of Hong Kong's most prominent pro-democracy leaders arrested on suspicion of organising and participating in unauthorised demonstrations, including Martin Lee, "Father" of the Democracy Movement, and newspaper publisher Jimmy Lai.

April 26—Small-scale democracy protests resume following coronavirus outbreak, many in shopping malls where people gather during lunch breaks.

May 6—Beijing issues warning to protestors, describing them as a "political virus".

May 8—Against background of moves to implement Phase One trade deal, US and China pledge not to allow coronavirus outbreak to push it off course.

May 15—Publication of long-awaited Independent Police Complaints Council report on policing of protests, finding that, aside from some minor problems, all police actions were lawful and appropriate.

May 18—Trump threatens permanent withdrawal of WHO funding on grounds of pro-China bias and says US will quit the organisation.

May 21—Beijing announces National People's Congress moving to impose a National Security Law (NSL) on Hong Kong.

May 28—National People's Congress passes NSL, to be imposed on Hong Kong without consulting Lam government or allowing amendment or discussion in Legco.

May 29—Trump says US will roll back some of the special preferences granted to Hong Kong; threatens sanctions on Chinese and Hong Kong officials "directly or indirectly involved in eroding Hong Kong's autonomy". UK states that, in wake of new national security legislation, it is looking at ways to grant citizenship to Hongkongers born before 1997 handover.

June 4—Legco passes legislation to outlaw disrespecting Chinese national anthem. For the first time in thirty-one years, Hong Kong government bans annual commemoration of Tiananmen Square massacre, using pretext of need to retain social distancing; thousands nevertheless mark the event in various locations.

June 18—Hong Kong scraps most social distancing regulations but maintains ban on gatherings of more than eight people, seen as a move to prevent demonstrations.

June 30—National People's Congress enacts NSL for Hong Kong.

July 1—NSL comes into force. Annual protest rally commemorating establishment of SAR banned; 370 people arrested as protests nevertheless held. First charges made under new NSL.

APPENDIX I

July 2—Nathan Law—one of the most prominent younger-generation democracy activists and a former legislator who was expelled—announces he has fled into exile abroad, where he will become a de-facto ambassador for democracy movement.

July 3—Canada becomes first country to suspend extradition agreements with Hong Kong in light of doubts over independence of the judiciary following introduction of NSL.

July 6—New Committee for Safeguarding National Security established to oversee implementation of NSL; 33-storey hotel commandeered to house the organisation from 8 July. Government announces that schools need to remove books that might breach new law.

July 8—Government announces all incoming civil servants will need to swear new pledge of allegiance.

July 10—Police raid offices of a polling organisation providing logistics for pro-democracy primaries to select candidates for September Legco election.

July 11–12—Over 600,000 voters turn out for the primaries, which government says may breach NSL.

July 14—Trump signs into law Hong Kong Autonomy Act, targeting officials deemed to have violated Hong Kong's constitutional freedoms with travel bans and banking restrictions.

July 16—Hong Kong forces expulsion of acting head of Taiwan office in Hong Kong after he refuses to pledge allegiance to "One China" policy.

July 28—Hong Kong University's governing body overrules university senate and fires Occupy organiser Benny Tai from his post as a tenured law professor.

July 29—Four student members of a disbanded pro-independence group arrested under NSL.

July 30—Twelve pro-democracy candidates disqualified from running in Legco election.

July 31—Government announces one-year postponement of Legco election on grounds of health dangers from the coronavirus pandemic. Warrants issued for arrest of six pro-democracy activists living overseas.

Aug 7—US imposes economic sanctions on Lam and ten other Hong Kong officials accused of undermining Hong Kong's autonomy.

Aug 10—Hong Kong police storm offices of opposition-supporting *Apple Daily* newspaper, arresting its founder Jimmy Lai, his two sons and four others.

Aug 11—Decision taken in Beijing to extend Legco members' term by one year, following postponement of election.

Aug 19—US joins UK, Germany, France, Canada, Australia and New Zealand in ending extradition agreements with Hong Kong.

Sept 1—Lam announces there is no separation of powers between executive, legislature and judiciary of Hong Kong government.

Sept 7—Beijing's HKMAO and Liaison Office double down on Lam's statement, declaring that lack of separation of powers was part of SAR's "guiding ideology" as laid down by Deng Xiaoping in 1987.

Sept 9—Police confirm over 10,000 people arrested in connection with protests between 9 June 2019 and 6 September 2020.

Sept 15—WTO rules that hundreds of billions of dollars' worth of US tariffs on Chinese goods violated international rules.

Oct 23—Britain confirms new scheme providing pathway to UK citizenship for Hongkongers holding British National (Overseas) passports and their dependants; 2.9 million are eligible for a BNO passport.

Nov 5—Police launch a "Stasi-style" hotline to receive tips from public on violations of NSL; two weeks later, police report 10,000 messages received in first week of operation.

Nov 11—Beijing orders disqualification from Legco of four sitting democrats, on grounds of endangering national security and seeking foreign intervention in Hong Kong affairs. The fifteen remaining pro-democracy legislators announce their resignation.

Nov 17—Mainland official announces moves to "perfect" Hong Kong's judicial system; says there must be more interpretation of Basic Law by Beijing.

Dec 2—Joshua Wong jailed for fourth time, related to 12 June 2019 demonstration outside police headquarters. Agnes Chow and Ivan Lam, long-time associates of Wong, also jailed.

Dec 3—After multiple arrests in 2019–20, publisher Jimmy Lai denied bail in a case of alleged fraud concerning use of his offices; a slew of other charges threaten lengthy incarceration.

Dec 5—Former legislator and Democratic Party member Ted Hui announces he has fled to exile in UK; police have told banks to freeze Hong Kong bank accounts of Hui and members of his family.

Dec 7—US imposes sanctions on fourteen Chinese officials accused of playing a role in expulsion of democrats from Legco.

Dec 11—Jimmy Lai appears in court on subversion charges under NSL, for "colluding with foreign powers". Hong Kong government announces purchase of 15 million Covid vaccine doses from Mainland manufacturers; Lam later says citizens won't be able to choose which vaccine they receive.

Dec 23—Following backlash, Lam announces U-turn on vaccine policy, allowing Hongkongers to choose their preferred vaccine.

2021

Jan 5—WHO announces abrupt postponement of investigation into the sources of the pandemic as China blocks visa issuance for some WHO investigators.

Jan 6—Arrest of fifty-three leading democrats charged with subversion under NSL: a law office raided, three media organisations ordered to hand over material in connection with arrests.

Jan 9—In a major reversal of diplomatic policy, United States removes all restrictions on contacts between American and Taiwanese government officials.

Jan 14—WHO investigation team finally arrive in the PRC after affirming that "this is not about finding China guilty".

APPENDIX II

WHO'S WHO IN HONG KONG POLITICS

This guide provides pen portraits of the people who have influenced, taken part in or had an impact on Hong Kong politics during the uprising. Names of Hong Kong personalities are rendered in Cantonese transliteration. The pinyin system is used for Mainland personalities. SAR officials subject to economic sanctions by the US for undermining Hong Kong's autonomy are marked as "(Sanctioned by US.)". Democrats arrested or charged under the National Security Law are marked as "(NSL target)".

Laura Cha Shih May–lung

Laura Cha, a Shanghainese by birth, is related by marriage to the powerful Cha family. She has a long history as a PRC trustee. Cha was appointed to Carrie Lam's Executive Council while serving as a delegate to the National People's Congress in Beijing. More more importantly, she was Vice-Chairman of the China Securities Regulatory Commission, a vice-ministerial rank. Cha was the first Hongkonger to join the Chinese government. A lawyer and securities regulator by trade and Chairwoman of the Stock Exchange, Cha is an active political player with hardline antidemocratic views. Among insiders, she is mentioned as a possible candidate for the post of Chief Executive.

Andy Chan Ho-tin

Born in 1990, Chan has the dubious distinction of leading the first political party to have been banned in Hong Kong. The Hong Kong National

Party is an outlier in the democracy movement, as it has openly advocated Hong Kong independence. It is hard to tell whether Chan is more interested in independence or in trying to influence the democracy movement to take a more militant stance. He has been arrested twice: once for assaulting a police officer and secondly for alleged involvement with an illegal weapons cache. At the time of writing, he has yet to be convicted on the weapons charge but was acquitted for assault, but remains high on the list of people the pro-China camp is keen to see behind bars.

Anson Chan Fang On-sang

Widely regarded as one of Hong Kong's most formidable civil servants, Chan is Shanghainese by birth, comes from a distinguished family and has spent her career in the civil service, rising to become the Chief Secretary: number two in the colonial government, the first woman and first ethnic Chinese to fill this role. She served under the last Governor, Chris Patten, and continued in post after the handover. Often described as the "Iron Lady", Chan has had a career marked by integrity and a willingness to take tough decisions. Her dismay over developments in Hong Kong led her, after retirement, to successfully run for the legislature and to become a leading representative of what might be described as the democracy movement's moderate wing. She has played a high-profile role in the movement's outreach to foreign states: to the fury of Beijing, Chan has access to the highest levels of governments overseas. Along with Albert Ho, Jimmy Lai and Martin Lee, she has been branded part of the "Gang of Four" by Mainland media, which regularly denounces this quartet for inviting foreign meddling in Chinese affairs. Following the death of her daughter in June 2020, Chan announced her retirement from public life.

Bernard Charnwut Chan

The Convenor of Lam's Executive Council, said to be a moderating voice among this non-official or non-civil-service group of advisors. Chan comes from an immensely rich Thai-Chinese family whose fortunes were founded on the Bangkok Bank. He remains heavily involved in the family's businesses alongside an impressive list of public appointments. Presumably because of his Thai background, Beijing will not trust him to become Chief Executive; but he remains highly influential, and is seen as one of the few members of the administration prepared to engage with the opposition. Amiable and cosmopolitan, Chan is a natural conciliator—but, in a political system where conciliation is not required, this is a wasted talent.

Margaret Chan Fung Fu-chun

With China's avid backing, Chan became the Director-General of the World Health Organization in 2006, making her Hong Kong's most prominent leader of a major international institution. She has had a career as a bureaucrat in the public health sector and was widely criticised for her work at the WHO. Since stepping down at the WHO in 2017, she has remained behind the scenes as part of the Mainland's United Front nexus, occasionally emerging to denounce the protests.

Teresa Cheng Yeuk-wah

In the ranks of Lam's widely disliked government, Cheng has achieved the unenviable distinction of being even more unpopular than other officials. Following a successful career as an arbitration specialist, she was appointed as Justice Secretary in 2018 and has been deeply involved in all the highly controversial legal decisions taken during the uprising. With more or less zero political instincts, she has very few friends in the legal fraternity. (Sanctioned by US.)

Matthew Cheung Kin-chung

Best described as the "bureaucrat's bureaucrat", in 2017 this civil service lifer rose to the number two job in the SAR government. Astonishingly, within the civil service he has a reputation for being a "Master of Communications"; his talents in this regard remain invisible to everyone else. Cheung is, however, a very loyal right hand to Carrie Lam, and the ultimate insider, who knows his way around the people and corridors of the civil service. As the uprising continued, he began sounding more and more like a Mainland official, able to read whatever script was put in front of him and never deviating from it.

Chi (Shih) Wing-ching

Chi is an unusual figure in tycoon circles because, despite his reliance on business in Mainland China, he is sufficiently independently minded to dare to criticise official policy. He is the founder of Centaline, one of the biggest property agencies in Hong Kong and China. He also founded a popular free daily newspaper called *AM730*, which has been boycotted by Mainland advertisers for not showing sufficient hostility to the democracy movement. Like many other tycoons, Chi is Shanghainese, but he does not come from a wealthy family and, even more unusually, was a Marxist in his youth, who became a teacher at a United Front school. Unlike other business leaders who have come to embrace the Communist Party, Chi's leftist background and lack of opportunism led him to take a distinctive and nuanced view of the protests.

Eddie Chu Hoi-dick

Chu had a long history as a social activist before winning a spectacular Legco election victory in 2016. For many years, he was an activist in the New Territories (NT) and earned the lifelong hatred of the powerful Heung Yee Kuk, which represents the interests of the NT barons. There is nothing typical about Chu, who mastered Farsi after attending Tehran University and becoming a journalist covering Iranian affairs. Born in 1977, he is considered too old to be part of the new generation of democracy activists, but is too young to be part of the older generation. He is, however, well-liked in both quarters, and admired both for his courage in confronting the Kuk and for refusing to conform, either in terms of dress or by bowing to the intense pressures he has faced as a result of his activism in the rural areas. (NSL target)

Philip Dykes

Dykes is a British-born barrister who has led the Hong Kong Bar Association for longer than any previous chairman. During the protests, he emerged as a highly vocal advocate for the rule of law. He is a constitutional and administrative law specialist who has been involved in a number of key cases where it was alleged that Hong Kong's mini-constitution was being undermined. The once British-dominated Bar has long disappeared, but Dykes has retained the strong support of his Chinese colleagues, despite a number of attempts to dislodge him. In 2020, before September's Legislative Council elections were postponed, he was nominated by the democrats to run for the legal functional constituency.

APPENDIX II

Rita Fan Hsu Lai-tai

Fan was once widely mocked as "Hong Kong's Jiang Qing", a reference to the hard-faced wife of Mao Zedong, infamous for her activities during China's Cultural Revolution. Fan moved seamlessly from being a pillar of the colonial establishment to becoming an ultra-loyalist pro-Beijing stalwart. The regime bestowed thanks by making her the first President of the SAR's Legislative Council; she also presided over its shadow body established before the handover. She went on to serve as Hong Kong's most senior member of China's rubber-stamp parliament and has become something of a semi-official spokeswoman for Beijing in Hong Kong. Her family background is interesting, as her father was involved in the notorious Shanghai-based criminal Green Gang, although she denies all knowledge of this. Fan herself took a break from politics to work for Albert Yeung, the boss of the Emperor Group.

Han Zheng

In 2018, Han, China's most senior Vice-Premier, was appointed as head of the Central Coordination Group for Hong Kong and Macau Affairs, effectively Beijing's point man for Hong Kong. His post had previously been occupied by the more senior Zhang Dejiang. As things have turned out, this offered Han the opportunity for political advancement. Events in Hong Kong have made this job far more activist than it was under Zhang. Both in public and in private, Han has been seen directing the affairs of the Hong Kong government, summoning Chief Executive Carrie Lam to public and private meetings and marshalling the senior figures within the SAR's pro-China camp. Han, a former Shanghai mayor who survived Party infighting that might have led to his demotion in the Hu Jintao era, places great emphasis on economic development. He was personally responsible for changing Beijing's narrative of events in Hong Kong, declaring the protests to be a product of economic discontent.

Aron Harilela

Following the death of his father Hari in 2014, Aron became head of Hong Kong's most influential Indian family, with diversified business interests and a long history of involvement in public affairs under both the British and Chinese administrations. Harilela Sr had maintained strong personal relationships with Hong Kong's first and second Chief Executives, having previously been close to British officials. The long-established Indian community in Hong Kong had looked to him to protect their affairs. When Aron, his eldest son, assumed responsibility for the family business, he also took on the political responsibilities and, by an accident of timing, became Chairman of the Hong Kong General Chamber of Commerce just as the 2019 protests were breaking out. This is the most influential of business organisations and Aron Harilela has used his influence to create distance between it and the unpopular Lam administration—never actually breaking ranks, but emerging as a force for moderation. He is untypical of his family, not least in having married outside the circle of Indian families originating from Sindh Province, and in bringing a more cosmopolitan outlook to the way business is conducted.

Albert Ho Chun-yan

Ho is one of the most prominent veterans of Hong Kong's democracy movement and part of the so-called "Gang of Four" demonised in the Mainland media. He managed to qualify as a solicitor despite his modest beginnings by working two jobs while studying for his law degree. He went on to become a founder of what became the Democratic Party, which he also chaired. He has twice been the subject of violent assaults, which have done nothing to dissuade him from his prominent role both in the Hong Kong democracy movement and in the wider campaign for democracy on the Mainland. In 2012, he ran for the post of Chief Executive in a pre-ordained election that he had no prospect of winning. A year later, he became internationally famous for his role as legal advisor to the American whistleblower Edward Snowden, who had sought temporary refuge in Hong Kong.

Charles Ho Tsu-kwok

A grandson of the founder of the highly lucrative Hong Kong Tobacco Corporation, Ho, a Beijing stalwart, seized the opportunity to take control of the Sing Tao newspaper group in 2001 to move himself into a position of greater political influence. His newspapers have become leading platforms for the views of the Chinese government, which regularly uses these outlets to disseminate sensitive information that, for various reasons, is not considered suitable for release via the official state-controlled media. Ho enjoys the limelight and, while remaining a firm supporter of the Party, often goes off script when airing his opinions of individuals within the pro-China camp; this is largely the result of personal disagreements, not least with Carrie Lam.

Denise Ho Wan-see

A famous singer and actress whose stellar career was stalled by her high-profile participation in the 2014 Umbrella Movement. One of the few prominent Hong Kong people to come out as a lesbian, she is also highly involved in the campaign for LGBT rights. Like all other artists in Hong Kong, Ho was dependent on performances in China and Mainland sponsorship, but has been banned from entry to the Mainland and blacklisted by all major entertainment companies for her role in the democracy movement. She remains hugely popular in Hong Kong, however, and attracts enthusiastic audiences on the rare occasions when she is allowed to perform. She has also emerged as a powerful pro-democracy advocate in the international arena.

Junius Ho Kwan-yiu

A former president of the Law Society, the fanatically pro-China Ho is constantly involved in controversies. He has deep roots in the New Territories, where he was elected as a legislator in 2016, and plays a key role in the Heung Yee Kuk, the advisory body supposed to represent indigenous Hongkongers. Taking the most hardline of anti-democratic positions, he has also proved to be a highly effective organiser for the pro-China camp, and in his private life is a prominent owner of race horses. The level of dislike he attracts from democrats is matched by the near adoration he enjoys from Beijing's supporters. Ho is, however, a more complex individual than his combative profile suggests. He was, for example, the only pro-China legislator to support a 2017 motion commemorating the Tiananmen Massacre.

Regina Ip Lau Suk-yee

A legislator who has twice attempted to become the Chief Executive, Ip has spent most of her career as a civil servant. She was always known in the service as an uncompromising and authoritarian figure, characteristics that brought her to the attention of the Chinese authorities. She left the service to become Hong Kong's Secretary for Security in 1998, and was responsible for the ill-fated plan to introduce national security legislation in 2003. Unlike the ministers who have been responsible for the equally ill-fated 2019 extradition bill, Ip resigned to take responsibility for this debacle. She subsequently ran for election to the legislature. Her first attempt, in a contest with Anson Chan, saw her soundly defeated; but Ip does not take defeat lightly and came back to win a subsequent contest. Despite evident independence of mind as an Exco member (her current position), she is careful to keep on the side of the Beijing authorities, and often adopts a leading role in advocating the most hardline of policies. Ip can be abrasive and severe, but is also known to be kind and highly supportive towards people who surround her.

Jimmy Lai Chee-ying

After arriving penniless from Shunde, Guangdong Province as a teenager, Lai worked his way up in Hong Kong and earned a fortune in the clothing business, establishing one of Asia's best-known retail clothing brands, Giordano. The Tiananmen protests spurred him to focus on politics and led him to found the mass-circulation *Next Magazine* and *Apple Daily* newspaper. Both publications have been uncompromising advocates for the democracy movement. When it became evident to Lai that his position as a publisher was undermining his other business interests, he sold his controlling stake in Giordano. Lai has suffered assaults, advertiser boycotts of his publications and even a particularly unsavoury campaign to get his Shunde relatives to disown him; yet he remains unflinching in his political and publishing activities. He is close to fellow "Gang of Four" member Martin Lee, who influenced his conversion to Catholicism. He has been subjected to a slew of arrests, most importantly for breaches of the National Security Law. The authorities finally managed to imprison him in December 2020.

Carrie Lam Cheng Yuet-ngor

Appointed Chief Executive in 2017, Lam has succeeded in becoming even more unpopular than her three unloved predecessors. A devout Catholic and believer in social justice for the underprivileged, she was loyal to the colonial regime and is even more loyal to the Mainland Communist regime. A diligent and hardworking official, she rose through the ranks of the civil service, occupying an impressive variety of jobs in key departments, but Lam is utterly devoid of charisma or empathy with the people. Her achievement in becoming Hong Kong's first female leader and her genuine commitment to public service are likely to be overshadowed by her failure in the job of Chief Executive, which has led most of the government's longest-standing allies to turn against her. However, they continue to nominally back her under orders from Beijing to do so—for now. (Sanctioned by US.)

Kenneth Lau Ip-keung

No one would be surprised if an empty car drew up and the unassuming Kenneth Lau stepped out. Yet, having inherited the chairmanship of the Heung Yee Kuk from his father Lau Wong-fat, he occupies a highly influential position as leader of the body supposedly representing the interests of Hong Kong's indigenous citizens. The word "supposedly" is appropriate because the Kuk only supports the rights of males. The organisation has influence totally disproportionate to its size. The former colonial power lavished privileges on this body, fearing its potential for stirring revolt among the rural population. When the prospect of Chinese rule loomed, the wily Lau Sr was quick to transfer allegiance to the new source of power and volunteer its membership as the shock troops of the new order. Kenneth Lau has stepped into his shoes—without an ounce of charisma, but taking on the major posts his father used to occupy in the legislature and on the Executive Council. As he rarely speaks in public, and sticks tightly to the script when he does, Lau's real views are unknown. He is mainly a figurehead, holding together a rather combustible coalition of village chiefs who tolerate him because their intense rivalry would get out of control if he stepped down. The Lau family's extensive land holdings have made him very rich.

Nathan Law Kwun-chung

Following his controversial self-exile to Britain in 2020, Law has become the protest movement's de-facto roving ambassador, interacting with a very wide range of leading foreign government officials, journalists and others. In September 2016, at the age of 23, he became the first leader of the

Umbrella Movement to be elected to the Legislative Council, the youngest ever legislator. The following year, he was expelled and subsequently jailed for his activities during the 2014 protests. Law is slightly older than the other new-generation protest leaders, notably shy on a personal level and more thoughtful than some of his firebrand colleagues. Born across the border in Shenzhen, he came to Hong Kong at the age of 6 and was brought up more or less single-handedly by his mother. Despite his family's modest means, he managed to enter university, where he quickly became a student leader. Although not a founder of Scholarism, the movement that propelled Joshua Wong to international fame, Law quickly became a key part of the pro-democracy leadership. A warrant for his arrest on grounds of breaching the National Security Law was issued in 2020. The UK, however, will not extradite him.

Lee Cheuk-yan

A veteran trade unionist and democracy advocate, he has also been a leading figure in support of the democracy movement on the Mainland, where he was detained by the authorities in 1989 for handing over cash to Tiananmen protestors. A co-founder of Hong Kong's Labour Party, he has always emphasised workers' issues. There is something indefatigable about Lee, who seems to be equally at home on the streets as protestor, working as a legislator and going to court, either to defend himself or other democrats. Although Lee is clearly a member of the "Old Guard", he seems to have a better rapport with the younger generation of protestors than some of his contemporaries.

John Lee Ka-chiu

As Carrie Lam's Secretary for Security and therefore nominally responsible for the police, he has scuttled away from exercising political control, yet has become the government minister vying with Teresa Cheng for top spot in the list of unpopular officials. A former Chief Superintendent of Police who has spent most of his career away from the frontlines, happily dealing with administration, Lee brings a clear police perspective to his role as a government minister. He was invisible most of the time during the uprising, only to pop up on occasion to echo whatever had been said by the police leadership. (Sanctioned by US.)

APPENDIX II

Mark Lee Po-on

The low-profile Lee figures on this list by virtue of his role as CEO of TVB, Hong Kong's dominant terrestrial broadcaster, which—despite regulations that do not permit control by non-residents—is firmly under the control of Mainland business entities. Lee, an accountant by trade, has no experience of the entertainment and news industries that are TVB's bread and butter, but he is a reliable front for the people who control the station. TVB has drawn increasingly close to Beijing and is regularly denounced by protestors for being little more than an extension of the state media apparatus. However, this is to ignore the station's rich history in Hong Kong's popular culture and its role as the main news provider for a large swathe of the population. Lee presides over a station with a fast-shrinking audience, especially among the young. If he has any big ideas for reviving the glory that was once TVB, he is keeping them firmly under wraps.

Martin Lee Chu-ming

Widely known as the "Father of Democracy" in Hong Kong, the patrician Lee has been a leading figure in the movement since the 1980s. He cofounded what was to become the Democratic Party and, with the late Szeto Wah, became the de-facto leader of the democratic camp. In the days before the handover, when Beijing officials were still talking to opposition figures, both Lee and Szeto had a role in drafting the Basic Law, though their involvement ground to a halt in the wake of the Tiananmen Square massacre. However, Lee, son of a Kuomintang Lieutenant-General, had maintained wary but consistent contacts with Chinese officials, partly based on his father's high standing with the Communist leadership, despite his intense anti-Communism. Lee became a dominant figure in the colonial legislature and worked closely with Chris Patten on electoral reform; he also chaired the Bar Association. He has become a familiar face on the international human rights circuit, maintaining contacts with the most senior levels of the British and American political systems. This high international profile also accounts for China castigating him as part of the "Gang of Four". By contrast, many of the younger protestors see him as a too-moderate relic of the past who is of declining relevance. However, having been arrested in April 2020 for involvement in an unauthorised demonstration, Lee declared himself relieved to be standing alongside the thousands of young people who had shared this fate.

Lee Shau-kee

Probably the richest man in Hong Kong, against stiff competition, Lee controls Henderson Land and a web of associated companies anchored by the profits of property development. He is affectionately known as Uncle Four, as he is famously the fourth-born in his immigrant family, who originate, like Jimmy Lai, from Shunde, Guangdong Province. In theory, Lee is now retired and has handed over the running of his businesses to his two sons in favour of focusing on his numerous philanthropic endeavours, but people like Lee never really retire. Although he is courted by politicians and plays a nominal role in Beijing bodies, he eschews direct political involvement; he simply maintains a sufficiently pro-China position to safeguard his business interests. He judiciously funds and gives support to United Front organisations, but by choice is not prominent in these endeavours.

Starry Lee Wai-king

Lee, the Chairwoman of Hong Kong's biggest political party, the Democratic Alliance for the Betterment and Progress of Hong Kong (DAB), has enjoyed a stellar political career. In 2015, she replaced the old-school Communist Party member Tam Yiu-chung (see below) as leader of the DAB, with the aim of giving it a fresher, less obviously "Party" image. Despite serving in a number of prominent roles, including membership of the Executive Council, it is hard to think of a single distinctive thing Lee has achieved. Although she is personally engaging, she appears to have had all signs of charisma surgically removed. But she is compliant, can be relied upon to only occasionally stumble when reading out a pre-prepared script, and is sufficiently amiable to maintain peace among the big egos vying for position in the DAB. Coming from a working-class family and being seen very much as a "local" provides her with credibility in a party that nominally supports the interests of working people.

Leung Chun-ying

Appointed as Hong Kong's third Chief Executive in 2012, both he and his wife are offspring of police officers. There has always been extensive speculation about whether Leung is a member of Hong Kong's underground Communist Party, but whether he has actually joined the ranks matters little: since his student days he has been a stalwart supporter. This is despite the fact that he studied in England, sent both his daughters overseas to study and has spent most of his working life in the employment of foreign companies. Such was the backlash against his first term as Chief Executive (2012–17) that Beijing declined to grant another, but kept him close and gave him face by making him one of the many Vice-Chairmen of the National Committee of the Chinese People's Consultative Conference, a tier down from China's rubber-stamp parliament. Since handing over to Carrie Lam, Leung has taken up the role of Beijing's attack dog, issuing a constant flow of statements via Facebook calling for hardline action against the democracy movement, offering rewards for the arrest of protestors, calling for all manner of public officials to be sacked, and launching a number of legal actions in relation to accusations against him of corruption in public office. Neither the accusations nor Leung's lawsuits have proved to be conclusive. Largely friendless, as he has a habit of falling out with allies, Leung remains in Beijing's good books as one of the most loyal of the loyal.

Edward Leung Tin-kei

Widely known as the spiritual leader of the 2019–20 uprising, despite having been incarcerated throughout. In 2018, he was given a six-year jail sentence for rioting and police assault. His influence on the protests stems from coining the slogan "Liberate Hong Kong, Revolution of Our Times!", and from having been an early advocate of stepping up direct action to assert Hong Kong's autonomy. As a founder of the movement called Hong Kong Indigenous, he has angered the authorities and inspired protestors by emphasising the particular identity of Hongkongers and their distinctiveness from the Mainland. Interestingly, he is one of the few younger-generation protest leaders to have been born across the border, although he grew up in Hong Kong. Leung may be cerebral and not obviously charismatic, but there is something about his strength of conviction and ability to put into words what many ordinary Hongkongers were thinking. After performing unexpectedly well in a 2016 byelection, he was among those barred from contesting that year's Legco election. Leung is somewhat distant from other prominent figures in the democracy movement, but his name was often evoked during the uprising.

Elsie Leung Oi-sie

Appointed as the Hong Kong SAR's first Justice Secretary, Leung is almost certainly one of the core members of the local underground

Communist Party. She is from a leftist family and was also one of the founders of the DAB. Leung has served on a great number of official Hong Kong committees as well as Mainland bodies. Ascending to the top legal job despite a largely unimpressive legal career specialised in matrimonial law, Leung has failed to win wide support within the legal community. A diminutive and graceful person, she has been steadfast in her allegiance to the Mainland, but is never aggressive in her support. Even her opponents concede that she is a civil and patient adversary. Unlike a number of other prominent Chinese flag-wavers who switched allegiance to the Mainland once the handover drew near, Leung had always been a supporter and is respected for her consistency.

Leung Kwok-hung

Better known as "Long Hair", Leung is, by any standards, an unusual figure: a Marxist from an early age, a full-time activist for most of his life, and an avid football supporter. Leung's signature look makes him unmissable in his natural habitat, out on the streets. He formed the League of Social Democrats, the most radical of the traditional political parties. Elected three times as a legislator and expelled from the chamber and jailed on multiple occasions, he has now effectively been barred from standing for election. As the radicalism of younger protestors has risen, Leung has appeared to be less radical, and faces criticism for his non-violent principles. However, by force of personality and his willingness to turn up to every protest, Long Hair continues to be a major figure in the democratic movement.

Andrew Li Kwok-nang

A distinguished and highly respected lawyer, Li was the SAR's first Chief Justice, from 1997 to 2010. His work in this post has had a lasting influence and his successors have been judged against the high benchmark he set. Li resigned before the end of his term, leading to speculation that this was the result of pressure from Beijing—something he has neither confirmed nor denied. He is reserved and has been sparing in making public comments since retirement; but when he does so, as he has in expressing concerns over the rule of law, his comments receive careful attention. He has also been a mentor to a number of lawyers who have become leaders in the profession. He is a member of the Li clan, one of

APPENDIX II

Hong Kong's most prominent old money families, whose fortune is based on the Bank of East Asia.

Li Ka-shing

Probably no longer Hong Kong's richest man, but undoubtedly its most influential business leader, who used to be known as "Superman". Starting from nothing, Li has established a conglomerate with interests in property, ports, retail and wholesale businesses, hotels, electricity supply and telecommunications. With his fractured English and heavily Chaozhou-accented Cantonese, Li could easily be underestimated as a less substantial figure than he is. But he is shrewd to the nth degree, a wily trader of assets and a highly successful investor. His Cheung Kong conglomerate has ventured where most other Hong Kong tycoons fear to tread, and the business has expanded, mainly by acquisition. Although his fortune is firmly rooted in Hong Kong, in recent years Li has increasingly shifted elsewhere, divesting heavily from Hong Kong and the Mainland in favour of overseas projects. This is one of the reasons he has largely but not entirely fallen out of favour with the authorities in Beijing. The other reason is that, unlike all of the other local tycoons, he has been ambiguous rather than fulsome in support of the Party line during the uprising. In theory, he has retired from running his listed companies, handing over control to his rather anaemic eldest son Victor and giving younger son Richard the resources to buy a clutch of business holdings. However, Li Sr is far from out of the game, and it is inconceivable that he does not still exercise control behind the scenes.

Stephen Lo Wai-chung

A police bureaucrat rather than a frontline officer, Lo found himself thrust into the headlines as the uprising erupted and he was expected, as Commissioner of Police, to be the face of the force. As government officials disappeared from view, the police became the most visible remnant of the administration; but Lo, incredibly, never once visited the protest frontlines. In November 2019, he retired, much to the relief of many of the people he was supposed to be leading. His departure was marked with none of the usual eulogies and ceremonies that might have been expected. He has since faded into well-deserved obscurity. (Sanctioned by US.)

Luo Huining

Luo was brought out of pending retirement in 2020 to run Beijing's Central Liaison Office in Hong Kong, taking over from Wang Zhimin, "punished" for his failures in tackling the protest movement. In July 2020 Luo was also appointed the "advisor" to the Hong Kong Committee for Safeguarding National Security, effectively becoming its political commissar overseeing its activities. He is an economist by training, but a lifelong bureaucrat by occupation, seen as a hardline enforcer. Since arriving in Hong Kong, Luo has adopted a high-profile interventionist role, at times openly bypassing the Lam government in issuing edicts. Like many young people during the Cultural Revolution, he was sent to the countryside to "learn from the masses". He has also spent some time as a steelworker, before joining the Party in 1982.

Geoffrey Ma Tao-li

The somewhat clubbable and Anglophile Ma became Chief Justice in 2010, having previously served as Chief Judge of the High Court and held a number of other judicial jobs. He is conservative by nature and adept at treading the fine line between not angering his political bosses and adhering to the principles of the rule of law. Ma is not notably energetic but is widely known as a safe pair of hands. The importance of his role increased tremendously during the uprising, when there were widespread fears that rule of law was becoming rule by law, as arrests of protestors mounted to unprecedented levels. Caught in the crossfire, Ma managed to retain the respect of both sides, but has often given the impression of yearning for his pending retirement.

Christopher Patten

The last Governor of Hong Kong, Lord Patten retains an intense interest in the SAR from his base in Britain. Better known as Chris Patten, he was one of the big beasts of British politics before coming to Hong Kong and had the kind of political clout that his Foreign Office predecessors as Governors lacked. Though sometimes accused of grandstanding by Hong Kong democrats, he had a close working relationship with them; and his reforms, designed to lay the groundwork for democracy after the handover, remain a key part of his legacy, although they were entirely expunged by the incoming regime. His approach led to unceasing conflict with the Chinese authorities, who famously named him as "a sinner for a thousand years". They remain mystified and aggravated by his continued involvement and popularity in Hong Kong. As a member of the House of Lords, Patten uses his position to influence the British government toward more active protection of Hong Kong's autonomy. Despite his love of visiting Hong Kong, he now believes that the authorities would bar him from entry.

Jimmy Sham Tsz-kit

As leader of the Civil Human Rights Front, Sham played a leading role organising the largest rallies during the uprising, mobilising literally millions of people. He has had a lifetime as a political activist. Born in 1987, he is one of the few openly gay political leaders in Hong Kong and has been a high-profile advocate for LGBT rights. In 2019, at the height of the protests, he was violently assaulted by a gang of thugs and hospitalised. Later that year, he won a seat in the district council elections that gave democrats an overwhelming victory. A member of Long Hair's League of Social Democrats, Sham is on the left of the democracy movement; but, in the fractious world of opposition politics, he has shown an unusual ability to co-ordinate and work with all shades of opinion. He was disqualified as a candidate for the now-postponed 2020 Legco election. (NSL target)

Benny Tai Yiu-ting

A legal academic, Tai was a leader of the civil disobedience Occupy Central movement that morphed into the 2014 Umbrella Movement. Deeply religious, he says he has been inspired by another Christian leader, Martin Luther King Jr. Tai is also heavily involved in co-ordination efforts among the democratic camp. As the initiator of Project Storm, he is widely credited with helping democrats secure victory in the 2019 district council elections. During the Umbrella protests, younger protestors were frustrated by his insistence on non-violence and often shunned him. However, his jailing in 2019 for causing a public nuisance has helped achieve a degree of reconciliation. In July 2020, he was fired from his post as a law professor at Hong Kong University, even before the completion of the appeal process. He is often the subject of attack by pro-China media, accusing him of inviting foreign intervention into Hong Kong affairs and acting as a front for foreign forces. (NSL target)

Maria Tam Wai-chu

Once a stalwart of the colonial establishment, Tam, a lawyer, has been transformed into a leading spokeswoman of the new order. She is the daughter of a police officer who became unusually rich, owning a range of businesses from night clubs to taxis and restaurants. She has maintained close links with the force. Tam has also been a member of a number of Mainland bodies and focuses on legal work, in particular matters relating to the Basic Law. Early in her career, she was a women's rights advocate. As a result of a conflict of interests arising from her undeclared involvement in the taxi business while serving as a member of the colonial government's transport advisory committee, she fell somewhat out of favour with the former rulers.

Tam Yiu-chung

A lifelong trade unionist, Tam is arguably the most senior Hong Kong representative in Mainland institutions. He serves as the only Hong Kong member of the National People's Congress Standing Committee, which means he was the only Hongkonger involved in drafting the National Security Law, a process that even excluded the Chief Executive. Tang was a founder and chairman of the DAB. There is little doubt that he is part of the inner circle of Hong Kong's underground Communist Party, but he declines to discuss this matter. A perennial survivor in the turbulent world of party politics, Tam has remained at the centre of Hong Kong politics for four decades. He comes from a Hakka family, the largest non-Cantonese minority in Hong Kong. (Sanctioned by US)

Chris Tang Ping-keung

A notably ambitious and hardline police officer, he finally succeeded in becoming the Commissioner of Police at the height of the uprising in November 2019. He is also the most political police chief ever seen in the SAR, as reflected in his many visits to the Mainland and by virtue of his central role in bodies implementing the National Security Law. Since taking on the top police job, Tang has increasingly involved himself in political affairs and is widely seen as Beijing's trusted implementor. He was long groomed for promotion, attending training courses in France and Britain and with the FBI in America. More important, however, is his training at the China Executive Leadership Academy, an elite school for

Communist Party cadres. He also studied at the People's Public Security University in Beijing. Unlike Stephen Lo, on becoming Commissioner, Tang headed straight for the protest frontlines and frequently returned. He has not only sanctioned more aggressive policing of protests but has taken to issuing statements that veer close to a political point of view. His personal attacks on protest leaders go down well both in Beijing and among the police rank and file. (Sanctioned by US.)

Henry Tang Ying-yen

Tang comes from a very wealthy family that made its first fortune in the textile business in Wuxi, before fleeing to Hong Kong in the wake of the Communist Revolution. His father later became well connected with the leaders of the new order. It is rumoured that the family was happier having Tang getting involved in politics than in the family business, and there is every indication that he was groomed for high office, which culminated in his appointment as Chief Secretary, number two in the government, until he resigned to contest the 2012 Chief Executive election. Tang, with Beijing's full backing, was set to win, until his campaign was disrupted by a scandal involving unauthorised structural alterations at his lavish home. Tang has a tendency never to take responsibility when things go wrong on his watch. Better known for his amiability than for his intellectual prowess, Tang has spent the years since the 2012 debacle rehabilitating himself and becoming a staunch member of the pro-China camp. His return to high office is therefore not ruled out.

James Tien Pei-chun

Son of the well-known Shanghainese industrialist Francis Tien and brother of Michael (below), he is one of the more distinctive members of the pro-China camp. Tien has been a central player in conservative political circles since the 1980s and has served in a number of capacities: as a legislator, an Executive Council member and a representative on Mainland political bodies. However, he is probably best known as the leader of the Liberal Party who withdrew support for the Tung government's draconian national security legislation after mass street protests in 2003. This effectively led to the shelving of the bill and began the process of Tien's distancing from the rest of the pro-government camp. His move infuriated the Beijing authorities, and he became the first person in history to be stripped of membership of the Chinese People's Political Consultative Conference. His more independent stance has led him further away from his former allies in the years since, but he still regards himself as part of the pro-China bloc. Without the burden of office, Tien has become a notably relaxed player in the political game, and one of the few able to cross the political divide.

Michael Tien Puk-sun

The younger brother of James Tien, Michael also cannot be described as a supporter of the pro-China bloc by reflex. He founded the successful G2000 cut-price clothing chain, but increasingly spends more time on politics. Though more aggressive than his brother, he is sufficiently independently minded not to be entirely trusted by the pro-Beijing camp, although he remains within its fold. He has developed a strong interest in transport matters following his controversial chairmanship of Hong Kong's railway corporation, during which he clashed frequently with the corporation's management.

Donald Tsang Yam-kuen

Following the meltdown of Tung Chee-hwa as Hong Kong's first Chief Executive, Beijing decided that it might be better to have him replaced by a safe pair of hands from within the civil service. Tsang had been Tung's number two, and had served as Financial Secretary among many other posts during his lifetime in the civil service. He is the son of a police officer and brother of a former chief of police—the kind of disciplinary background that appeals to the hard men in Beijing. More problematic, from their point of view, was his slavish participation in the old colonial order, to the point of having accepted a knighthood just before the handover. However, Tsang has worked unceasingly to prove that he can be equally slavish towards the Communist Party. Once in office (2005–12), Tsang largely did as he was told and adopted a very high-handed way of dealing with subordinates and others, which may well have contributed to his downfall. He is known for his love of Rolex watches and vintage Mercedes-Benz cars. Shortly after retirement, when he was replaced by Leung Chun-ying (who was not a friend), Tsang was charged with two counts of misconduct in public office, and convicted of one. It is widely but inaccurately believed that, following twenty months in jail, he was found innocent after three appeals. The reality is that the Court of Final Appeal eventually declared his first trial a mistrial, rather than an acquittal. Prosecutors were theoretically able to bring fresh charges, but did not do so as Tsang had served his sentence during the long judicial process. He has since become largely a non-person as far as Beijing is concerned, despite his tentative attempts to regain position.

Jasper Tsang Yok-sing

Tsang, a former President of the Legislative Council, is the only pro-Beijing leader who is widely respected in opposition circles, while remaining a stalwart of the pro-China camp. Unlike most members of this largely opportunist camp, he is a well-read Marxist. Both he and his older brother Tsang Tak-sing have been involved in Communist politics since their school days, although it was Tak-sing who was jailed by the British during the 1960s protests against the Cultural Revolution (he went on to edit the Communist *Ta Kung Pao* newspaper, and became an SAR government minister, the only Party veteran to have done so). The reason for Jasper Tsang's popularity is that few people doubt his sincerity or courage. Offered the prospect of a good career under the British, he chose instead to teach at a leftist school; given the chance to be a high-flyer under the new order after the handover, he was constrained by his independence of mind and refusal to pursue an opportunistic path for personal advancement. He was a founder of the DAB and became its first chairman. Despite Beijing's distrust of independently minded individuals, Tsang remains an influential figure in pro-China circles and has lines of communications with the opposition. Many people believe that Tsang is the best Chief Executive Hong Kong never had. He was prepared to run for the job in 2017, but the idea was nixed in Beijing.

John Tsang Chun-wah

In a sea of grey civil servants displaying all the charisma of ticket collectors on a damp day, Tsang, with his trademark moustache, always stood out. Maybe this was because he spent most of his youth living in the United States, working in a number of jobs as an architect and educator. He returned to Hong Kong in 1982, joining the colonial civil service and enjoying a stellar career, culminating in his stint as the SAR's longest serving Financial Secretary. In 2017, he stepped down in a bid to become Chief Executive, vying with Carrie Lam. If anything, Tsang's high popularity ratings persuaded the bosses on the Mainland not to trust him, as they feared that popular support might encourage Tsang to be more assertive in defending Hong Kong's interests. His deep interest in local culture and avid support for the Hong Kong football team were also strikes against him. Inevitably, the majority of Election Committee members took their cue from Beijing and supported Lam. Since then, Tsang has been sparing in his public appearances and pronouncements, but is widely seen as one of the few leaders capable of straddling the political divide and negotiating some form of consensus.

Tung Chee-hwa

The eldest son of the wealthy Shanghainese shipping magnate Tung Chao yung, Tung became Hong Kong's first Chief Executive at the handover in 1997. Realising that Beijing had earmarked him for the post, Governor Chris Patten had appointed him to serve on the colonial Executive Council to gain experience of government, and in the hope that he would engage with the political process. Tung accepted the appointment but did not engage. Although his family had a history of stalwart support for the anti-Communist Kuomintang, Tung turned the other way after his late father's company was rescued by Beijing via local businessman Henry Fok. At this point, Tung became an ultra-loyalist for his new business partners—a classic case of the success of Beijing's United Front efforts. Once installed in office, Tung demonstrated an almost unbelievable inability to do the job: rarely consulting with anyone besides Mainland officials; micro-managing government departments, but reluctant to take decisions; and seemingly oblivious to what was going on outside his office. His downfall was triggered in 2003 by the failed attempt to push through a national security law despite widespread street protests. He hung on for another year or so before allegedly resigning on grounds of ill health. Although Tung's failure in the job embarrassed Beijing, he has remained a close ally; because of his cosmopolitan background, global business connections and fluent English, he has become a de-facto roving ambassador for the PRC. During the 2014 and 2019–20 movements, he took an increasingly high profile in Hong Kong, urging a hardline response and mobilising support for the Party.

APPENDIX II

Wang Zhimin

An identikit Beijing bureaucrat, Wang had the misfortune in 2017 to be appointed as head of Beijing's Central Liaison Office in Hong Kong, and to be kicked out in 2020 for failing to handle the uprising—specifically, for misjudging the pro-China camp's prospects in the 2019 district council elections, failing to foresee its spectacular defeat. Originating from nearby Fujian Province, Wang has a long history of involvement in Hong Kong and Macau affairs. However, he has departed the Liaison Office without leaving an identifiable legacy, and has been demoted to a relatively insignificant research post.

Joshua Wong Chi-fung

If Hong Kong's democracy movement has one universally recognised face, it is that of Joshua Wong. A skinny, fast-talking, self-described nerd with dyslexia, he hardly seems an obvious candidate for this role. However, by the age of 15 he had led a successful protest movement against a government plan to impose patriotic education on the school curriculum, and has not stopped since. He comes from a religious middle-class family of Lutherans with a strong sense of social justice. His father is also one of Hong Kong's most prominent anti-gay rights campaigners, views not shared by his son. Some people close to Wong wonder if he ever sleeps, as he appears to be working day and night for the movement. Although he was well known back in 2011, he became far better known during the Umbrella protests of 2014, along with Agnes Chow, Ivan Lam, Nathan Law and Lester Shum. Despite protestations to the contrary, these five young people effectively led the movement, with Wong emerging as the most outstanding leader. Although his political activism has clearly cost him educational opportunities, he is impressively quick to learn: by sheer willpower, he rapidly mastered English and got himself up to speed with other protest leaders and movements around the world. He helped form the Demosisto political party in 2016, propelling the new-generation democracy movement towards elective politics despite the fact that he has been barred from standing for office. The party has since been dissolved. Undaunted by four spells in jail (the latest since 2 December 2020), and more in the pipeline, Wong has a kind of charisma which is hard to define but is staggeringly effective. Members of the pro-China camp remain convinced that he is somehow being manipulated by foreign powers, mainly because they can offer no other explanation for his impact. (NSL target)

Wu Chi-wai

Chairman of the Democratic Party, the largest of Hong Kong's pro-democracy parties. Wu has been rather overshadowed by his predecessors in this role such as Martin Lee and Emily Lau, but his dogged determination has earned the respect of colleagues and an intense dislike from political opponents. He has essentially been in politics all his working life. In December 2020, he stepped down to be replaced by Lo Kin-hei, a member of the party's younger generation. (NSL target)

Xia Baolong

When heads rolled in 2020 among the senior Chinese officials handling Hong Kong affairs for their failure to end the uprising, Xi Jinping turned to a trusted ally and old colleague to assume leadership of the Hong Kong and Macau Affairs Office in Beijing. Xia's appointment also signals an elevation in the office's role, because he is the first cabinet-level state leader to be put in charge of Hong Kong and Macau affairs. At the time of his appointment, he was also the secretary-general of the Chinese People's Consultative Conference, a post he relinquished in May 2020 to focus on Hong Kong. Xia has approached this job with the kind of determination that is to be expected from the man who had a role in vigorously suppressing Christian churches in Zhejiang, where he served as Party chief. In 2003, when Xia first arrived in the province, Xi Jinping was his immediate boss. Since taking over the HKMAO, Xia has busied himself issuing edicts from his office in Beijing. He has tended to brush the Hong Kong government to one side and has made it clear who is pulling the strings. As he is beyond the customary retirement age for Chinese officials, it is widely assumed that he is on a fast clean-up mission, clearing the way for a new incumbent once the job has been done.

Alvin Yeung Ngok-kiu

A barrister by profession and leader of the Civic Party, Yeung comes from a middle-class background. This is appropriate for the Civic Party, which grew out of the 2003 protests against the proposed national security legislation, and was largely formed by lawyers. Born in 1981, Yeung is part of a younger generation of democrats, but is regarded as somewhat senior by the very young activists of the 2019–20 uprising. Although his opponents regularly criticise him for not knowing enough about the mother country, he is in fact a postgraduate from Peking University. In a political world dominated by dowdy personalities, Yeung cuts a dashing figure; he always seems relaxed, though he is notably hardworking. In November 2020, he was expelled from the Legislative Council on orders from Beijing; he subsequently resigned as party leader. (NSL target)

Allan Zeman

Zeman has a habit of popping up all over the place—sometimes in commerce, at other times in show business, and very frequently at government and political events. He was born to one of the few Jewish families who remained in Germany after the defeat of the Nazis; they moved to Canada, where he grew up and started his business career at a very early age. In Hong Kong, he founded a successful clothing company, but is better known for buying up the Lan Kwai Fong area of central Hong Kong and turning it into a famous entertainment district. This venture was so successful that the name and concept were exported to the Mainland. Respected as a businessman on an international level, he became chairman of the Wynn Resorts gambling empire after it ran into major difficulties in Macau. He is equally well known as a political insider, close to the government yet friendly with the opposition. In 2008, it was assumed that Donald Tsang would appoint him to the Executive Council, which required him to relinquish his Canadian citizenship and become one of the few non-ethnic Chinese nationals. However, Beijing's paranoid suspicion of foreigners prevented his appointment from materialising—but Zeman continued to serve on a number of official committees and was notably successful as Chairman of the government-owned Ocean Park, a maritime theme park. He is an inveterate showman, shrewd businessman and proud Hongkonger, who bobs around between political movements, counselling the kind of moderate approach that has few takers these days.

Cardinal Joseph Zen Ze-kiun

The wafer-thin and diminutive Zen poses enormous problems for the leaders of the SAR, many of whom, including Carrie Lam, are observant Catholics. He became a cardinal in 2006, making him the most senior

Chinese in the Church. This elevation came despite bitter opposition from Beijing and the government-supporting members of the Church within Hong Kong. They were all too aware of his relentless activism for democracy and human rights, and his staunch opposition to moves to reconcile the Vatican with the Communist Party on the Mainland. He remains an avid supporter of the Mainland's Underground Church, which is increasingly beleaguered. Born in Shanghai, Zen entered the priesthood as a young man, studying in Italy and working as an educator in Hong Kong. Many of the older members of the democracy movement are also Catholic, notably Martin Lee and Jimmy Lai, whom Zen helped to convert. His influence on them has been substantial. He retired as a cardinal in 2009, but remains active in both the Church and the democracy movement. Although he is widely seen as a radical, Zen is a social conservative, sharing mainstream Catholic views on issues of social reform.

Zhang Xiaoming

Young and suave by the standards of Chinese bureaucrats, Zhang was another victim of the purge of officials in 2020, standing accused of having failed to deal with the Hong Kong protests. Most of his career has focused on Hong Kong affairs, becoming the head of the Central Liaison Office and then Director of the Hong Kong and Macau Affairs Office, but only briefly before his 2020 demotion to deputy. At one time, he appeared to be the new face of Chinese officialdom: smart and quick on his feet, he outshone his predecessors at the Liaison Office. However, he was never anything but a hardliner in terms of policy. Chillingly, he became famous for telling the opposition legislator Leung Yiu-chung: "The fact that you are allowed to stay alive already shows the country's inclusiveness." His hardline stance was not enough, however, to save him from his 2020 humiliation.

Zheng Yanxiong

A former secretary-general of the Guangdong Communist Party, Zheng was a surprise choice as head of the Office for Safeguarding National Security, established to enforce the new National Security Law in the summer of 2020. This office is effectively the Chinese secret police's headquarters in Hong Kong; however, Zheng does not come from a security background. He established a hardline reputation for putting down a widely publicised revolt in Wukan township in 2011, after citizens had managed to elect their own leader. He was subsequently promoted within Guangdong Province, and is the only leading Chinese official operating in Hong Kong who is fluent in Cantonese.

ACKNOWLEDGEMENTS

In order to write this book, I have interviewed a great many people on the streets and elsewhere during the protests. Aside from public figures, none of them are identified by their real names as, in the circumstances of Hong Kong in 2021, they would be exposed to risks. For the same reason, I have been unable to name here a number of people who have contributed a great deal to this book. I am nevertheless extremely grateful for the generosity of interviewees in finding the time to talk to me, and to many others who have provided all manner of assistance.

Kristina Pérez, my agent, was an early supporter of this project and has gone far beyond what is normally expected of a literary agent. Throughout this tortuous process, I have been helped by Eric Sze in ways too numerous to mention. I am delighted that the cover features an image by the fearless photographer May James. I would also like to thank all of my colleagues at the television news programme *The Pulse*: Executive Producer Diana Wan, and the other producers I have worked with over a long period of time, including Nina Loh and Liz Yuen. They have often provided insights and information that had a habit of passing me by.

This book was edited with meticulous attention by Lara Wu and greatly benefited as a result. I would also like to extend thanks to everyone else at Hurst who has done so much to bring this book into being.

NOTES

INTRODUCTION

1. Li Keqiang, Premier of the State Council, "Report on the Work of the Government", delivered at the First Session of the 13th National People's Congress of the People's Republic of China, 5 March 2018, available online at http://online.wsj.com/public/resources/documents/NPC2018_GovtWorkReport_English.pdf (last accessed 9 Nov. 2020).

3. Charley Lanyon, "Trump says White House will 'do something' about Hong Kong issue by end of week", *South China Morning Post (SCMP)*, Hong Kong, 27 May 2020, https://www.scmp.com/news/china/diplomacy/article/3086198/us-senators-move-pressure-china-hong-kong-sanctions-bill (last accessed 9 Nov. 2020).

4. *Stand News*, "Lam Cheng: There is no separation of powers in Hong Kong, only the 'division of labour' checks and balances the executive-led structure; 'the core is the Chief Executive'", Hong Kong, 1 September 2020 (in Chinese).

5. Kimmy Chung and Tony Cheung, "Hong Kong protests have 'obvious characteristics of colour revolution', top Beijing official warns amid 'worst crisis since 1997 handover'", *SCMP*, Hong Kong, 8 August 2019, https://www.scmp.com/news/hong-kong/politics/article/3021877/protests-colour-revolution-threatening-hong-kong-abyss-top (last accessed 9 Nov. 2020).

1. AN UNHAPPY FAMILY

1. Xinhua, "Xi lauds Macao's 'shining chapter' of 'one country, two systems' practice", Macau, 20 December 2019, http://www.xinhuanet.com/english/2019-12/21/c_138647103.htm (last accessed 9 Nov. 2020).

2. Devin O'Connor, "Macau Gaming Industry Responsible for 86 Percent of Enclave Government Tax Revenue", Casino.org, 19 December 2019, https://www.casino.org/news/macau-gaming-industry-responsible-for-86-percent-of-tax-revenue/ (last accessed 17 Nov. 2020).

3. Guo Rui, "Why China's Greater Bay Area plan fails to capture the imagination of young Hongkongers", *SCMP*, Hong Kong, 15 January 2020, https://www.scmp.com/news/china/politics/article/3046086/why-chinas-greater-bay-area-plan-fails-catch-imagination-young (last accessed 19 Nov. 2020).

4. Frank Welsh, *A History of Hong Kong*, HarperCollins, London, 1993, p. 1.

5. Deng Xiaoping, "Our Basic Position on the Question of Hong Kong", 24 September 1982, available online at https://dengxiaopingworks.wordpress.com/2013/03/08/our-basic-position-on-the-question-of-hong-kong/ (last accessed 9 Nov. 2020).

6. This highly truncated version of the negotiations leading up to the transfer of power is largely based on research I undertook for my book: Stephen Vines, *Hong Kong: China's New Colony*, Orion, London, 1999.

7. Hong Kong Basic Law Drafting Committee, *The Basic Law of the Hong Kong Special Administrative Region of the People's Republic of China*, adopted by the National People's Congress 4 April 1990, available at https://www.cmab.gov.hk/doc/en/documents/policy_responsibilities/Racial_Discrimination/AnnexI-Eng.pdf (last accessed 9 Nov. 2020).

8. *Deng Xiaoping on the Question of Hong Kong*, New Horizon Press, Hong Kong, 1995, p. 52.

9. Kathy Chen, Urban C. Lehner and Marcus W. Brauchli, "Qian Says Hong Kong Faces Curbing of Political Freedom", *Asian Wall Street Journal*, Hong Kong, 16 October 1996, https://www.wsj.com/articles/SB8454063306679000 (last accessed 4 Dec. 2020).

10. Vines, *Hong Kong*, Chapter 6.

11. The history of the Chinese "Great State" is laid out with some skill in Timothy Brook, *Great State: China and the World*, Profile, London, 2019.

12. PRC Taiwan Affairs Office and the Information Office of the State Council, *The One-China Principle and the Taiwan Issue*, February 2000, Beijing, available online at http://english1.english.gov.cn/official/2005-07/27/content_17613.htm (last accessed 20 Nov. 2020).

13. *Hong Kong Economic Journal*, "Tsai rejects 'one country, two systems', saying it failed in HK", *EJ Insight*, Hong Kong, 10 October 2019, https://www.ejinsight.com/eji/article/id/2272634/20191010-tsai-rejects-one-country-two-systems-saying-it-failed-in-hk (last accessed 4 Dec. 2020).

14. Sarah Zheng, "Beijing vows to 'fully respect' Taiwanese way of life ... after reunification", *SCMP*, Hong Kong, 7 November 2019, https://www.scmp.com/news/china/politics/article/3036618/beijing-vows-fully-respect-taiwanese-way-life-after (last accessed 20 Nov. 2020).

15. Lily Kuo, "'All necessary means': Xi Jinping reserves right to use force against Taiwan", *The Guardian*, London, 2 January 2019, https://www.theguardian.com/world/2019/jan/02/all-necessary-means-xi-jinping-reserves-right-to-use-force-against-taiwan (last accessed 20 Nov. 2020).

16. Richard McGregor, *Xi Jinping: The Backlash*, Penguin Australia, Melbourne, 2019, p. 8.

17. Ibid., p. 11.

18. Vivienne Zeng, "Beijing's liaison chief under fire after saying separation of powers 'does not suit Hong Kong'", *Hong Kong Free Press (HKFP)*, Hong Kong, 14 September 2015, https://hongkongfp.com/2015/09/14/beijings-liaison-chief-under-fire-after-saying-separation-of-powers-does-not-suit-hong-kong/ (last accessed 20 Nov. 2020).

19. A full transcript is to be found under the heading "Press conference on the fourth plenary session of the 19th CPC Central Committee" at China.org.cn, Beijing, 5 November 2019 (in Chinese).

20. Willy Lam, interview with the author, "CPC's fourth plenary session, Xi Jinping met Carrie Lam: discussion with Willy Lam", *The Pulse*, Radio Television Hong Kong, 9 November 2019, available online at

https://podcast.rthk.hk/podcast/item.php?pid=205&eid=147945&yea
r=2019&lang=en-US (last accessed 20 Nov. 2020).

21. Tony Cheung, William Zheng and Gary Cheung, "'No other authority has right to make judgments': China slams Hong Kong court's ruling on anti-mask law as unconstitutional", *SCMP*, Hong Kong, 19 November 2019, https://www.scmp.com/news/hong-kong/politics/article/3038325/hong-kong-judges-slammed-chinas-top-legislative-body (last accessed 20 Nov. 2020).

22. Ibid.

23. Tony Cheung and Lilian Cheng, "Beijing right to condemn opposition lawmakers blocking Hong Kong legislative work, Lam says", *SCMP*, Hong Kong, 14 April 2020, https://www.scmp.com/news/hong-kong/politics/article/3079885/beijing-criticisms-opposition-lawmakers-not-interference (last accessed 20 Nov. 2020).

24. Gary Cheung and Kimmy Chung, "Beijing's attack on Hong Kong opposition viewed as 'taste of what's to come' as attention pivots from coronavirus to city's legislative elections", *SCMP*, Hong Kong, 15 April 2020, https://www.scmp.com/news/hong-kong/politics/article/3079962/beijings-attack-hong-kong-opposition-viewed-taste-whats (last accessed 20 Nov. 2020).

25. Lee Yee, "Ways of the World: The Dust has Settled", *Be Water*, Hong Kong, 9 September 2019 (in Chinese).

2. A FARCICAL POLITICAL SYSTEM

1. Stephen Vines, *Hong Kong: China's New Colony*, Orion, London, 1999, pp. 209–10.

2. Reporters from the Reuters news agency first broke the story of Bauhinia Villa, and provided much of the material for its discussion in this chapter: Keith Zhai, James Pomfret and David Kirton, "Exclusive: China sets up Hong Kong crisis center in mainland, considers replacing chief liaison", Reuters, Hong Kong, 26 November 2019, https://www.reuters.com/article/us-hongkong-protests-shenzhen-exclusive-idUSK-BN1Y000P (last accessed 20 Nov. 2020).

3. Demosisto press conference, Hong Kong, 20 April 2020.

4. Xinhua, "Central gov't agency, liaison office have power to supervise major affairs in HK: spokesperson of liaison office", Beijing, 17 April 2020.

5. *Stand News*, "The Hong Kong and Macao Affairs Office issued three statements in a row", Hong Kong, 21 April 2020 (in Chinese).

6. Kathleen Magramo, "Hong Kong leader Carrie Lam admits to being caught out by protests: 'I'm an administrator that doesn't understand politics'", *SCMP*, Hong Kong, 28 August 2020, https://www.scmp.com/news/hong-kong/politics/article/3099226/hong-kong-leader-carrie-lam-admits-being-caught-out-civil (last accessed 23 Nov. 2020).

7. Elizabeth Cheung and Christy Leung, "One in five Hongkongers living below the poverty line in 2018, as concern groups warn falling economy may cause situation to get worse", *SCMP*, Hong Kong, 13 December 2019, https://www.scmp.com/news/hong-kong/society/article/3042039/one-five-hongkongers-living-below-poverty-line-2018 (last accessed 23 Nov. 2020).

8. A detailed account of how this gerrymandering works is to be found in *Webbsite*, "Getting to 601: How Beijing controls the HK Chief Executive election", Hong Kong, 28 January 2020, https://webb-site.com/articles/gettingTo601.asp (last accessed 23 Nov. 2020).

9. Government of the Hong Kong Special Administrative Region, "2020 final registers of electors published today", press release, 17 July 2020, https://www.info.gov.hk/gia/general/202007/17/P2020071700177.htm (last accessed 25 Nov. 2020).

10. Census and Statistics Department, Hong Kong Special Administrative Region, "Quarterly Report of Employment and Vacancies Statistics", June 2020, https://www.statistics.gov.hk/pub/B10500032020QQ02B0100.pdf (last accessed 25 Nov. 2020), p. 2.

11. Kelly Ho, "Hong Kong gov't studying voting in China plan, as minister casts doubt on public survey", *HKFP*, Hong Kong, 28 October 2020, https://hongkongfp.com/2020/10/28/hong-kong-govt-studying-voting-in-china-plan-as-minister-casts-doubt-on-public-survey/ (last accessed 25 Nov. 2020).

12. Despite its centrality in Hong Kong's political life, there is markedly little written about the Communist Party in Hong Kong, especially in

English. The best English-language source of information is Christine Loh, *Underground Front: The Chinese Communist Party in Hong Kong*, Hong Kong University Press, Hong Kong, 2010.

13. Author's notes taken at the event.

3. A MALFUNCTIONING ECONOMY

1. *Global Times*, "Resentment against rich exaggerated in China", op-ed, Beijing, 23 April 2015, https://www.globaltimes.cn/content/918235. shtml (last accessed 12 Nov. 2020).

2. Stephen Vines, "China takes aim at Hong Kong tycoons", *The Sunday Times*, London, 29 September 2019, https://www.thetimes.co.uk/article/china-takes-aim-at-hong-kong-tycoons-5nh3zfv5v (last accessed 24 Nov. 2020).

3. Cited in Gary Cheung, "Scapegoats or scoundrels? Why ties between Beijing and Hong Kong's property tycoons are unravelling amid protest crisis", *SCMP*, Hong Kong, 25 September 2019, https://www.scmp. com/news/hong-kong/politics/article/3030209/scapegoats-or-scoundrels-why-ties-between-beijing-and-hong (last accessed 24 Nov. 2020).

4. Cheng Qingqing, Bai Yunyi and Zhao Juecheng, "HK property moguls urged to shoulder responsibility in easing tensions", *Global Times*, Beijing, 29 September 2019, https://www.globaltimes.cn/content/ 1165852.shtml (last accessed 24 Nov. 2020).

5. Gary Cheung, "HK protests: how tycoons went from trusted advisors to Beijing's 'bogeymen' who refused to step up", *SCMP*, Hong Kong, 15 June 2020, https://www.scmp.com/news/hong-kong/politics/article/3089018/hong-kong-protests-how-tycoons-went-trusted-advisers (last accessed 24 Nov. 2020).

6. Chinayearbooks.com, *2020 China Statistical Yearbook*, Beijing, 1 May 2020.

7. Ibid.

8. Question in the Legislative Council from Jimmy Ng and written response from the Secretary for Development, Michael Wong, "LCQ15: Improving average living floor area per person", press release from the Hong Kong government, 20 June 2018, available at https://www.info.

gov.hk/gia/general/201806/20/P2018062000367.htm (last accessed 24 Nov. 2020); Sophie Hui, "More than 40pc of salary goes on rent for subdivided flats", *The Standard*, Hong Kong, 24 June 2019, https://www.thestandard.com.hk/section-news/section/4/208931/More-than-40pc-of-salary-goes-on-rent-for-subdivided-flats#:-:text=The%20average%20rent%20of%20a,feet%20in%20public%20rental%20housing (last accessed 25 Nov. 2020).

9. Shrink That Footprint, "How big is a house? Average house size by country", November 2014, http://shrinkthatfootprint.com/how-big-is-a-house (last accessed 24 Nov. 2020).

10. Government of the Hong Kong Special Administrative Region, "Hong Kong Poverty Situation Report 2018", Hong Kong, 13 December 2019, available at https://www.statistics.gov.hk/pub/B9XX0005E2018AN1 8E0100.pdf (last accessed 24 Nov. 2020).

11. Ibid.

12. Law Chi-kwong, interview with the author, "Budget 2020–2021: Discussion with Law Chi-kwong, Secretary for Labour and Welfare", *The Pulse*, Radio Television Hong Kong, 7 March 2020, https://podcast.rthk.hk/podcast/item.php?pid=205&eid=155453&year=2020&lang=en-US (last accessed 24 Nov. 2020).

13. Eswar S. Prasad, "Why China No Longer Needs Hong Kong", *The New York Times*, New York, 3 July 2019, https://www.nytimes.com/2019/07/03/opinion/hong-kong-protest.html (last accessed 24 Nov. 2020).

14. *The Economist*, "Hong Kong remains crucially important to mainland China", London, 8 August 2019, https://www.economist.com/briefing/2019/08/08/hong-kong-remains-crucially-important-to-mainland-china (last accessed 25 Nov. 2020)

15. Tianlei Huang, "Why China Still Needs Hong Kong", Peterson Institute for International Economics, Washington DC, 15 July 2019, https://www.piie.com/blogs/china-economic-watch/why-china-still-needs-hong-kong (last accessed 25 Nov. 2020).

16. Hong Kong Monetary Authority, "The Three-tier Banking System", Hong Kong, 2 November 2020, https://www.hkma.gov.hk/eng/key-functions/banking/banking-regulatory-and-supervisory-regime/the-three-tier-banking-system/ (last accessed 30 Nov. 2020).

17. Wen Simin, Liu Yanfei and Timmy Shen, "In Depth: After Cash Splash, Mainland Property Developers Flounder in Hong Kong", *Caixin*, Beijing, 5 March 2019, https://www.caixinglobal.com/2019-03-05/in-depth-after-cash-splash-mainland-property-developers-flounder-in-hong-kong-101387861.html (last accessed 25 Nov. 2020).

18. Sandy Li, "One in 10 new Hong Kong homes to be built by mainland Chinese developers in three years", *SCMP*, Hong Kong, 27 January 2016, https://www.scmp.com/property/article/1905877/one-10-new-hong-kong-homes-be-built-mainland-chinese-developers-three-years (last accessed 25 Nov. 2020).

19. Eric Lam and Yue Qiu, "Hong Kong's Stock Market Tells the Story of China's Growing Dominance", Bloomberg News, New York, 23 June 2017, https://www.bloomberg.com/graphics/2017-hang-seng-index/ (last accessed 25 Nov. 2020).

20. An English-language report of this story appeared as Michael Forsythe, David Enrich and Alexandra Stevenson, "Inside a Brazen Scheme to Woo China: Gifts, Golf and a $4,254 Wine", *The New York Times*, New York, 14 October 2019, https://www.nytimes.com/2019/10/14/business/deutsche-bank-china.html (last accessed 25 Nov. 2020).

21. Orange Wang and Zhou Xin, "China cements Communist Party's role at top of its SOEs, should 'execute the will of the party'", *SCMP*, Hong Kong, 8 January 2020, https://www.scmp.com/economy/china-economy/article/3045053/china-cements-communist-partys-role-top-its-soes-should (last accessed 25 Nov. 2020).

22. Tom Mitchell and Xinning Liu, "Chinese Communist party asserts greater control over private enterprise", *Financial Times*, London, 29 September 2020, https://www.ft.com/content/582411f6-fc3b-4e4d-9916-c30a29ad010e (last accessed 25 Nov. 2020).

4. CHINA'S NIGHTMARE: THE BIRTH OF A HONG KONG IDENTITY

1. Government of the Hong Kong Special Administrative Region, "Transcript of remarks by CE at media session (with video)", press release, 9 August 2019, https://www.info.gov.hk/gia/general/201908/09/P2019080900869.htm (last accessed 26 Nov. 2020).

2. *Apple Daily*, "Shenzhen's GDP leapfrogging Hong Kong is not an issue: Carrie Lam", Hong Kong, 13 October 2020, https://hk.appledaily.com/news/20201013/EX4DSW7Q4RALFHDZ32JZWM2MKU/ (last accessed 26 Nov. 2020).

3. Kris Cheng, "Carrie Lam's right to reside in EU through her husband does not affect her candidacy, gov't says", *HKFP*, Hong Kong, 22 March 2017, https://hongkongfp.com/2017/03/22/carrie-lams-right-reside-eu-husband-not-affect-candidacy-govt-says/ (last accessed 26 Nov. 2020).

4. Public Opinion Programme, University of Hong Kong, "HKU POP final farewell: Rift widens between Chinese and Hongkong identities, national pride plunges to one in four", press release, Hong Kong, 27 June 2019, https://www.hkupop.hku.hk/english/release/release1594.html (last accessed 26 Nov. 2020). The University closed down its opinion polling operation following publication of this survey.

5. Mark Magnier, "Taiwanese support closer ties with US over China, few identify as solely Chinese, Pew Research survey finds", *SCMP*, Hong Kong, 12 May 2020, https://www.scmp.com/news/china/politics/article/3084068/taiwanese-support-closer-ties-us-over-china-few-identify-solely (last accessed 26 Nov. 2020).

6. Census and Statistics Department, Government of the Hong Kong Special Administrative Region, "2016 Population By-census: Snapshot of the Hong Kong Population", Chart 3, p. 5, https://www.bycensus2016.gov.hk/data/snapshotPDF/Snapshot01.pdf (last accessed 27 Nov. 2020).

7. Alfred M. Wu and Kee-Lee Chou, "Public Attitudes towards Income Redistribution: Evidence from Hong Kong", *Social Policy & Administration*, 2017, vol. 51, no. 5, pp. 738–54 (first published 3 November 2015).

8. Joshua Wong with Jason Y. Ng, *Unfree Speech*, Penguin Books, London, 2020, p. 12.

5. HUBRIS

1. Given the very high number of arrests, charges and court cases, it is hard

to keep track of what is happening on this front. A useful and frequently updated source of information is to be found at Kong Tsung-gan, "Arrests and trials of Hong Kong protesters", https://medium.com/@KongTsungGan/arrests-and-trials-of-hong-kong-protesters-2019-9d9a601d4950 (last accessed 4 Dec. 2020).

2. *HKFP*, "Interview: Ex-head of legislature Jasper Tsang says the gov't is weakest player of four in Hong Kong's struggle", Hong Kong, 16 November 2019, https://hongkongfp.com/2019/11/16/interview-ex-head-legislature-jasper-tsang-says-govt-weakest-player-four-hong-kongs-struggle/ (last accessed 26 Nov. 2020).

3. Isabella Steger and Echo Huang, "Hong Kong's latest strong-arm tactics are fueling a growing independence movement", *Quartz*, New York and London, 3 August 2016, https://qz.com/748956/hong-kongs-government-is-fueling-an-independencemovement-by-banning-a-philosophy-student-from-politics/ (last accessed 26 Nov. 2020).

5. Kelly Ho, "Hong Kong's Carrie Lam says she is 'immune' to criticism; hails 'instant results' of security law", *HKFP*, Hong Kong, 20 October 2020, https://hongkongfp.com/2020/10/20/hong-kongs-carrie-lam-says-she-is-immune-to-criticism-hails-instant-results-of-security-law/ (last accessed 26 Nov. 2020).

6. *The Standard*, "Fugitive bill was Lam's idea", Hong Kong, 23 December 2019, https://www.thestandard.com.hk/section-news/section/4/214744/Fugitive-bill-was-Lam%27s-idea (last accessed 27 Nov. 2020). This newspaper is part of the *Sing Tao* group and, with its sister Chinese-language papers, often acts as a semi-official mouthpiece for Beijing, especially in matters where the official state media is instructed to stand back.

7. Embassy of the People's Republic of China in the United Kingdom, "Ambassador Liu Xiaoming Gives Exclusive Live Interview to BBC Newsnight", press release transcript of 12 June interview with the BBC's Mark Urban, 13 June 2019.

8. Melinda Liu, "Hong Kong's Future: Police State or Mob State?", *Foreign Policy*, New York, 25 October 2019, https://foreignpolicy.com/2019/10/25/hong-kong-protests-future-china-police-mob/ (last accessed 27 Nov. 2020).

9. *HKFP*, "Interview: Ex-head of legislature Jasper Tsang says the gov't is weakest player of four in Hong Kong's struggle", Hong Kong, 16 November 2019, https://hongkongfp.com/2019/11/16/interview-ex-head-legislature-jasper-tsang-says-govt-weakest-player-four-hong-kongs-struggle/ (last accessed 27 Nov. 2020).

10. Author interview with Martin Lee (member of the Basic Law Drafting Committee until 1989, when he resigned following the Tiananmen Square massacre), 22 November 2019, Hong Kong.

11. Interview with *TVB News*, Hong Kong, 10 June 2019. The station subsequently stated that the interview had been recorded on 5 June but, for reasons not explained, was only aired five days later.

12. I have spoken to a large number of Carrie Lam's past and present colleagues. For obvious reasons, they do not wish to be named. Their views are reflected elsewhere in this work.

6. BE WATER

1. *Sing Tao Daily*, "Exclusive: Han Zheng, Lam Cheng, Hong Kong officials at late-night meeting are expected to announce the suspension of the law", Hong Kong, 14 June 2019 (in Chinese).

2. Sum Lok-kei, "Nearly a fifth of Hong Kong voters say they support violent action by protesters, such as attacking opponents or hurling petrol bombs and bricks", *SCMP*, Hong Kong, 21 December 2019, https://www.scmp.com/news/hong-kong/politics/article/3043073/nearly-fifth-voters-say-they-support-violent-actions (last accessed 30 Nov. 2020).

3. RTHK English News, "Police admit to being in Yuen Long before attack", Hong Kong, 15 July 2020, https://news.rthk.hk/rthk/en/component/k2/1537993-20200715.htm (last accessed 30 Nov. 2020).

4. I have written more extensively about the role of Triads in Hong Kong in Stephen Vines, *Hong Kong: China's New Colony*, Orion, London, 1999. For the quotations here, see pp. 247–54.

5. AFP, "China warns Hong Kong protesters not to mistake gov't 'restraint for weakness'", *HKFP*, Hong Kong, 6 August 2019, https://hongkongfp.com/2019/08/06/china-warns-hong-kong-protesters-not-mistake-govt-restraint-weakness/ (last accessed 30 Nov. 2020).

6. Government of the Hong Kong Special Administrative Region, "CE announces withdrawal of Fugitive Offenders Bill among 'four actions' to help society move forward", press release, Hong Kong, 4 September 2019, available at https://www.info.gov.hk/gia/general/201909/04/P2019090400704.htm (last accessed 1 Dec. 2020).

7. Reuters, "Exclusive: 'If I have a choice, the first thing is to quit'—Hong Kong leader Carrie Lam—transcript", Hong Kong, 3 September 2019, https://www.reuters.com/article/us-hongkong-protests-carrielam-tran-scrip-idUSKCN1VO0KK (last accessed 17 Nov. 2020).

7. REVENGE

1. Christy Leung, "Exclusive: New Hong Kong police chief Chris Tang tells residents: the force cannot end protests alone", *SCMP*, Hong Kong, 19 November 2019, https://www.scmp.com/news/hong-kong/law-and-crime/article/3038305/incoming-police-chief-chris-tang-tells-hong-kongers (last accessed 1 Dec. 2020).

2. *Ming Pao*, "Chinese University Survey: 50% of respondents have zero trust in the police", Hong Kong, 20 September 2019 (in Chinese).

3. Jeffie Lam, "Police reputation in tatters across the political divide according to online survey of Hong Kong voters", *SCMP*, Hong Kong, 21 December 2019, https://www.scmp.com/news/hong-kong/politics/article/3043030/police-reputation-tatters-across-political-divide-according (last accessed 1 Dec. 2020).

4. Shibani Mahtani et al., "In Hong Kong crackdown, police repeatedly broke their own rules—and faced no consequences", *The Washington Post*, Washington DC, 24 December 2019, https://www.washington-post.com/graphics/2019/world/hong-kong-protests-excessive-force/ (last accessed 1 Dec. 2019).

5. BBC News, "Simon Cheng: Former UK consulate worker says he was tortured in China", London, 20 November 2019, https://www.bbc.com/news/av/world-asia-50481937 (last accessed 1 Dec. 2020).

6. Interview with the author, Hong Kong, 4 October 2019.

7. Echo Xie, "Hong Kong court sent wrong signals to radical protesters over face mask ban, say mainland Chinese analysts", *SCMP*, Hong Kong,

19 November 2019, https://www.scmp.com/news/china/politics/article/3038302/hong-kong-court-sent-wrong-signals-radical-protesters-over-face (last accessed 1 Dec. 2020).

8. These figures were supplied by the police and are contained in BBC News, "Hong Kong Polytechnic University: Protesters still inside as standoff continues", London, 19 November 2019, https://www.bbc.com/news/world-asia-china-50465337 (last accessed 2 Dec. 2020).

9. Danny Mok, "Hong Kong protests: more petrol bombs and offensive weapons found at Polytechnic University on Sunday", *SCMP*, Hong Kong, 2 December 2019, https://www.scmp.com/news/hong-kong/politics/article/3040136/hong-kong-protests-more-petrol-bombs-and-offensive-weapons (last accessed 2 Dec. 2020).

10. James Pomfret and Clare Jim, "Exclusive: Hong Kongers support protester demands; minority wants independence from China—Reuters Poll", Reuters, Hong Kong, 31 December 2019, https://www.reuters.com/article/us-hongkong-protests-poll-exclusive-idUSKBN1YZ0VK (last accessed 2 Dec. 2020).

11. Ng Kang-chung, "Take 'public interest' into account on whether to bring cases to court, instead of just sufficient evidence, head of Hong Kong Bar Association says in speech", *SCMP*, Hong Kong, 13 January 2020, https://www.scmp.com/news/hong-kong/law-and-crime/article/3045884/take-public-interest-account-whether-bring-cases-court (last accessed 2 Dec. 2020).

12. The history of these events has been widely covered, but the best and most succinct account is to be found in Chapter 4 of Nigel Collett, *A Death in Hong Kong: The MacLennan Case of 1980 and the Suppression of a Scandal*, CITYUHK Press, Hong Kong, 2018.

13. Independent Police Complaints Council, "A Thematic Study by the IPCC on the Public Order Events arising from the Fugitive Offenders Bill since June 2019 and the Police Actions in Response: Volume 1", Hong Kong, May 2020, available at https://www.ipcc.gov.hk/doc/en/report/thematic_report/Volume%201%20(CH1-CH4).pdf (last accessed 2 Dec. 2020).

14. Clement Chan, interview with the author, "IPCC thematic study: discussion with Clement Chan of IPCC", *The Pulse*, Radio Television

Hong Kong, 22 May 2020, available at https://podcast.rthk.hk/pod-cast/item.php?pid=205&eid=159413&year=2020&lang=en-US (last accessed 2 Dec. 2020).

15. Lilian Cheng, "National security law: Hong Kong leader calls on oppo-sition camp not to demonise legislation", *SCMP*, Hong Kong, 16 June 2020, https://www.scmp.com/news/hong-kong/politics/article/3089 241/national-security-law-hong-kong-leader-calls-opposition (last accessed 2 Dec. 2020). At a press conference reported in this story, Lam clarified that she was "not a party to the lawmaking institution" drafting the law and lacked "any details about the provisions in the legislation, and how they are going to be applied".

8. REVOLUTION OF OUR TIMES

1. Jeffie Lam, "'Liberate Hong Kong; revolution of our times': Who came up with this protest chant and why is the government worried?", *SCMP*, Hong Kong, 6 August 2019, https://www.scmp.com/news/hong-kong/politics/article/3021518/liberate-hong-kong-revolution-our-times-who-came-protest (last accessed 2 Dec. 2020).

2. Kimmy Chung, "Aspiring election candidates insist their use of 'Liberate Hong Kong; revolution of our times' protest slogan does not mean they advocate independence", *SCMP*, Hong Kong, 16 October 2019, https://www.scmp.com/news/hong-kong/politics/article/3033100/aspiring-election-candidates-insist-their-use-liberate-hong (last accessed 2 Dec. 2020).

3. The results (in Chinese only) can be found on the Hong Kong Public Research (HKPR) Institute website, 31 July 2019, https://www.pori.hk/report/antiextraditionbillfreq (last accessed 4 Dec. 2020).

4. Shelly Banjo and Natalie Lung, "How Fake News and Rumors Are Stoking Division in Hong Kong", Bloomberg News, New York, 11 November 2019, https://www.bloomberg.com/news/articles/2019-11-11/how-fake-news-is-stoking-violence-and-anger-in-hong-kong (last accessed 4 Dec. 2020), citing HKPR poll taken in August 2019.

5. Victor Ting, "Survey reveals widening rift between generations of Hongkongers over anti-government protests", *SCMP*, Hong Kong,

9 December 2019, https://www.scmp.com/news/hong-kong/politics/article/3041298/survey-reveals-widening-rift-between-generations (last accessed 3 Dec. 2020).

6. *The Lancet*, "The Lancet: Study suggests mental health impact of ongoing social unrest in Hong Kong", press release, London, 9 January 2020, available at https://www.eurekalert.org/pub_releases/2020-01/tl-tls010820.php (last accessed 3 Dec. 2020).

7. Carine Chow, "Tourism, design and medical staff hit the worst by stress", *The Standard*, Hong Kong, 3 August 2020, https://www.thestandard.com.hk/section-news/section/4/221495/Tourism,-design-and-medical-staff-hit-the-worst-by-stress (last accessed 3 Dec. 2020).

8. Lam Ka-shing, "Best Mart 360 shuns 'war zone' Hong Kong for mainland China in growth plan after protesters trash 75 of its 102 stores", *SCMP*, Hong Kong, 28 November 2019, https://www.scmp.com/business/companies/article/3039803/best-mart-360-flees-war-zone-hong-kong-mainland-china-after (last accessed 4 Dec. 2020).

9. *Dimsum Daily*, "Deloitte, auditor of debt-ridden Next Digital Group which owns Apple Daily resigns due to professional risks related to auditing and its fees", Hong Kong, 17 December 2019, https://www.dimsumdaily.hk/deloitte-auditor-of-debt-ridden-next-digital-group-which-owns-apple-daily-resigns-due-to-professional-risks-related-to-auditing-and-its-fees/ (last accessed 3 Dec. 2020).

10. Kimmy Chung, "'Black Blorchestra' crew behind music video of protest anthem 'Glory to Hong Kong' voice fears about being identified", *SCMP*, Hong Kong, 18 September 2019, https://www.scmp.com/news/hong-kong/politics/article/3027744/black-blorchestra-crew-behind-music-video-protest-anthem (last accessed 4 Dec. 2020).

11. Ng Kang-chung, "Anti-government activists' plan to win key Legislative Council seats in 2020 election suffers blow as minister reveals huge backlog to trade union approval", *SCMP*, Hong Kong, 12 April 2020, https://www.scmp.com/news/hong-kong/politics/article/3079547/anti-government-activists-plan-win-key-legislative-council (last accessed 3 Dec. 2020).

12. As early as September 2019, Amnesty International gathered a mass of evidence to this effect. See the first of a series of statements: Amnesty

International, "Hong Kong: Arbitrary arrests, brutal beatings and torture in police detention revealed", Hong Kong, 19 September 2019, https://www.amnesty.org/en/latest/news/2019/09/hong-kong-arbitrary-arrests-brutal-beatings-and-torture-in-police-detention-revealed/ (last accessed 3 Dec. 2020).

13. *Stand News* compiled statistics and testimonies of mistreatment under arrest during the first nine months of the protests; these were published under the following headline: *Stand News*, "At least 100 defendants were absent from hearing for the first time due to injuries. 20 people complained of being beaten by the police with obvious injuries. 8 people's beatings caused fractures", Hong Kong, 13 March 2020 (in Chinese).

14. Alvin Lum, "Hong Kong police 'systematically infringed' human rights of protest arrestees, local group argues in report destined for UN", *SCMP*, Hong Kong, 13 May 2020, https://www.scmp.com/news/hong-kong/politics/article/3084050/hong-kong-police-systematically-infringed-human-rights (last accessed 3 Dec. 2020).

15. *SCMP*, "'Exodus' from Hong Kong? Those who fear national security law mull best offers from welcoming countries", Hong Kong, 12 July 2020, available at https://newscolony.com/exodus-from-hong-kong-those-who-fear-national-security-law-mull-best-offers-from-welcoming-countries/ (last accessed 24 Nov. 2020).

16. Cindy Wang and Chinmei Sung, "Hong Kong Immigration to Taiwan Surges as Protests Grind On", Bloomberg News, New York, 19 August 2019, https://www.bloomberg.com/news/articles/2019-08-19/hong-kong-immigration-to-taiwan-surges-as-protests-grind-on (last accessed 3 Dec. 2020).

17. Selina Cheng, "4 out of 10 HongKongers would emigrate if given the opportunity—survey", *HKFP*, Hong Kong, 8 October 2020, https://hongkongfp.com/2020/10/08/4-out-of-10-hongkongers-would-emigrate-if-given-the-opportunity-survey/ (last accessed 3 Dec. 2020).

18. *Dimsum Daily*, "Only 20% plan to migrate and leave Hong Kong, latest poll shows", Hong Kong, 20 September 2020, https://www.dimsumdaily.hk/only-20-plan-to-migrate-and-leave-hong-kong-latest-poll-shows/ (last accessed 3 Dec. 2020).

9. VIRUS AND CRISIS

1. Quoted by Ching Cheong in Hong Kong Journalists Association, *2020 Annual Report: Freedom in Danger*, 2020, "Chapter 4: Press freedom a matter of life and death—A reflection on the Wuhan pneumonia", p. 52, https://drive.google.com/file/d/1JBoaxj-J9TfLaLVfxLkq_9-JkwZZ ewmF/view (last accessed 30 Nov. 2020).

2. Guo Rui, "Coronavirus: Why did China's multimillion-dollar early warning system fail?", *SCMP*, Hong Kong, 13 March 2020, available at https://malaysia.news.yahoo.com/coronavirus-why-did-china-multimillion-025333317.html (last accessed 30 Nov. 2020).

3. *Apple Daily*, "Xi Jinping claims COVID victory to rally loyalty: critic", Hong Kong, 8 August 2020.

4. Ben Westcott and Steven Jiang, "Chinese diplomat promotes conspiracy theory that US military brought coronavirus to Wuhan", CNN, New York, 14 March 2020, https://edition.cnn.com/2020/03/13/asia/china-coronavirus-us-lijian-zhao-intl-hnk/index.html (last accessed 30 Nov. 2020).

5. Natasha Khan, "New Virus Discovered by Chinese Scientists Investigating Pneumonia Outbreak", *The Wall Street Journal*, New York, 8 January 2020, https://www.wsj.com/articles/new-virus-discovered-by-chinese-scientists-investigating-pneumonia-outbreak-11578485668 (last accessed 30 Nov. 2020).

6. Amy Qin and Javier C. Hernández, "China Reports First Death From New Virus", *The New York Times*, New York, 10 January 2020, https://www.nytimes.com/2020/01/10/world/asia/china-virus-wuhan-death.html (last accessed 30 Nov. 2020).

7. Christopher A. Mouton et al., "COVID-19 Air Traffic Visualization: COVID-19 Cases in China Were Likely 37 Times Higher Than Reported in January 2020", RAND Corporation, Santa Monica, CA, 2020, https://www.rand.org/pubs/research_reports/RRA248-3.html (last accessed 30 Nov. 2020).

8. Emily Rauhala, "China's claim of coronavirus victory in Wuhan brings hope, but experts worry it is premature", *The Washington Post*, Washington DC, 25 March 2020, https://www.washingtonpost.com/

world/asia_pacific/china-wuhan-coronavirus-zero-cases/2020/03/25/ 19bdbbc2-6d15-11ea-a156-0048b62cdb51_story.html (last accessed 30 Nov. 2020).

9. Dali L. Yang, "China's early warning system didn't work on covid-19. Here's the story", *The Washington Post*, Washington DC, 24 February 2020, https://www.washingtonpost.com/politics/2020/02/24/chinas-early-warning-system-didnt-work-covid-19-heres-story/ (last accessed 30 Nov. 2020).

10. James Kynge, Sun Yu and Tom Hancock, "Coronavirus: the cost of China's public health cover-up", *Financial Times*, London, 6 February 2020, https://www.ft.com/content/fa83463a-4737-11ea-aeb3-95583 9e06441 (last accessed 30 Nov. 2020).

11. Stephanie Hegarty, "The Chinese doctor who tried to warn others about coronavirus", BBC News, London, 6 February 2020, https:// www.bbc.co.uk/news/world-asia-china-51364382 (last accessed 30 Nov. 2020).

12. Linda Lew, "Coronavirus pandemic shows global consequences of China's local censorship rules", *SCMP*, Hong Kong, 7 June 2020, https://www.scmp.com/news/china/society/article/3087866/corona-virus-pandemic-shows-global-consequences-chinas-local (last accessed 30 Nov. 2020).

13. Ibid.

14. *The Guardian*, "Ren Zhiqiang—who called Chinese president a 'clown'—jailed for 18 years", London, 22 September 2020, https:// www.theguardian.com/world/2020/sep/22/ren-zhiqiang-who-called-chinese-president-a-clown-jailed-for-18-years (last accessed 30 Nov. 2020).

15. Quoted in Geremie R. Barmé, "China's Coronavirus Crisis Is Just Beginning", *The New York Times*, New York, 3 March 2020, https:// www.nytimes.com/2020/03/03/opinion/coronavirus-china-xi-jinping. html (last accessed 30 Nov. 2020).

16. Ibid.

17. BBC News, "Coronavirus: Chinese citizen journalist faces jail for Wuhan reporting", London, 17 November 2020, https://www.bbc. co.uk/news/world-asia-china-54969682 (last accessed 30 Nov. 2020).

18. Ai Weiwei, "China is ill, but it goes much deeper than the coronavirus", *The Guardian*, London, 8 March 2020, https://www.theguardian.com/commentisfree/2020/mar/08/china-ill-not-only-coronavirus-communist-party-control (last accessed 30 Nov. 2020).

19. *Stand News*, "Hong Kong government schemes to create 'favourable atmosphere' for the Pro-establishment camp amidst anti-epidemic work", Hong Kong, 22 February 2020 (in Chinese).

20. Chinese University Centre for Communication and Public Opinion, "Survey of 847 Hong Kong respondents aged 15 and above", 19–27 March 2020. See Tony Cheung and Natalie Wong, "Coronavirus: Hong Kong residents unhappy with Covid-19 response—and surgical masks one big reason why, Post survey shows", *SCMP*, Hong Kong, 1 April 2020, https://www.scmp.com/news/hong-kong/politics/article/3077761/coronavirus-post-poll-shows-hong-kong-residents-unhappy (last accessed 30 Nov. 2020).

21. Government of the Hong Kong Special Administrative Region, "Transcript of remarks of press conference (with photo/video)", Hong Kong, 5 February 2020, https://www.info.gov.hk/gia/general/202002/05/P2020020500740.htm (last accessed 30 Nov. 2020). (These remarks were subsequently removed from another government website.)

22. Ng Kang-chung, "Coronavirus: more than 6 million masks procured by Hong Kong government found to be fake", *SCMP*, Hong Kong, 3 July 2020, https://www.scmp.com/news/hong-kong/law-and-crime/article/3091616/coronavirus-more-6-million-masks-procured-hong-kong (last accessed 30 Nov. 2020).

23. Government of the Hong Kong Special Administrative Region, "Economic situation in the Third Quarter of 2020 and Latest GDP and Price Forecasts for 2020", press release, Hong Kong, 13 November 2020, https://www.hkeconomy.gov.hk/en/pdf/20q3_pr.pdf (last accessed 4 Dec. 2020).

24. Ng Kang-chung, "Tax breaks, goodies in HK$120 billion package aimed at keeping 'still fertile' Hong Kong afloat through social unrest and coronavirus outbreak", *SCMP*, Hong Kong, 26 February 2020, https://www.scmp.com/news/hong-kong/hong-kong-economy/article/3052482/hong-kong-budget-cash-handouts-tax-breaks-and (last accessed 30 Nov. 2020).

25. Sophia Ankel, "A construction expert broke down how China built an emergency hospital to treat Wuhan coronavirus patients in just 10 days", *Business Insider*, New York, 5 February 2020, https://www.businessinsider.com/how-china-managed-build-entirely-new-hospital-in-10-days-2020-2?r=US&IR=T (last accessed 30 Nov. 2020).

26. BBC News, "Coronavirus: How NHS Nightingale was built in just nine days", London, 17 April 2020, https://www.bbc.co.uk/news/health-52125059 (last accessed 30 Nov. 2020).

27. Ralph Jennings, "Why Taiwan Has Just 42 Coronavirus Cases while Neighbors Report Hundreds or Thousands", *VOA News*, Washington DC, 4 March 2020, https://www.voanews.com/science-health/coronavirus-outbreak/why-taiwan-has-just-42-coronavirus-cases-while-neighbors-report (last accessed 30 Nov. 2020).

28. Interview with Bruce Aylward, "Coronavirus situations in New York city, London and Lombardy, Italy & interview with WHO Bruce Aylward", *The Pulse*, Radio Television Hong Kong, 28 March 2020, 19:54, https://www.rthk.hk/tv/dtt31/programme/thepulse/episode/619602 (last accessed 30 Nov. 2020).

29. Courtney J. Fung and Shing-Hon Lam, "China already leads 4 of the 15 U.N. specialized agencies—and is aiming for a 15th", *The Washington Post*, Washington DC, 3 March 2020, https://www.washingtonpost.com/politics/2020/03/03/china-already-leads-4-15-un-specialized-agencies-is-aiming-5th/ (last accessed 30 Nov. 2020).

30. Mitt Romney, "America is awakening to China. This is a clarion call to seize the moment", *The Washington Post*, Washington DC, 23 April 2020, https://www.washingtonpost.com/opinions/global-opinions/mitt-romney-covid-19-has-exposed-chinas-utter-dishonesty/2020/04/23/30859476-8569-11ea-ae26-989cfce1c7c7_story.html (last accessed 30 Nov. 2020).

31. Associated Press, "China delayed releasing coronavirus info, frustrating WHO", New York, 2 June 2020, https://apnews.com/article/3c061794970661042b18d5aeaaed9fae (last accessed 30 Nov. 2020).

32. AFP/JIJI, "WHO says it was first alerted to coronavirus by its office, not China", *Japan Times*, Tokyo, 4 July 2020, https://www.japantimes.co.jp/news/2020/07/04/world/who-coronavirus-alert-china/ (last accessed 30 Nov. 2020).

33. For a forensic examination of these matters, see Claudia Rosett, "A Chinese Communist Virus at the World Health Organization", in Fred Fleitz et al., *Defending Against Biothreats: What We Can Learn from the Coronavirus Pandemic to Enhance U.S. Defenses Against Pandemics and Biological Weapons*, Centre for Security Policy Press, Washington DC, 2020, available online at https://www.centerforsecuritypolicy.org/wp-content/uploads/2020/08/BioDefense_Rosett_080720.pdf (last accessed 4 Dec. 2020).

34. Christian Shepherd, Katrina Manson and Jamie Smyth, "Failure by WHO team to visit Wuhan sparks concerns over virus probe", *Financial Times*, London, 26 August 2020, https://www.ft.com/content/f9dea077-66fb-4734-9d1d-076dc93568e1 (last accessed 30 Nov. 2020).

35. Shi Jiangtao, "China denies coronavirus cover-up and insists relations with rest of world have not been damaged", *SCMP*, Hong Kong, 7 June 2020, available at https://malaysia.news.yahoo.com/china-denies-coronavirus-cover-insists-094634178.html (last accessed 30 Nov. 2020).

36. Rhoda Kwan, "'Health and safety' of Canadians in Hong Kong jeopardised by Ottawa's acceptance of Hong Kong refugees, says Chinese envoy", *HKFP*, Hong Kong, 16 October 2020, https://hongkongfp.com/2020/10/16/health-and-safety-of-canadians-in-hong-kong-jeopardised-by-ottawas-acceptance-of-hong-kong-refugees-says-chinese-envoy/ (last accessed 30 Nov. 2020).

37. Reuters, "Exclusive: Internal Chinese report warns Beijing faces Tiananmen-like global backlash over virus—sources", Beijing, 4 May 2020, https://uk.reuters.com/article/uk-health-coronavirus-china-sentiment-ex/exclusive-internal-chinese-report-warns-beijing-faces-tiananmen-like-global-backlash-over-virus-sources-idUKKBN22G198 (last accessed 1 Dec. 2020).

38. Josh Rogin, "The coronavirus crisis is turning Americans in both parties against China", *The Washington Post*, Washington DC, 8 April 2020, https://www.washingtonpost.com/opinions/2020/04/08/coronavirus-crisis-is-turning-americans-both-parties-against-china/ (last accessed 1 Dec. 2020).

39. François Godement, *Europe's Pushback on China*, policy paper, Institut Montaigne, Paris, June 2020, https://www.institutmontaigne.org/res-

sources/pdfs/publications/europes-pushback-china-intention-policy-paper.pdf (last accessed 1 Dec. 2020).

40. Juliet Eilperin et al., "U.S. sent millions of face masks to China early this year, ignoring pandemic warning signs", *The Washington Post*, Washington DC, 18 April 2020, https://www.washingtonpost.com/health/us-sent-millions-of-face-masks-to-china-early-this-year-ignor-ing-pandemic-warning-signs/2020/04/18/aaccf54a-7ff5-11ea-8013-1b6da0e4a2b7_story.html (last accessed 1 Dec. 2020).

41. Wendy Wu, "Coronavirus: don't politicise medical supply problems, China says", *SCMP*, Hong Kong, 30 March 2020, available at https://sg.news.yahoo.com/coronavirus-don-t-politicise-medical-060459186.html?guccounter=1&guce_referrer=aHR0cHM6Ly93d3cuZ29vZ2xlL mNvbS88&guce_referrer_sig=AQAAACIm6ln1mWamE0UNvUVLb-tbN_9Nv3c7-RyA_W4VRDafI-JpPG31cui37QigeMb8skD3HSaUk7 cp7kFlgmg3Z8YCrcd5ETKfEKceQphK7LMvnCeg8PytejTxotQvZnd-BSaGQtQTuhTSKUkB76b61lJbbiPbtjf_FUZiTGaClqaa9 (last accessed 1 Dec. 2020).

42. Amber Athey, "Italy gave China PPE to help with coronavirus—then China made them buy it back", *The Spectator*, London, 4 April 2020, https://spectator.us/italy-china-ppe-sold-coronavirus/ (last accessed 24 Nov. 2020).

43. Stuart Lau, "Coronavirus: China gets defensive during high-level EU event on fundraising and vaccine development", *SCMP*, Hong Kong, 5 May 2020, https://www.scmp.com/news/world/europe/arti-cle/3082841/coronavirus-china-gets-defensive-during-high-level-eu-event (last accessed 1 Dec. 2020).

44. Stuart Lau, "EU leaders talk tough to Beijing over long list of unmet promises", *SCMP*, Hong Kong, 23 June 2020, https://www.scmp.com/news/china/diplomacy/article/3090198/eu-leaders-talk-tough-beijing-over-long-list-unmet-promises (last accessed 23 Nov. 2020).

45. Philip Blenkinsop and Robin Emmott, "EU leaders call for end to 'naivety' in relations with China", Reuters, Brussels, 22 March 2019, https://uk.reuters.com/article/us-eu-china/eu-leaders-call-for-end-to-naivety-in-relations-with-china-idUKKCN1R31H3 (last accessed 23 Nov. 2020).

46. Bloomberg, "Coronavirus: no 'business as usual' with China after pandemic, Britain says", *SCMP*, Hong Kong, 17 April 2020, https://www.scmp.com/news/world/europe/article/3080304/coronavirus-no-business-usual-china-after-pandemic-britain-says (last accessed 1 Dec. 2020).

47. John Bolton, "Online Zoom Event: John Bolton: The Man in the Room Where It Happened", Foreign Correspondents' Club, Hong Kong, 15 July 2020, https://www.fcchk.org/event/club-online-zoom-event-john-bolton-the-man-in-the-room-where-it-happened/ (last accessed 1 Dec. 2020).

48. Isabel Reynolds and Emi Urabe, "Japan to Fund Firms to Shift Production Out of China", Bloomberg News, New York, 8 April 2020, https://www.bloomberg.com/news/articles/2020-04-08/japan-to-fund-firms-to-shift-production-out-of-china (last accessed 1 Dec. 2020).

49. Statista, "China's share of global gross domestic product (GDP) adjusted for purchasing-power-parity (PPP) from 2009 to 2019 with forecasts until 2025", New York, 2020, https://www.statista.com/statistics/270439/chinas-share-of-global-gross-domestic-product-gdp/ (last accessed 4 Dec. 2020).

50. Charlie Campbell, "'How Can I Get Through This?' The Impact of Coronavirus on China's Economy Is Only Just Beginning", *Time*, New York, 21 April 2020, https://time.com/5824599/china-coronavirus-covid19-economy/ (last accessed 1 Dec. 2020).

51. Frank Tang, "Is China's second quarter GDP as rosy as it seems?", *SCMP*, Hong Kong, 17 July 2020, available at https://malaysia.news.yahoo.com/china-second-quarter-gdp-rosy-115623912.html (last accessed 1 Dec. 2020).

52. *China Daily*, "First into the virus slump, China is proving the fastest out", Beijing, 17 August 2020; copy available at Bloomberg News, "First Into the Virus Slump, China Is Proving the Fastest Out", New York, 15 August 2020, https://www.bloomberg.com/news/articles/2020-08-15/first-into-the-virus-slump-china-is-proving-the-fastest-out (last accessed 1 Dec. 2020).

53. Evelyn Cheng, "Unemployment ticks higher in China as coronavirus

shock to economy persists", CNBC, New York, 15 May 2020, https://www.cnbc.com/2020/05/15/unemployment-rises-in-china-as-corona-virus-shock-to-economy-persists.html (last accessed 1 Dec. 2020).

54. Amanda Lee, "China's banking system begins to crack at its grass roots as two bank runs take place within a week", *SCMP*, Hong Kong, 23 June 2020, https://www.scmp.com/economy/china-economy/article/3090266/chinas-banking-system-begins-crack-its-grass-roots-two-bank (last accessed 1 Dec. 2020).

55. Reuters, "China's debt tops 300% of GDP, now 15% of global total: IIF", London, 18 July 2019, https://www.reuters.com/article/us-china-economy-debt-idUSKCN1UD0KD (last accessed 24 Nov. 2020).

10. HONG KONG IS NOT ALONE: THE WORLD IS WATCHING

1. Quoted in Ben Blanchard, "UPDATE 3-Chinese paper says 'foreign forces' using Hong Kong havoc to hurt China", Reuters, London, 10 July 2019, https://uk.reuters.com/article/hongkong-extradition-march-china/update-3-chinese-paper-says-foreign-forces-using-hong-kong-havoc-to-hurt-china-idUKL4N23G0MR (last accessed 1 Dec. 2020).

2. Frank Chen, "US NGOs, local tycoon funding HK protests: report", *Asia Times*, Bangkok, 13 November 2019, https://asiatimes.com/2019/11/us-ngos-local-tycoon-funding-hk-protests-report/ (last accessed 1 Dec. 2020).

3. Matt Clinch, "Carrie Lam suggests foreign influence in Hong Kong protests: 'Perhaps there is something at work'", CNBC, New York, 21 January 2020, https://www.cnbc.com/2020/01/21/carrie-lam-suggests-foreign-influence-in-hong-kong-protests.html (last accessed 1 Dec. 2020).

4. Alan MacLeod, "The Revolution Isn't Being Televised", FAIR, New York, 26 October 2019, https://fair.org/home/the-revolution-isnt-being-televised/ (last accessed 1 Dec. 2020).

5. *Dimsum Daily*, "Is United States involved in the current civil unrest in Hong Kong via its National Endowment for Democracy?", Hong Kong, 25 August 2019, https://www.dimsumdaily.hk/is-united-states-involved-in-the-current-civil-unrest-in-hong-kong-via-its-national-

endowment-for-democracy-ned/ (last accessed 1 Dec. 2020). Interestingly, this outlet, with an enthusiasm for bizarre theories, takes pains to disguise its ownership. According to a statement it published on 20 September 2019, *Dimsum* is run by a British Virgin Islands-registered company "backed by local Hong Kong investors". (*Dimsum Daily*, "Clarification to quash rumours with regards to ownership of Dimsumdaily and our pro-Beijing stance", Hong Kong, 20 September 2019, https://www.dimsumdaily.hk/clarification-to-quash-rumours-with-regards-to-ownership-of-dimsumdaily-and-our-pro-beijing-stance/ (last accessed 1 Dec. 2020).)

6. National Endowment for Democracy (NED), "National Endowment for Democracy responds to threat of Chinese government sanctions", Washington DC, 2 December 2019, https://www.ned.org/national-endowment-for-democracy-responds-to-threat-of-chinese-government-sanctions/ (last accessed 1 Dec. 2020).

7. NED, "2019 Annual Report", Washington DC, 2019, https://www.ned.org/annual-report/2019-annual-report/ (last accessed 24 Nov. 2020).

8. Alvin Lum, "Hong Kong protesters raise US$1.97 million for international ad campaign as they accuse police of 'war crimes' and using 'chemical weapons'", *SCMP*, Hong Kong, 12 August 2019, https://www.scmp.com/news/hong-kong/politics/article/3022498/hong-kong-protesters-raise-us197-million-international-ad (last accessed 1 Dec. 2020).

9. Maurice Glasman, "In the heart of Baghdad, a new vision for Iraq is emerging", *New Statesman*, London, 29 November 2019, https://www.newstatesman.com/world/2019/11/heart-baghdad-new-vision-iraq-emerging (last accessed 1 Dec. 2020).

10. *The Washington Post*, "How China corralled 1 million people into concentration camps", editorial, Washington DC, 29 February 2020, https://www.washingtonpost.com/opinions/global-opinions/a-spreadsheet-of-those-in-hell-how-china-corralled-uighurs-into-concentration-camps/2020/02/28/4daeca4a-58c8-11ea-ab68-101ecfec2532_story.html (last accessed 1 Dec. 2020).

11. UK Home Office News Team, "Media factsheet: Hong Kong BN(O)s",

Home Office blog, 29 May 2020, https://homeofficemedia.blog.gov.uk/2020/05/29/media-factsheet-hong-kong-bnos/ (last accessed 24 Nov. 2020).

12. Reuters, "China says Sino-British Joint Declaration on Hong Kong no longer has meaning", London and Beijing, 30 June 2017, https://uk.reuters.com/article/uk-hongkong-anniversary-china/china-says-sino-british-joint-declaration-on-hong-kong-no-longer-has-meaning-idUKKBN19L1IR (last accessed 1 Dec. 2020).

13. UK Secretary of State for Foreign & Commonwealth Affairs, *The Six-Monthly Report on Hong Kong: 1 January to 30 June 2019*, London, 31 October 2019, https://assets.publishing.service.gov.uk/government/uploads/system/uploads/attachment_data/file/856991/Hong_Kong_Six-monthly_Report_Jan-Jun19.pdf (last accessed 1 Dec. 2020).

14. "Hong Kong National Security Legislation", statement by Foreign Secretary Dominic Raab, *Hansard* HC Deb., vol. 678, col. 329 (1 July 2020).

15. Stephanie Dalzell, "Scott Morrison says Australia won't respond to Chinese 'coercion' over warning about universities", *ABC News*, Canberra, 11 June 2020, https://www.abc.net.au/news/2020-06-11/australia-morrison-china-respond-coercion-on-universities/12342924 (last accessed 23 Nov. 2020).

16. Will Jennings, "Support for helping British passport-holders in Hong Kong is rising", YouGov, London, 1 July 2020, https://yougov.co.uk/topics/politics/articles-reports/2020/07/01/support-helping-british-passport-holders-hong-kong (last accessed 1 Dec. 2020).

17. Jeremiah Cha, "People in Asia-Pacific regard the U.S. more favorably than China, but Trump gets negative marks", *Fact Tank*, Pew Research Center, Washington DC, 25 February 2020, https://www.pewresearch.org/fact-tank/2020/02/25/people-in-asia-pacific-regard-the-u-s-more-favorably-than-china-but-trump-gets-negative-marks/ (last accessed 1 Dec. 2020).

18. Global Voices, "Beijing constructs an 'independence' plot for Hong Kong protests through information operations", *HKFP*, Hong Kong, 5 November 2019, https://hongkongfp.com/2019/11/05/beijing-con-structs-independence-plot-hong-kong-protests-information-opera-

tions/ (last accessed 1 Dec. 2020), based on a public talk by Fu King-wa of the Journalism and Media Studies Centre of the Hong Kong University on *Matters.news*, Hong Kong, 1 November 2019.

19. A detailed account of this activity by Chinese media organisations is to be found in Louisa Lim and Julia Bergin, "Inside China's audacious global propaganda campaign", *The Guardian*, London, 7 December 2018, https://www.theguardian.com/news/2018/dec/07/china-plan-for-global-media-dominance-propaganda-xi-jinping (last accessed 1 Dec. 2020).

20. Jim Waterson and Dean Sterling Jones, "Daily Telegraph stops publishing section paid for by China", *The Guardian*, 14 April 2020, https://www.theguardian.com/media/2020/apr/14/daily-telegraph-stops-publishing-section-paid-for-by-china (last accessed 1 Dec. 2020).

21. Kimmy Chung and Alvin Lum, "Hong Kong government spends HK$7.4 million in global advertising blitz, but PR experts question effectiveness of campaign", *SCMP*, Hong Kong, 24 September 2019, https://www.scmp.com/news/hong-kong/politics/article/3030020/hong-kong-government-spends-hk74-million-global-advertising (last accessed 1 Dec. 2020).

22. *China Daily*, "'Gang of four' 'incited' unrest in Hong Kong", Beijing, 1 November 2019, https://www.chinadaily.com.cn/a/201911/01/WS5dbb89faa310cf3e35574d6e.html (last accessed 1 Dec. 2020).

23. Quoted in James Kynge, "China, Hong Kong and the world: is Xi Jinping overplaying his hand?", *Financial Times*, London, 10 July 2020, https://www.ft.com/content/a0eac4d1-625d-4073-9eee-dcf1bacb749e (last accessed 1 Dec. 2020).

24. Channel News Asia, "Trump: Hong Kong would have been 'obliterated in 14 minutes' if not for me", Singapore, 22 November 2019, https://www.channelnewsasia.com/news/world/trump-hong-kong-protests-obliterated-14-minutes-xi-jinping-trade-12118468 (last accessed 1 Dec. 2020).

11. FOLLOW THE MONEY

1. Tax Justice Network, "Financial Secrecy Index—2020 Results", London,

2020, https://fsi.taxjustice.net/en/introduction/fsi-results (last accessed 1 Dec. 2020).

2. Tax Justice Network, "Financial Secrecy Index 2020: Narrative Report on Hong Kong", London, 2020, https://fsi.taxjustice.net/PDF/HongKong.pdf (last accessed 1 Dec. 2020).

3. Alexa Olesen, "Leaked Files Offer Many Clues To Offshore Dealings by Top Chinese", International Consortium of Investigative Journalists (ICIJ), Washington DC, 6 April 2016, https://www.icij.org/investigations/panama-papers/20160406-china-red-nobility-offshore-dealings/ (last accessed 1 Dec. 2020).

4. Stuart Lau, "Chinese dominate list of people and firms hiding money in tax havens, Panama Papers reveal", *SCMP*, Hong Kong, 10 May 2016, https://www.scmp.com/news/hong-kong/article/1943463/chinese-dominate-list-people-and-firms-hiding-money-tax-havens-panama (last accessed 1 Dec. 2020).

5. Reuters, ""Hong Kong takes aim at middlemen in wake of Panama Papers scandal", *The Edge Markets*, Selangor, Malaysia, 15 February 2017, https://apps.theedgemarkets.com/article/hong-kong-takes-aim-middlemen-wake-panama-papers-scandal (last accessed 4 Dec. 2020).

6. Ibid.

7. Hong Kong Securities and Futures Commission, *Asset and Wealth Management Activities Survey 2018*, Hong Kong, July 2019, https://www.sfc.hk/-/media/EN/files/ER/PDF/Asset-and-Wealth-Management-Activities-Survey-2018_EN.pdf (last accessed 4 Dec. 2020).

8. BBC News, "'One million' Chinese officials punished for corruption", London, 24 October 2016, https://www.bbc.com/news/world-asia-china-37748241 (last accessed 1 Dec. 2020).

9. James T. Areddy, "Report: Corrupt Chinese Officials Take $123 Billion Overseas", *The Wall Street Journal*, New York, 16 June 2011, https://www.wsj.com/articles/BL-CJB-13932 (last accessed 11 Dec. 2020).

10. Eeo.com.cn, Beijing, 19 January 2013 (in Chinese).

11. BBC News, "China corruption: Life term for ex-security chief Zhou", London, 11 June 2015, https://www.bbc.com/news/world-asia-china-33095453 (last accessed 1 Dec. 2020).

12. Benjamin Kang Lim and Ben Blanchard, "Exclusive: China seizes $14.5 billion assets from family, associates of ex-security chief: sources", Reuters, London, 30 March 2014, https://www.reuters.com/article/us-china-corruption-zhou-idUSBREA2T02S20140330 (last accessed 1 Dec. 2020).

13. William Zheng, "China reveals mountain of bribes seized from fallen Communist Party boss Zhao Zhengyong", *SCMP*, Hong Kong, 14 May 2020, available at https://sg.news.yahoo.com/china-reveals-mountain-bribes-seized-133611417.html?guccounter=1&guce_referrer=aHR0c HM6Ly93d3cuZ29vZ2xlLmNvbS8&guce_referrer_sig=AQAAA C2tOWGOsEJge_AlYR53lSd4oHCyXhqzmB2TVngWJ2xQl9Wwd8 GqSwd0PxbV9HjQkUPQKEAkk3UvowTVS0xoLOIy7fJB8gGjRUnu OHF-t-QbLALV9o1_pBe47TxHQgt8F3O7im5FV7vqzss185ewD-buh6eoPMqm256pfAI1NiiF0 (last accessed 2 Dec. 2020).

14. Juliette Garside and David Pegg, "The Panama Papers and the French villa at the heart of a Chinese scandal", *The Guardian*, London, 7 April 2016, https://www.theguardian.com/news/2016/apr/06/panama-papers-french-villa-heart-chinese-scandal-bo-xilai (last accessed 2 Dec. 2020).

15. David Barboza, "As China Official Rose, His Family's Wealth Grew", *The New York Times*, New York, 23 April 2012, https://www.nytimes.com/2012/04/24/world/asia/bo-xilais-relatives-wealth-is-under-scrutiny.html (last accessed 2 Dec. 2020).

16. Sally Gainsbury, "Gu's sister fronted property company", *Financial Times*, London, 8 August 2012, https://www.ft.com/content/2ea37758-e162-11e1-9c72-00144feab49a (last accessed 2 Dec. 2020).

17. Bloomberg News, "Xi Jinping Millionaire Relations Reveal Fortunes of Elite", New York, 29 June 2012. The fallout from this detailed investigation was so severe that Bloomberg had to remove stories from its website, staff were sacked or resigned, and intensive negotiations were held with officials in Beijing to keep other aspects of the company alive in China. Part of the deal involved undertakings from Bloomberg that it would desist from further stories of this kind, according to agency staffers. Bloomberg's reports on its investigation are available at https://2013.sopawards.com/wp-content/uploads/2013/05/45-Bloomberg-News1-Revolution-to-Riches.pdf (last accessed 3 Dec. 2020).

18. Ibid.

19. Michael Forsythe, "As China's Leader Fights Graft, His Relatives Shed Assets", *The New York Times*, New York, 17 June 2014, https://www.nytimes.com/2014/06/18/world/asia/chinas-president-xi-jinping-investments.html (last accessed 2 Dec. 2020).

20. Bloomberg News, "Xi Jinping Millionaire Relations".

21. Bloomberg News, "Immortals Beget China Capitalism From Citic to Godfather of Golf", New York, 12 December 2012. Again available at https://2013.sopawards.com/wp-content/uploads/2013/05/45-Bloomberg-News1-Revolution-to-Riches.pdf (last accessed 3 Dec. 2020).

22. ICIJ, "Li Peng", *Offshore Leaks Database*, Washington DC, undated, https://offshoreleaks.icij.org/stories/li-xiaolin (last accessed 3 Dec. 2020).

23. ICIJ, "Trend Gold Consultants Limited", *Offshore Leaks Database*, Washington DC, undated, https://offshoreleaks.icij.org/nodes/151840 (last accessed 3 Dec. 2020).

24. *Apple Daily News Special Reports*, Hong Kong, 10 August 2018 (in Chinese).

25. Marina Walker Guevara et al., "Leaked Records Reveal Offshore Holdings of China's Elite", ICIJ, Washington DC, 21 January 2014, https://www.icij.org/investigations/offshore/leaked-records-reveal-offshore-holdings-of-chinas-elite/ (last accessed 3 Dec. 2020).

26. Deloitte Monitor, *The Deloitte International Wealth Management Centre Ranking 2018: The winding road to future value creation*, third edition, Zurich, 2018, available at https://www2.deloitte.com/ch/en/pages/financial-services/articles/the-deloitte-wealth-management-centre-ranking-2018.html (last accessed 3 Dec. 2020).

27. Mao Zedong, "The Role of the Chinese Communist Party in the National War", in *Selected Works of Mao Zedong*, Vol. II, Foreign Languages Press, Beijing, 1975, p. 198.

28. Tax Justice Network, "Financial Secrecy Index 2020: Narrative Report on Hong Kong".

12. ENDGAME?

1. Markus B. Liegl, *China's Use of Military Force in Foreign Affairs: The Dragon Strikes*, Routledge, London, 2017, p. 164.

2. Chris Buckley, "'Clean Up This Mess': The Chinese Thinkers Behind Xi's Hard Line", *The New York Times*, New York, 2 August 2020, https://www.nytimes.com/2020/08/02/world/asia/china-hong-kong-national-security-law.html (last accessed 23 Nov. 2020).

3. Arjun Neil Alim and Francesco Loy Bell, "Ai Weiwei: China's national security law 'finished' Hong Kong's autonomy, says artist", *The Independent*, London, 28 July 2020, https://www.independent.co.uk/news/world/asia/ai-weiwei-interview-cracking-down-minority-groups-china-domestic-policy-a9641386.html (last accessed 23 Nov. 2020).

6. *China Digital Times*, "Translation: Former party professor call CCP a political zombie", Berkeley, CA, 12 June 2020, https://chinadigitaltimes.net/2020/06/translation-former-party-professor-calls-ccp-a-political-zombie/ (last accessed 23 Nov. 2020).

7. Li Fan, "Don't Give Up on Chinese Democracy", *Foreign Policy*, New York, 8 July 2020, https://foreignpolicy.com/2020/07/08/chinese-democracy-civil-society-coronavirus/ (last accessed 23 Nov. 2020).

8. Andrew Collier, "Hong Kong's not so special status as China's financial centre", *Financial Times*, London, 27 September 2019, https://www.ft.com/content/2c4c56bd-1c40-3261-8ba8-f3ce8c83e8d2 (last accessed 24 Nov. 2020).

9. Hong Kong Monetary Authority, "HONG KONG: The Global Offshore Renminbi Business Hub", Hong Kong, January 2016, https://www.hkma.gov.hk/media/eng/doc/key-functions/monetary-stability/rmb-business-in-hong-kong/hkma-rmb-booklet.pdf (last accessed 23 Nov. 2020).

10. Richard McGregor, *Xi Jinping: The Backlash*, Penguin, Melbourne, 2019, p. 8.

11. Minxin Pei, "The Political Logic of China's Strategic Mistakes", *Project Syndicate*, Prague, 8 July 2020, https://www.project-syndicate.org/commentary/china-strategic-mistakes-reflect-communist-party-mind-set-by-minxin-pei-2020-07?barrier=accesspaylog (last accessed 23 Nov. 2020).

12. Wen Xian, "China needs to get used to US jealousy", *Global Times*, Beijing, 28 July 2016, https://www.globaltimes.cn/content/997101.shtml (last accessed 23 Nov. 2020).

13. Voice of America, "China Poses Biggest Threat to U.S. National Security", editorial, Washington DC, 24 July 2020.

14. Robert Muller, "Economic clout makes China tougher challenge for U.S. than Soviet Union was—Pompeo", Reuters, Prague, 12 August 2020, https://www.reuters.com/article/us-czech-usa-pompeo-idUSK CN258204 (last accessed 23 Nov. 2020).

15. Finbarr Bermingham, "China-EU investment treaty talks hit crunch time, as Europeans bemoan seven years of 'promise fatigue' from Beijing", *SCMP*, Hong Kong, 23 July 2020, https://www.scmp.com/economy/global-economy/article/3094048/china-eu-investment-treaty-talks-hit-crunch-time-europeans (last accessed 23 Nov. 2020).

16. Eric Rosenbaum, "1 in 5 corporations say China has stolen their IP within the last year: CNBC CFO survey", CNBC Global CFO Council, New York, 1 March 2019, https://www.cnbc.com/2019/02/28/1-in-5-companies-say-china-stole-their-ip-within-the-last-year-cnbc.html (last accessed 3 Dec. 2020).

17. *Global Times*, "GT investigation: A battle to save exports, jobs", Beijing, 28 April 2020, https://www.globaltimes.cn/content/1187059.shtml (last accessed 4 Dec. 2020).

18. Statista, "Share of exports in gross domestic product (GDP) in China from 2009 to 2019", New York, 2020, https://www.statista.com/statistics/256591/share-of-chinas-exports-in-gross-domestic-product/ (last accessed 4 Dec. 2020).

19. American Chamber of Commerce in Hong Kong, "AmCham Temperature Survey Findings: OFAC's Sanction on Hong Kong & National Security Law", Hong Kong, 13 August 2020, https://www.amcham.org.hk/sites/default/files/content-files/WOI%20Judge%20Bios/WOI%20Judge%20Bios%202019/Survey%20Findings/OFAC's%20Sanction%20on%20Hong%20Kong%20%26%20National%20Security%20Law.pdf, (last accessed 3 Dec. 2020).

20. Joshua Wong with Jason Y. Ng, *Unfree Speech*, Penguin Books, London, 2020, p. 231.

21. Lester Shum, "Tomorrow will not be the end of Hong Kong", republished in *Stand News*, Hong Kong, 30 June 2020 (in Chinese).

22. Reuters, "Exclusive: HK survey shows increasing majority back pro-

democracy goals, smaller support for protest movement", Hong Kong, 30 August 2020, https://uk.reuters.com/article/uk-hongkong-security-poll-exclusive/exclusive-hong-kong-survey-shows-increasing-majority-back-pro-democracy-goals-smaller-support-for-protest-movement-idUKKBN25Q00Y?il=0 (last accessed 3 Dec. 2020).

23. Ramona Diaz, *A Thousand Cuts*, PBS Distribution, New York, 2020.
24. Richard Youngs, *Civic Activism Unleashed: New Hope or False Dawn for Democracy?*, OUP, Oxford, 2019.

INDEX

INDEX

INDEX

INDEX

INDEX

INDEX

INDEX

INDEX

INDEX

INDEX

INDEX

INDEX

INDEX

INDEX

INDEX